TEXTXET

Studies in comparative literature 39

Series Editors
C.C. Barfoot and Theo D'haen

MYTH, TELOS, IDENTITY
THE TRAGIC SCHEMA IN GREEK AND SHAKESPEAREAN DRAMA

IVÁN NYUSZTAY

Amsterdam - New York, NY
2002

ISBN 90-420-1540-3

The paper on which this book is printed meets the requirements of
'ISO 9706: 1994, Information and documentation - Paper for
documents - Requirements for permanence'.

© Editions Rodopi B.V., Amsterdam - New York, NY 2002
Printed in The Netherlands

CONTENTS

ACKNOWLEDGEMENTS   3

INTRODUCTION   5

I   *MODES OF THE TRAGIC IN GREEK DRAMA*   14

II   *MODES OF THE TRAGIC IN SHAKESPEAREAN DRAMA*   43

III   *CHARACTER AND IDENTITY*   63

IV   *ON THE THRESHOLD OF THE TRAGIC: THE TELEOLOGICAL FOUNDATIONS OF GREEK AND SHAKESPEAREAN TRAGEDY*   80

V   *FROM CHARACTER TO SELF*   104

VI   *FORMS OF ACTION AND PASSIVITY*   129

VII   *FORMS OF INACTION: SPEECH ACTS*   150

EPILOGUE   171

APPENDIX: HISTORY ASIDE IN RICHARD THE THIRD: *MIMESIS OR POIESIS?*   175

BIBLIOGRAPHY   184

INDEX   199

Acknowledgements

This book is to a large extent the result of my four-year research in Belgium, carried out at the *Katholieke Universiteit Leuven*. I am very grateful first of all to the English Department. Guido Latré did much to help my research work attain its present form. From the very beginning of our acquaintance he sought to secure all conceivable means to enhance the completion of my project. I am more than grateful to Ortwin de Graef for his inspiring criticism that compelled me to revise my methodology. His provoking remarks and original insights often led me to rethink the presuppositions of the individual chapters and helped to reformulate them in a way that proved most productive. I have gained much from Luke van der Stockt (Classical Philology), and also from William Desmond and Arnold Burms (Department of Philosophy).

Part of this research, however, had been carried out at *ELTE University of Budapest*. I am especially indebted to Géza Kállay, István Géher and Péter Dávidházi (Department of English Studies); Tibor Fabiny (*Pázmány Péter Catholic University,* Department of English Studies); and László Tengelyi (*ELTE,* Department of Philosophy), for their meticulous reading and criticism of the individual chapters and their constant encouragement, intellectual or otherwise.

Besides personal support I owe much to two grants. Thanks to a grant from *Peregrinatio* I had the chance to spend five months in Stratford-upon-Avon in 1994-1995, at the *Shakespeare Institute*, where the exceptional wealth of literature and the kind assistance of the director, Stanley Wells, greatly enhanced my work. A special debt is owed to the generous joint grant of the *Hungarian Soros Foundation* and the K. U. Leuven, which provided the financial means for the last years of my research.

I owe much to my friends and colleagues whose presence was a contribution in itself. Let me extend my warmest thanks to Ágnes Juhász and Rob Ormsby, Augustijn Callewaert, Michel Gillain, Prabhat Avasare, Annelein Masschelein, Ágnes Orzóy, Áron and Gábor Buzási, Péter Szalai, Ágoston Schmelowszky, András Monori, Aakash Sing, Serena Parekh, László Komorjai, Gabriella Somlyai, Katalin Almássy and András Kiséry.

Introduction

The concepts indicated in the title of this book specify the main reference points of an approach to tragic experience in Greek and Shakespearean drama. Such an approach takes as its starting point the presupposition that there is a tragic experience as such, common to both historical variants of the genre.

The interrelatedness of the conceptual triad of *myth*, *telos* and *identity* will be illustrated by what I call the tragic schema, introduced in Chapter 1. The tragic schema in its difference from alternative schematic ways of thinking proves essential for handling tragic experience. Its specific attribute is reflection, a term I adopt to mark the process of adaptation of myth in drama. I take dramatic reflection to be the domain, which necessitates the reassessment of characterological criteria and the reconsideration of dramatic action *per se*.

It is on these grounds, along the isolation of particular schemata (or different levels of problematization), that the comparative survey of the tragic will commence. I will focus on the most outstanding and frequent modes of the tragic as they appear in drama. The respective discussions of these modes take place with constant reference to the perspective of myth. The architectonic survey of Greek and Shakespearean plays takes these modes as means to expose crucial discrepancies between what I call pure tragedy on the one hand, and melodrama on the other. This generic distinction is the more justified when the incompatible ways of plot-construction are highlighted. As I will try to show, they derive from the diverse dramatic applications of the analysed concepts.

The tragic schema of Greek and Shakespearean drama presupposes the deep embeddedness of genre in myth, the Greek and the Christian. Both worldviews, the tragic and the ethic, respectively, can be said to include variants of the genuinely tragic experience. If this is so, it follows that the use of the term "Christian tragedy" is justifiable. Those who consider the term as a meaningless oxymoron, a contradiction in terms, tend to take the adjective "Christian" as a totality and refrain from seeing it in its historicity. I try to defend a de-totalizing view by showing how the basic concepts of pure tragedy, isolated in Greek drama, are reborn within Christianity. This rebirth is due to prevalent Calvinist and Lutheran doctrines. Christian tragedy will then be understood in a different light. It will pose itself as a valid genre in Shakespeare's England.[1]

The rootedness of tragedy in myth renders attempts at the moralization of the analysed modes questionable. In a continuous debate with such claims and especially with Aristotle's appertaining tenets, I will resort to the relevance of myth in the isolation of tragic experience. This, however, does not mean that ethical orientation is entirely absent from tragedy. On the contrary, it is precisely the insistence on ethical orientation on the part of characters in tragic drama that creates tragic experience (Chapters 1 and 2).

This Utopian insistence on the ethical approach brings about an internal dividedness, which I explore in a debate with Hegel's and Schelling's views on character. Their accounts of Greek and Shakespearean drama in general and of the relation between fate and character in particular, concentrate on pinpointing certain discrepancies and incompatibilities. It is only regrettable that this is done at the expense, to my understanding, of significant overlaps (Chapter 3).

The duplicity of directions implied by the breaking down of ethical orientation and the unfolding of an unforeseen development, display parallel vantage points and purposes with regard to action. This leads to the necessary step of sequestering perspectives and differentiating between teleological directions determining action. The teleological foundations of Greek and Shakespearean tragedy are based on the detailed findings of the architectonic survey of individual plays (carried out in Chapters 1 and 2). They also provide a possible account for the convergences of these findings (Chapter 4). It is along these foregoing analyses that the problem of tragic identity will present itself in a new light.

I address the question of tragic identity by introducing a form of contextualism specific to drama. This contextualism extends beyond ideas of conventionalism. It surpasses the distinction between contextualized modes of being and the being true to life by doubting the possibility of a non-contextualized truth to life. The comprehensive formula of contextualism will serve to contrast tragic identity with Alasdair MacIntyre's and Paul Ricoeur's versions of narrative identity. Tragic identity, as a prerogative of drama, is delineated along with discussions of related dramatic phenomena: *to pathei mathos* (learning through suffering) and *katharsis* (Chapter 5).

---

[1] For the influence of Protestant teachings on the religious consciousness of Elizabethan England, cf. John Stachniewsky, *The Persecutory Imagination: English Puritanism and the Literature of Religious Despair*, Oxford: Clarendon Press, 1991.

In the final chapters I return to the problem of fate and action in tragedy. I approach tragic identity or self-constitution from another aspect. If, as I argue throughout the preceding chapters, action is determined by fate (through myth), the only sphere where intention is manifest is the sphere of inaction. Still, under specific circumstances inaction is liable to be considered as action. As the result of a tentative modelling of action in Shakespearean drama, and the consequent recapitulation of the basic constituents of action, the borderline between action and inaction will appear blurred (Chapter 6).

Since inaction seems to be just as problematic as action itself, I discuss speech act theory as well as action-theory and apply the findings to particular scenes from *Hamlet*. Here, as elsewhere, the dialogue between philosophy and drama is supposed to be mutually enriching (if not disturbing). Philosophical texts help us to grasp and formulate the problem inherent in the dramatic situation and conversely, the dramatic situation may challenge the feasibility of philosophical arguments. The chosen scenes from *Hamlet* are therefore both read against and by these foregoing theorizations. What these analyses reveal in Shakespearean tragedy are those moments of inaction, when a reflecting self crystallizes in opposition to the character-actant. Agency and selfhood appear to be radically severed from each other. This leads to the undermining of the exclusive application of Aristotle's concept of *ethos* to drama, since, I believe, it answers merely for agency and hardly for selfhood (Chapter 7).

This way Chapters 1 and 2 inform Chapters 6 and 7, the make-up of different genres reveals different forms of self-constitution. The generic isolation of pure tragedy, carried out in what seems a structuralist bias,[2] thus prepares the instruction of ethics by tragedy, to speak with Paul Ricoeur.[3]

Instruction of ethics by tragedy is, without reservations, as obscure and misleading as can be. First, one has to determine what kind of ethics one is preparing to instruct; second, by what sense of tragedy; and third, how instruction can really remain instructive or constructive without becoming destructive. Not that these latter antinomies can easily be set apart. Instruction, in a sense, is always necessarily destruction and vice versa: the elusive character of these terms is as conspicuous as promising. Deconstruction, I should say, renders this

---

[2] Seems, since I frequently attack totalizing critical stances characteristic of structuralist thought.
[3] Cf. Paul Ricoeur, *Oneself as Another,* trans. Kathleen Blamey, Chicago: University of Chicago Press, 1992, 243.

elusiveness promising. It points to what is menacing in instruction, thereby justifying a certain sense of destruction. Instruction, turned tragic, may become a threat in undermining the ethical basis. But what kind of ethics is threatened thus by tragedy?

I believe that it is of paramount importance that the art of tragedy was systematically elaborated for the first time together with the first systematic foundation of ethics. The man responsible for both was, of course, Aristotle. Hence the constant moralization about tragedy in philosophy and literary criticism ever since (with a few exceptions, needless to say). Hence the all too willing taking for granted of the applicability of ethical concepts to tragedy. My approach to tragedy will radically question these procedures by pinpointing occurrences and modes of the tragic, which can hardly be accounted for by Aristotelian ethics. This will involve detailed discussions of the pillars of Aristotelian ethics, first and foremost of autonomy. Autonomy itself is not thematized by Aristotle. Still, it is precisely this lack that will prove most illuminating, as I shall try to point out. For Aristotle autonomy implicitly provides the basis for the scaffolding of ethical principles in the *Nicomachean Ethics*. Without a certain sense of this basis, the ethical norm of following the required mean would lose much of its appeal.

The example of explicit autonomy in the history of philosophy is, of course, Kant, which is of some interest, because the construction of his entire system on explicit autonomy goes together with a telling silence on tragedy. This silence is the more telling when juxtaposed with the verbosity of (more or less) contemporary German philosophy with regard to tragic drama. Hegel, Schelling, Schopenhauer (not to mention Nietzsche somewhat later) have contributed to our understanding of tragedy, thoroughly influencing literary scholarship. This contribution, I believe, could not have been as penetrating as it undoubtedly was, had their respective treatments of drama been mere literary allusions, interesting references, or colourful appendices. On the contrary, tragedy appears in Kant's German contemporaries as representative of a whole system of philosophical thinking.

If Kant is silent, Aristotle is also silent, I will argue, on certain components of drama that shatter autonomy. However, there is one such component that Kant introduces in his late *Religion within the Bounds of Reason Alone*: radical evil (*radikale Böse*). This concept threatened to undermine the whole idea of autonomy and freedom as expounded in the *Critique of Practical Reason*. The established bond between freedom and morality, the great Kantian project in the second

Critique, was broken, thus testifying to an unmasterable incompatibility.[4]

The way Kantian ethics is uprooted by the intervention of radical evil is exemplary of the way ethical systems of autonomy are uprooted by tragedy. Today these obsolete systems of ethical thought would usually be labelled collectively as ethics of modernity. Contrasted to the ethics of modernity, a large field of ethical thinking, abbreviated as postmodern ethics, appears to gain a foothold. Zygmunt Bauman sets up this crucial opposition in his book, *Postmodern Ethics.*[5] His approach is marked by the cardinal distinction he makes between ethics and morality, arguing that moral choice in modernity was degraded to comply with a compelling ethical code. Modern ethical thought, according to Bauman, exercised its power under the "twin banners of *universality* and *foundation*" (8). Linked to legislative practices, both universality and foundation served to promote coercion and obedience. It is to Bauman's credit that he takes a "non-aporetic, non-ambivalent morality, an ethics that is universal and "objectively founded", to be a practical impossibility; perhaps also an *oxymoron*, a contradiction in terms". By contrast, the postmodern moral condition is defined by Bauman as essentially "ambivalent", "non-rational", "aporetic" and "not universalizable" (10-11). The moral ambivalence and uncertainty is, emphatically, incurable in the postmodern perspective, unlike in modernity, where, the experienced aporetic situation (fate) was regarded as repairable. For Bauman it was the achievement of the postmodern perspective to unmask illusions and to regain morality from ethics, the moral self from the code, autonomy from heteronomy (14).

Bauman's differentiation between morality and ethics is in many ways reminiscent of *Sittlichkeit* and *Moralität*. The dichotomy was set up by Hegel to criticize Kant's too abstract *Moralität*. Still, Bauman's conclusions reach far beyond. The concept of moral uncertainty disqualifies previous ethical codes and calls for a radical reassessment of foundations. Bauman's moral inquiry into postmodern ethics at the same time can hardly be considered exceptional. We find important parallels in contemporary moral philosophy, most notably in the work of Bernard Williams and Thomas Nagel.

What these philosophers mean by moral luck comes close to Bauman's moral uncertainty. In all three cases (though in various ways) modernity is discarded as a conglomerate of obsolete and no

---

[4] Cf. László Tengelyi, *Kant,* Budapest: Kossuth, 1988, 133.
[5] Zygmunt Bauman, *Postmodern Ethics* Oxford: Blackwell, 1995.

longer effective ethical doctrines. The starting point of the debate with modernity, both for Williams and Nagel, is Kant's aversion to contingency. It is in his *Groundwork of the Metaphysics of Morals*, where Kant defines the good will as good in itself, free from external influences, contingencies (first section, third paragraph). Accomplishment belongs to worthiness and utility, which Kant dissociates from the goodness of the will. Thus is the latter made to "sparkle like a jewel in its own right".[6] Williams counters this view by what may be called a result-centred ethics, according to which choice is justified by success.[7] I shall not go into details in respect to the diverse ways Williams and Nagel go about discrediting the inherited Kantian notions. Let this example of the extreme disparity of moral premises suffice. What is important for our present purposes is, rather, the intrusion of luck into contemporary moral theory and practice. As Williams puts it: "the aim of making morality immune to luck is bound to be disappointed" (36). The relevance of this intrusion is in bringing ethics closer to tragedy, to a never before conceived extent. For where does the problem of luck most blatantly come into focus if not in the realm of tragedy? It was Martha C. Nussbaum, who discovered the inexhaustible wealth of tragic experience for moral philosophy.

In *Fragility of Goodness* Nussbaum starts by reaffirming the irreducible role of luck in human experience and picks up the anti-Kantian thread. Turning to Greek tragedy involves the rehabilitation of the ancient texts from the misunderstandings that, she argues, have been generated by the "Kantian approach to problems of luck" (9). It is important to note, nevertheless that for Nussbaum, the consideration of tragic poetry remains a part of an ethical investigation (14). If for Bauman moral phenomena were inherently non-rational, Nussbaum turns to tragedy for the emotional response it is supposed to elicit. What this procedure amounts to is a confessedly Aristotelian ethicization of tragedy. The adaptation of the emotional elements of tragedy for ethical reflection. Though Nussbaum's approach is original and highly challenging, her method is not suited to the following discussions. In these discussions I will assume an emphatically anti-Aristotelian standpoint and will engage in a laborious rehabilitation of tragedy from the manipulations of Aristotelian ethics. I will look at ethics from the point of view of tragedy (instead of vice versa) and lay down the schemata of diverse perspectives on human experience.

---

[6]Quoted in full by Nagel in *Moral Luck,* ed. Daniel Statman, New York: State University of New York Press, 1993, 57.
[7]*Moral Luck*, 38.

It seems that the interaction between tragedy and contemporary moral philosophy or postmodern ethics, can take place only with certain reservations. In my view, moral philosophers like Williams and Nussbaum have taken tragic experience too lightly in order to be able to include it in their respective ethical reflections. The concept of luck (not to mention fortune)[8] itself betrays these procedures.[9] Tragedy allows no luck, nor fortune (as its synonym), but fate and necessity. I am aware that this needs some illustration and I am also aware that my understanding of tragedy may be condemned by readers of Greek literature like Williams and Nussbaum, as exaggerated and one-sided. Nevertheless, to substantiate my point I will take tragedy as seriously as possible, both in Greek and Shakespearean drama, in constant debate with excessively inclusive accounts. Polemics with totalizing views on tragedy (which include Aristotle's and Hegel's theories of drama), prepare the establishment of certain generic subdivisions. These will be seen as expressing incompatible forms of human experience.

Attempting to expose the distinctive, specific elements of a particular genre or paradigmatic experience, as it were, naturally entails isolating the encountered phenomena. This is the arduous route at the end of which, I hope the ontological specificity of pure tragedy in Greek and Shakespearean drama begins to present itself.

Finally, I will consider Shakespeare's presumed knowledge of Greek tragedy. This question of influence is seldom raised by comparative studies; its precariousness mostly encourages silence on the topic.[10] Others in favour of influence underline the importance of the Senecan tradition in its role of mediating Greek mythology and tragic vision.[11] An opposing view, the notion of direct influence, is held by

---

[8]The pertinent passages by Williams make clear his similar standpoint – "a deeper sense of exposure to fortune is expressed elsewhere in Greek literature, above all in tragedy", and a little further – "Greek philosophy, in its sustained pursuit of rational self-sufficiency, does turn its back on kinds of human experience and human necessity of which Greek literature itself offers the purest, if not the richest, expression" (quoted by Nussbaum, *Fragility of Goodness*, Cambridge: Cambridge University Press, 1993, 18).

[9]In fact, the concept of luck, as well as the Greek *tukhe* is the organizing principle of tragicomedy and comedy, as I will show in the following analyses.

[10]Cf. Lewis Campbell, *Tragic Drama in Aeschylus, Sophocles and Shakespeare*, London: Smith Elder and Co., 1904; Tom F. Driver, *The Sense of History in Greek and Shakespearean Drama*, New York: Columbia University Press, 1960; Adrian Poole, *Tragedy: Shakespeare and the Greek Example*, Oxford: Basil Blackwell, 1987.

[11]Advocates of Senecan influence include John W. Cunliffe, *The Influence of Seneca on Elizabethan Tragedy*, Hamden, CT: Archon Books, 1965; F. L. Lucas, *Seneca and*

critics like Emrys Jones, who stresses the availability of Greek tragedy in Renaissance England.[12] The number of editions and Latin translations, especially those of Euripides (Erasmus's translation of *Iphigeneia in Aulis* included), is regarded as providing a source of such immediate influence. Apart from the accessibility of Greek drama through translation, Jones points to another route of infiltration, Book 13 of Ovid's *Metamorphoses*, where the recounted stories are adopted from Euripides.

While outlining the possible sources of direct influence, nevertheless I would like to stress its relative insignificance for the present undertaking. The conceptual analyses of the particular details of tragic experience in Greek drama and their resonance in Shakespeare go far

---

Elizabethan Tragedy, New York: Haskell House Publishers, 1922; Kenneth Muir, *The Sources of Shakespeare's Plays*, London: Methuen & Co., 1977; T. S. Eliot, *Essays on Elizabethan Drama*, New York: Harcourt, Brace & Co., 1956; H. B. Charlton, *The Senecan Tradition in Renaissaince Tragedy*, Manchester: Manchester University Press, 1946; Braden Gordon, *Renaissance Tragedy and the Senecan Tradition: Anger's Privilege*, New Haven: Yale University Press, 1985; Robert S. Miola, *Shakespeare and Classical Tragedy: The Influence of Seneca*, Oxford: Clarendon, 1992. For further details see E. T. Klett, *The Meaning of Tragedy: Shakespeare and the Spirit of Euripides*, M.A. thesis, University of Birmingham, 1997. According to most of these studies, as summarized by Klett, the elements of Shakespearean drama which suggest a Senecan influence are: the five-act structure; certain stock characters; melodramatic narration of events; rhetorical set-pieces, such as the self-analytical soliloquy; *stichomythia*; lurid violence; and general topics such as madness, passion, vengeance and the supernatural interference (10). It is conspicuous in this series of presumable inheritance, that apart from the five-act structure (for the English five-act morality plays, the plays at universities and John Lyly's influence, see T. W. Baldwin, *Shakspere's Five-act Structure,* Urbana: University of Illinois Press, 1947, 493-544) there is nothing Renaissance tragedians could not have adapted from a possible Greek influence. Moreover, when citing Polonius' "Seneca cannot be too heavy, nor Plautus too light" (*Hamlet*, II.ii.401) to substantiate their view, there seems to be less critical attention to the nature of this influence than to its *factum brutum*. The fact that it is Polonius who reveals this infiltration, also shows us how to conceive of it within the context of the play. A study of the nature of influence therefore cannot but content itself with the repetition of the brute fact if it refuses to see it in relation to the sayer, i. e., to Polonius' character. Here I tend to take up T. S. Eliot's critical stance, which is not "so much concerned with the influence of Seneca on Shakespeare as with Shakespeare's illustration of Senecan and stoical principles" (40). Proceeding along this difference between Senecan influence on the one hand, and Shakespeare's own illustration of this influence on the other, would lead to a better understanding of the status of any influence within the Shakespearean corpus.

[12]Emrys Jones, *The Origins of Shakespeare*, Oxford: Clarendon, 1977. Jones' standpoint is defined in a debate with the conventional pro-Senecan arguments by Virgil K. Whitaker, *Shakespeare's Use of Learning: An Inquiry into the Growth of His Mind*, San Marino: Huntington Library, 1953, and H. B. Charlton, *The Senecan Tradition in Renaissaince Tragedy.*

beyond the contingency of dramatic adaptations. What is at stake in the following comparative survey is, rather, the metahistorical prevalence of the tragic, its eternal kinship with an unalterable human factor, with finitude itself.

I. Modes of the Tragic in Greek Drama

The present chapter seeks to approach the intricate problem of the tragic through the diversification of schematic modes of understanding. The questions that gave birth to such an undertaking can be subsumed under three points. Firstly, can ethics account for the different forms of the tragic? Secondly, what perspective does myth add to a merely ethical orientation? Thirdly, what is the proper schematic approach to the tragic? In this quest I take the phenomenon of the tragic as it is given in the two greatest manifestations of tragedy, the Greek and the Shakespearean. In both versions I attempt to identify the schematic belonging of the tragic. It will be argued that in both cases the origin of this belonging can be found along the same route, namely from the extolling of man and human capacities to his ultimate exposure and dethronement.

The close examination of the basic modes of the tragic in ethical orientation and beyond takes the direction offered by diverse schemata. The order of presented schemata by no means follows a historical chronology, or any subjective claims of priority. It is oriented, rather, towards the field of my main focus: tragedy. The identification of a comprehensive formula will be carried out by grasping the common denominator of the analysed modes. This "being necessarily wrong in action" will then be claimed to have been recapitulated in Shakespearean tragedy by the dramatic paradigmatic shift of theological doctrines. The decisive transformation of Christian conceptual thought reinstates the counterpart of the common denominator in the comprehensive formula of inherent deprivation. The formula will be introduced together with its crucial consequences on human endeavours.

The second part deals with the reappearance of the comprehensive formula in Calvinist and Lutheran teachings. By breaking away from the medieval governing concept of sin, certain Protestant doctrines re-establish the platform for the renascence of pure tragedy. The basic modes of the tragic in Greek tragedy then will finally be pinpointed in the individual texts of Shakespearean-Christian tragedy.

The schemata of evil

The present investigations locate the modes of the tragic at the junction of perspectives. Along with identifying them in the two distinct manifestations of the genre we find ourselves immediately confronted with the problem of evil. Accounting for evil appears right away as bearing necessary precedence over any discussion of the tragic. Through the phenomenon of the tragic a potential evil is realized, revealed, activated, brought onto the surface. The origin of this hidden presence, which, as such, evades human understanding as well as the basic motives of individual deliberation: these are the foregrounding metaphysical and ethical queries with which I will be primarily concerned. The constant reciprocity of dramatic and philosophical quests creates a fertile relationship built upon the simultaneous confirmation and challenging of one another. There is an apparent difficulty in the dramatic re-enactment of philosophical problems. The sphere of practical orientation on the one hand, faces the quest for theoretical knowledge on the other. The dramatic hero cannot content himself with an outsider's contemplative assessment of the situation, to the passive, disinterested reflection on events, he has to act, *draó*. He is a hero only insofar as he acts, that is, through the personification of human aspiration. The role itself he is allotted cuts short the profound analysis of his given situation entitling and at the same time compelling him as an insider to participate in the observed course of events. This observed course of events, structured as already involving the dramatic role of the hero as insider and representative of a human aspiration, is what we call plot.

To bridge the gap that presents itself for a textual hermeneutics including both dramatic and philosophical quests, I will include the order or schema of myth as mediator. Though in itself it precedes all theoretical understanding, myth, historically does lend itself to theorization. In its pre-theoretical form it is partly conceived of as preserved in shared knowledge, in the memory of general consciousness and in the written tradition, but also as practice, as far as it is represented on stage. Representation on stage, the animation of plot, however, is not yet drama, since it is void of the latter's basic grounding element: reflection.

Reflection in drama is first to be seen in relation to dramatic conflict which has gained primary significance in tradition. I see reflection as characterized by not only including conflict, but also embracing extra layers of meaning. Among these layers of meaning we find a form of conflict which presents itself between levels of discourse. The conflict animated in the plot seems to be accompanied by the conflict inherent in decoding, verbal-communicative presentation and assessment. The same plot structure will be estimated and assessed in contradictory ways by the hero, the chorus, the gods or the seer (*mantis*), etc.[13] This abundance of perspectives crystallizes in the collision between heroic discourse on one side and the divine discourse with its representatives, on the other.

Reflection in drama, apart from being reflection on the other, i.e., on a situation, an event or another character, is also reflection on oneself. Self-reflection constitutes another mode of conflict in which the character is animated in a desperate struggle with its role allotted in myth. Reflection in drama therefore harbours at least three modes of conflict, the conflict with the other, the conflict with oneself and the conflict between levels of discourse. This comprehensive term prerogative of drama thus bears a generically distinctive significance and it is in this form that it will be schematically applied.

Considering the question of evil and the modes of the tragic I first follow the path offered by philosophical reasoning, then proceed along towards a mythological approach, and, finally, address a dominant phenomenon in drama: reflection. The analysis thus outlined will bear on three diverse but often complementary schemata (or levels of understanding): first, on that of philosophical reasoning which I prefer to call the ethical schema; second, on that of the mytho-schematic confrontation; and third, on the level of reflected confrontation, the tragic schema.

The ethical schema

The foundation of the ethical schema follows Aristotelian ethics for several reasons. There is no available systematic theory of tragedy before the *Poetics* of Aristotle, yet we may find consolation in having recourse to his other works which provide the schematic context. For the lack of pre-Hellenic systematization of Attic tragedy we can hardly expect to be ever compensated. The fact that Aristotle's understanding of tragedy is deeply rooted in the Hellenistic period and the fundamental change of values is most convincingly maintained by A.

---

[13] The range of perspectives are here restricted to those of the insiders. Outsider perspectives on the other hand may include the perspective of the audience, the reader or even (con)textual perspectives, like parallel references from the same genre or outside.

W. H. Adkins.[14] However, the irremediable loss is somewhat attenuated by its consistent assertion. The true understanding of the loss may lead to truer insight. Such insight will be expected to evolve as the result of a schematic differentiation. The ethical schema will be based upon the *Nicomachean Ethics*[15] so that other schemata like the tragic, expected from the *Poetics* (in vain, as it will be seen shortly), may be measured against it. The conceptual relations revealed in such an application of intertextual cross references are illuminating for identifying and isolating the distinctive movements or lack thereof from one schema to another. Before treating the *Poetics* as a constant reference point in understanding tragedy one should therefore consider it in the context of the more comprehensive *Ethics*.

In Aristotelian ethics evil belongs to the realm of extreme actions that violate the rule of the mean. This is the realm of excessive or deficient actions (1106b). Virtue, *arete* on the other hand is in adherence to the mean, the due mean, *mesotes* followed by the wise man. The ethical norm, however, according to his own restrictions, cannot be applied to all forms of actions. Feelings and deeds of envy, shamelessness, malice, murder, fornication, etc. are evil in themselves and in these cases one can only be wrong, *aiei hamartanei* (1107a). Virtue, *arete,* then, as follows, is not opposed to these forms of behaviour, but to those that fail to hit the mean, *meson* and are in this sense actions of excess or deficiency, *hyperbole kai elleipsis,* joined under the label *hamartia* (1106b). The concept of moral virtue in this context embraces these alternatives of emotions and actions. In the elaboration of the concept of moral virtue Aristotle links the term with choice, *prohairesis* (1107a), a crucial step receiving detailed analysis in Book III.

Choice in the *Nicomachean Ethics* is subsumed under the wider field of voluntary actions, *hekousion,* "it is the choice of good or evil that determines our character", *prohaireisthai tagatha e ta kaka poioi tines esmen* (1112a). The alignment of choice with character, *ethos* is made explicit right from the beginning of the passage centred on choice (1111b) and is one of the dominant steps that take beyond the limits of *Ethics*. Needless to say, the same juxtaposition, not to mention the coincidential rendering of character and choice, is a decisive element in the argumentation of the *Poetics*, "character, *ethos* is that

---

[14] A. W. H. Adkins, *Merit and Responsibility: A Study in Greek Values,* Oxford: Clarendon, 1960.
[15] Aristotle, *Nicomachean Ethics*, The Loeb Classical Library, English trans. H. Rackham, Cambridge, Mass. and London: Harvard University Press, 1994 (1926).

which reveals moral choice, *prohairesis*" (1450b).

The concept of *prohairesis* in the *Ethics,* however, is not defined merely as being a voluntary action based on choice between good and evil. Rather, it is further restricted to the scope of actions preceded by deliberation or assent, *bouleuton* (1112a and 1135b). There is no deliberation about necessity, *ananke,* nature, *physis* and chance, *tyche*, consequently there can be no question of choice in relation to these forces, either. We deliberate about things within our control and uncertain in their issue (1112a). Choice is, then, a voluntary act preceded by deliberation understood in this sense.

In the crucial passage where Aristotle defines the range of voluntary actions, we find the essential criteria for establishing ethical autonomy. The origin of a voluntary act lies in the agent, "who knows the particular circumstances in which he is acting" (1111a). The most important circumstances are claimed to be the nature of the act itself and its effect.

If, however, the origin of the act lies outside the agent, as in the case of the workings of necessity or chance or if the individual is merely used by another individual as a means to an end outside his deliberation or even further, if he acts voluntarily in particular circumstances he seems to understand, but happens to be wrong in retrospect, action is defined as involuntary, *akousion.* The key terms discussed in relation to involuntary action are compulsion and ignorance. An action is compulsory when the origin of the act lies outside the agent and he contributes nothing to it (1110b). Action based on ignorance, *agnoia* on the other hand, allows for the differentiation between two classes within the ascription "not voluntary". Action is deemed involuntary only when it is regretted, whereas the lack of contrition renders the terms voluntary and involuntary inapplicable and in this case the label non-voluntary, *oukh hekousion* is used instead (*ibid*). Oedipus' murdering of his father would belong to the former class, to regretted action committed in ignorance. Ignorance here would denote unfamiliarity with the two outstanding circumstances mentioned, the nature of the act and its outcome.

In a step taken toward the delineation of the interrelated concepts of justice and responsibility Aristotle says that involuntary actions cannot be called just or unjust, *dikaios* or *adikos,* except incidentally (1135b). It is only when the act is voluntary that the agent can be blamed and his act called injustice. Through this roundabout way I finally return to the general premise of Book III, namely the introductory juxtaposition of virtue and voluntary action: it is only voluntary actions, *hekousioi* that merits either praise or blame. The Aristotelian doctrine confirming this premise, i.e., that virtue and vice depend on us is a conclusion reached via the outlined differentiation between voluntary and involuntary actions. We are entitled to call an action virtuous or vicious only on the condition that it has been committed willingly, intentionally. The road is cleared to introduce socially relevant factors of communal life,[16] like aspects of responsibility, forms of justice. A sense of symmetry and proportion is apparent in the Aristotelian treatment of justice, *to dikaion,* as an exercise of the mean, namely between the excesses and defects of injustice, *to adikon* (1134a). The range of choices preceded by deliberation and their due judgements are centred around their respective conceptions of the mean.

The ethical schema delineated above soon found itself having to face the problem of individual autonomy, the criterion for voluntary action. For the agent to act voluntarily awareness of the actual circumstances was considered necessary. Ethical autonomy may be extracted from the arguments of the *Nicomachean Ethics* as a premise involving the free choice of the individual between alternatives of action in a given situation. In perceiving and understanding the given situation as a necessary prerequisite of any choice based on deliberation, ethical autonomy finds itself deeply embedded in epistemological autonomy.

Epistemological autonomy means the free, independent assessment of the situation, without any external bias, influence or pressure. The finitude of the understanding individual, in the words of Paul Ricoeur, is manifest in the "perspectival limitation of perception".[17] The here-and-now of perception is a crucial hindrance for the objective understanding of the thing perceived. The limits of viewpoint, the finitude of bodily existence are given limiting factors of knowledge, the problem of which is central to a philosophical reflection on epistemological autonomy. For us, in so far as the question of ethical autonomy is concerned, let it suffice that in the relation between the application of the elusive term voluntary and the necessarily restricted understanding of circumstances, there seems to be some disproportion.

Such disproportion includes something amoral or premoral, a reference to human finitude threatening with an early explosion of the

---

[16] Aristotle's ethical reasoning is closely bound to social demands, cf. Alasdair MacIntyre's *A Short History of Ethics*, London: Routledge, 1993, 68.
[17] Paul Ricoeur, *Fallible Man*, trans. Charles A. Kelbley, New York: Fordham University Press, 1986, 20.

symmetrical structure of the ethical schema, the underlying pattern of crime and punishment. In elaborating his doctrine of *mesotes*, however, Aristotle evades the question, only remarking that "the truly good and wise man will bear all kinds of fortune in a seemly way and will always act in the noblest manner that the circumstances allow" (1101a). Further elaboration of the circumstantial determination is of course, missing due to the impending groundlessness of a detailed ethical reflection. The prepared situation, the situatedness of the assessing consciousness cannot receive greater emphasis than the ethically autonomous individual's actions. Only the latter can be held responsible; in such a way that the judgement be proportionate to the actions. This is the symmetry of the ethical schema.

Evil for Aristotle, then, is manifest in the extreme actions of the moral being and is avoidable by following the rule of the mean. The supreme good is happiness *eudaimonia*, which is the ultimate purpose of all actions (1097b): "happiness is won by virtue and by some kind of study or practice" (1099). The happiness of the individual living by the moral *habitus* also depends on external goods. Bodily health and external advantages are indispensable for acquiring happiness, with which one should be "moderately equipped" (1179a). Happiness, thus far interpreted as teleological activity, here forsakes grounds for external circumstances that hardly come under individual influence. While happiness does not originate wholly from our will, wickedness does. The perpetrator of evil deeds is held entirely responsible, since he has diverted from the rule represented by the moral being. Evil arising from the violation of a rule or law will recur in myth and tragedy, where instead of the symmetry of the ethical schema we find the asymmetry of the mythic and the tragic schemata.

The schema of myth

The philosophical analysis of the origin of evil in Aristotle remains limited to the field of ethics and it is only in the works of Plotinos and the NeoPlatonists that we find its subtle undertaking as a metaphysical problem. This is the era of the philosophy of materia, the theory of *privatio boni*, the negative approach to the existence of evil.[18] The *mytho-schematic* investigations of the origin of evil, however, add new perspectives to the present analysis. In myth man is confronted with evil in contrast with the moral being who either complies with or di-

---

[18] Cf. László Tengelyi, "Malum est privatio boni", in *A bun mint sorsesemény* Budapest: Atlantisz, 1992, 21.

verts from the rule. The active character of compliance-diversion stands in sharp contrast with the passive form of the being-confronted-with and as such, refers to man's vulnerability and the threatening presence of primordial evil.

Myth is the register of the tripartite interrelation of man-God-fate. In myth the relation of man to man is also explained with constant reference to God and fate. Compliance, in myth, one could say, means proper self-location within the hierarchy, the displacement of man's initiative and the recognition of the dependence of human status as such. In myth self-displacement is thus the unconditional surrendering of a metaphysically restricted vantage point. This mythological phenomenon points to an essential characteristic in the human assessment of history, namely the secondariness of human judgement and personal perspective. Secondariness does not necessarily mean subordination, because this would entail a previous superordination and a chronological dependence between ethics and myth, but it clearly indicates the deficiency of an exclusively ethical approach. Myth testifies that evil is primordial, always already present. Man in myth finds evil as already given, prepared, as something outside himself waiting for him, something which is *there*.

Paul Ricoeur looks at the roots of primordial evil in outlining the basic structure of Sumer-Accadian theogonical Urmyths, Babylonian dramas of creation and Greek myths. Evil in these narratives presents itself already in the process of divine creation. In the birth of gods themselves and their battle against each other we find the manifestation of primordial evil, the indirect consequence of which is human existence itself. Ricoeur contrasts the theogonical myths with the anthropogonical creation myth of the biblical Genesis, where primordial evil is replaced by man's disobedience, from which sin derives.[19]

Primordial evil is therefore ethically inconceivable since it is indifferent to the symmetrical ethical schema. It presents itself to man in its totality only when he had taken it upon him, that is, committed it. To know evil as evil is to realize it, the act of committing is necessary for understanding. Ethics cannot differentiate between potential and committed evil, the presence in hiddenness and an actualised, revealed presence. In a comprehensive encompassing of primordial good and evil the ethical schema fails to serve as vantage point.

---

[19]"The Myth of Adam", in Paul Ricoeur, *Symbolism of Evil*, trans. Emerson Buchanan, Boston: Beacon Press, 1967.

The schema of myth, however, locates evil in a prehuman network of relations, the sphere of the gods, and is therefore primordially inseparable from the divine will on the one hand and the pre-ordinance of fate on the other. The distinctively human thirst to know evil is transformed in the larger context of relations. If the good is the ultimate goal in the ethical sense, the ultimate goal in myth is god's will or the pre-ordinance of fate. The desire to know evil becomes secondary to the obedience to higher organizing principles. This is the above-mentioned secondariness, which formulates in myth a universal habit, the higher counterpart of the Aristotelian moral *habitus*, the so-called mytho-schematic habitus. The distinctive feature of the mytho-schematic habitus is the unique way in which it treats primordial evil first in its possible or actual relation to the gods and fate and secondly in its relation to man. What is secondarily good or bad is primarily the polarized totality of divine will. In this sense the concept of the good and the wicked God may be defined, but this is already the sphere of tragedy.

According to the above, man is confronted in myth with something that is god's will viewed in terms of the schema of myth. Primordial evil itself is immediately subsumed in that divine will, just as primordial good is. Polarized evaluation is derivative, secondary within the hierarchy of myth. The schema of myth mediates this secondariness into tragedy, where the concepts of good and evil integrated in the hierarchy of myth collide with their ethico-schematic assessment. The point of collision is the tragic hero himself who, unlike the mythical hero, is endowed with the capacity of reflection. Due to this endowment the tragic hero is more than his mythical antecedent, but at the same time his deeds and judgements cannot be fully understood if we simply regard him as a moral being, forgetting about the significant role he plays in myth. The schizophrenic state of the tragic hero is the consequence of being confronted with evil in myth and being endowed with the ability to reflect on it in the ethical schema. This is the final state in the schemata of evil: reflected confrontation.

The tragic schema

The tragic schema is the reflected schema of myth. In tragedy myth is animated; the interactive relations of mythical figures are brought into tangible closeness by the dramatic plot. It follows that in the tragic plot it is not the mythological story as such that receives primal significance, but rather the ways in which the characters fulfil the divine will of God(s) in their respective roles. Here a distinction should be made between divine will and the pre-ordinance of fate.

The imputation of will to gods is the consequence of anthropomorphization, as are the concepts of good and evil. Divine intervention in human affairs in Greek tragedy leads to the presupposition of a preceding intent of the same order. Preceding intent is conceived of as necessary by the hero, the sufferer of its consequences and whenever he fails to detect the will in the actual context, instead of a spontaneous substitution, he is convinced of the presence of its most threatening mode: deception.

The pre-ordinance of fate, however, does not bear the characteristics of an anthropomorphic divine will, but is primarily mechanic. It is an automatic mechanism indifferent to man, the fulfilment of which in the plot is nothing else but what actually (and finally) takes place. The preserver of the sound totality of myth. Occasionally, when fate is mediated through divine will, we find the dramaturgical reunion of the two organizing principles. It is in this sense that we can say that in the *Libation-Bearers* the adherence to Apollo's commands is also obedience to a supreme authority. Mechanic plot government may in many cases exclude divine will or be indifferent to it in the same way as it is indifferent to human aspirations.

The questions of plot government lead to the necessary differentiation between subjective and objective teleology, two parallel vantage points. Differentiated teleology, the underlying sense and essence of tragedy, involves contrasting perspectives on the plot, that of the hero on the one hand, and that of the representatives of fate, on the other. The crucial difference between Oedipus' and Teiresias' knowledge about the real plot is didactic in this sense, since the king's error on which his subjective teleological sequence of actions is based is clearly revealed by the blind seer. Teiresias sees through the void and finally, in *anagnórisis* teaches Oedipus himself to see through the void, through complete darkness. The fateful error which caused irreparable consequences is also the starting point of differentiated teleology, the absence of which, namely the premature reconciliation of subjective and objective *telos* would be responsible for another genre, that of melodrama.

In what follows I attempt to analyse the structure of the dramatic plot from the point of view of the reflected confrontation with evil. The ethico-schematic reflection of the hero is necessarily part of his self-made subjective teleological sequence of actions. At the same time the reflection on objective teleology is the task of the outsider, the audience, the reader. The question of evil in tragedy is foremost that of the tragic, in which we find a blend between the ethical and the mythological schemata. From the possible forms of the tragic I select and examine the most important and frequent modes: the mode of *kakos* (evil), of *miasma* (defilement, pollution), of *hamartia* (error) and, finally, of *hybris* (pride).

Modes of the Tragic: *Kakos and miasma*

The collective concept of *kakos* encompasses the most decisive experiences of evil of the heroes in pure tragedy. If all the individual experiences of evil were to be summed up in an all-embracing negative state, then this frustrating grounding experience would be *dusdaimonia*, preordained despair, opposite of *eudaimonia*, deserved, merited happiness. This is not the Aristotelian version of *eudaimonia*, that is happiness realized in an activity determined by virtue, since this is beyond the tragic hero's alternatives.[20] In tragedy *eudaimonia* becomes *eutukhe*, good fortune, the self-moderation of fate, which is created by divine collaboration through debt. This mechanism of owing is also the divine justification of the subjective *telos*, "after this relief from woes / I bring you tidings of a happy lot", says Athena in the *Ion* (1604-605). We find the same sort of completion in the end of *Iphigeneia in Taurica*, where it is also Athena's intervention due to which tragic fulfilment is evaded. Thus the Chorus is entitled to say, "speed with fair fortune, in bliss speed on / for the doom reversed, for the life re-won", *moiras eudaimones ontes* (1490-91). Here too, the dominance of the experience of *kakos* is transformed into *eudaimonia* and therefore the world of tragedy is shattered and in its stead we find the sequence of fortunate events triggered by divine compensation. This compensation is responsible for the degradation of pure tragedy dominated by *kakos* and for the rise of a new genre, that of melodrama.

The lack of the dominance of *kakos* in melodrama is manifest in its delibility.[21] The offence of the traveller arriving in Taurica is matricide, the most abominable of sins, *miasma*, which according to Iphi-

---

[20] Cf. Euripides, *Medeia*, "for no mortal ever attains to blessedness, *thneton gar oudeis estin eudaimon aner*" (1228). In the references to Euripides' plays I rely on the complete bilingual edition of The Loeb Classical Library, ed. and trans. Arthur S. Way, Cambridge, Mass. and London: Harvard University Press, 1958.

[21] I coin the word delibility from the words "indelibility" and "delible" (cf. the OED), to denote an abstract form of washability.

geneia seems to be washed away in seawater, just as all evil deeds, "*thalassa kludzei panta tanthrópon kaka*" (1193).[22] *Kakos* in the drama refers to murder, *fonos* and is a synonym for defilement, *miasma* and dirt, *musos* (1225, 1229-30). Delibility as a genre-threatening element occurs in the *Eumenides*, too, where Orestes is acquitted from matricide, his defilement washed away through divine compensation. The inexorable God of tragedy is attenuated and transformed through the paradox of divine debt into the responsible deity of melodrama. Parker reminds us of the etymological link between Phoibos and purification in pointing to an explicit reference in *Eumenides* 62.[23]

In pure tragedy, however, *miasma* is indelible. The intensity of pollution is the more apparent when it is the consequence of an involuntary act.[24] The two exemplary illustrations in tragedy of this overwhelming defect are the cases of Oedipus and Hercules, whose deeds in Parker's words engender "permanent stain".[25]

Oedipus Tyrannus may be called tragedy of *miasma*, since indelible pollution is the decisive experience of evil in the play, "King Phoebus bids us straitly extirpate / a fell pollution [*miasma*] that infests the land." Oedipus' question is not yet hopeless, but belongs to the same order, "*poioi katharmoi?*" ["with what cleansing",[26] my translation]. The prophecy suggests an apparently easy solution, "banishment or the shedding blood for blood", *fonoi fonon palin luontas* (96-101). Oedipus' offence is thus dirt, pollution, *musos* (138), which would be a "scandal ye should leave unpurged" (256).

The act of self-blinding following *anagnórisis* is not the washing away of defilement, but the bitter irony of a hero discovering and ac-

---

[22] Robert Parker describes pollution in Euripides as being already internalized and devoid of its sting, Cf. *Miasma, Pollution and Purification in Early Greek Religion*, Oxford: Clarendon, 1983, 310.
[23] *Ibid.*, 139.
[24] Cf. Parker, 317. The act of Oedipus in the *Oedipus Tyrannus* is more emphatically referred to as being involuntary by nature than in another play, the *Oedipus at Colonus*. The passage quoted by Parker is from the latter, "Pure by law, unknowing did I come to this" (548). This metadramatic treatment of Oedipus, however, reinstalls him in the status of the mythical hero by stripping him of the dramatic context and is heedless that in doing this perhaps it is losing sight of him in his role as a tragic hero.
[25] *Ibid.*, 317.
[26] The English translation here, "what expiation means he" lacks the essential meaning of the original, which is to purge, to cleanse. All references to Sophocles' plays are from the bilingual edition of the Loeb Classical Library, ed. and trans. Francis Storr, Cambridge, Mass. and London: Harvard University Press, 1962.

knowledging the uselessness of his aspirations before the mechanism of fate activated by the prophecy and his own curse.

The tragic phenomenon of permanent stain is specified as crucial in the *Seven Against Thebes*, "Death dealt thus one to other by two of one blood, of that pollution there is no growing old" says the Chorus referring to the duel between Eteokles and Polyneikes (681-82).[27] Oedipus' curse is in that way the indirect cause of *miasma*, both serving the fulfilment of fate, one through its ineluctability, the other through its indelibility. The hopelessness of the latter is emphasized by the rhetorical question, "who can wash away their stain, [*katharmos*]?" (738). Hopelessness in that sense is the dominant emotional state of pure tragedy. The mechanism of fate thus activates itself through the mechanism of curse and prophecy. It is within this scope of objective teleology that the mechanism of *kakos-for-kakos*, the dispensation of revenge can be understood.[28]

"Righteous? How not? To requite an enemy evil for evil", *ekhthron antameibesthai kakois,* says the Chorus leader in the *Libation-Bearers* (123), that is, to "take life for life" (121) is still justifiable in the second part of the trilogy. This mechanism of *kakos* sanctifies revenge, *timória*, which is murder, *phonos* prepared by Electra, committed by Orestes. The causal chain of the series of vengeances is interrupted by the anthropomorphic intervention of the gods in the *Eumenides*, where deities finally give up their indifference, which is necessitated by the phenomenon of debt rising to its structurally dominant role in Euripides.[29] This mechanism of owing, the paradox of divine debt replaces the dominance of *kakos* and represents the underlying structural basis of melodrama. At the same time let us bear in mind that outside the *Eumenides* the difference between divine will and the pre-ordinance of fate is maintained, since Orestes is persecuted by the Erynes (cf. *Iphigeneia in Taurica*).[30]

---

[27] All quotations from Aeschylus' plays are taken from the Loeb Classical Library, ed. and trans. Herbert Weir Smyth, Cambridge, Mass., and London: Harvard University Press, 1963.
[28] Here I am concerned with the mechanism of *kakos* in pure tragedy. Revenge may be fulfilled through the gods' collaboration: in melodrama.
[29] In the *Ion* the God Apollo has to answer for his impregnating Creusa, the plot closure is shaped by divine attenuation, the appeasement of conflict motivated by the debt of a previous interference.
[30] Hugh Lloyd-Jones is alert enough to recognize the double perspective of the closure in the *Eumenides*, Apollo's ceremony of purification is somewhat darkened by the fact that it still remains to appease the Erinyes. Cf. *The Justice of Zeus*, London: University of California Press, 1971, 77.

Reciprocated evil is also prevalent in *Electra*, testifying to the plot-governing force of the mechanism, "Vengeance for wrong", *amoibai kakon*, (1147) here too, refers to the righteous retaliation of Klutaimnestra, what is more, vengeance is here equated with justice, "the tide of justice [*dike*] whelmeth, refluent-roaring, / the wanton wife" (1155).

The human execution of revenge may be encouraged by the gods themselves, who as divine accomplices, create the context for due retaliation. Zeus and Hebe rejuvenate Iolaos to capacitate him to take his revenge on Eurustheus, *neos genestai kapotisasthai diken ekhthrous*. As a consequence of a miraculous transformation "from out that murky gloom / he flashed – a youth with mighty-moulded arms!" (848-55). This is the dramatic foregrounding of Eurusteus' fate, but owing to the unification of divine and human will, which is also the reconciliation of the subjective and the objective teleological sequences or in other words, to the divine justification of the subjective *telos*, what we get is the quenching of a melodramatic thirst for revenge and not tragic fulfilment.

In *The Madness of Hercules,* however, the revenge against King Lycus is tragic fulfilment, as it is only apparently the result of divine collaboration, *dika kai theon palirrous potmos* (736), the outcome of a process fostered by god's will. Lussa, goddess of madness destroys an impending melodramatic closure by restoring the dominance of differentiated teleology, the prerequisite of pure tragedy. D. J. Conacher deems the divine destruction unreasonable and attributes its arbitrariness to the mechanism of *tukhe*.[31] *Tukhe* is behind the random succession of events, which runs contrary to Aristotle's statement that "the elements should emerge from the very structure of the plot, so that they ensue from the preceding events by necessity or probability, *e anankaion e heikos*."[32] In the case of Hercules, however, it is the excessive glorification and idolization that is the cause of the intervention of the jealous gods: "else the gods must wane / and mortals wax, if he taste not her vengeance" (841-42). Here the proximate cause of massacre is divine *phthonos*, jealousy, to which I shall return later.

Tragic fulfilment is achieved by Aphrodite's revenge in *Hippolytos*. Here divine retribution is an example of the entire lack of melo-

---

[31] D. J. Conacher, *Euripidean Drama, Myth, Theme and Structure*, Toronto: University of Toronto Press, 1967, 17.
[32] Aristotle, *Poetics*, The Loeb Classical Library, ed. and trans. Stephen Halliwell, Cambridge, Mass. and London: Harvard University Press, 1995, 1452a.

dramatic collaboration and of a plot governed by a wicked, hostile God intervening theomorphically from an inconceivable distance. Divine intervention is always problematic, since it is at once the abridgement of a bottomless gulf and its reinforcement. Theomorphic intervention attests to the comprehensive tragic mode of divine existence, that of non-intervention in the subjective teleological direction. For human perspective therefore it is tragic insofar as it is theomorphic, autotelic and melodramatic insofar as it is merely (not just apparently) anthropomorphic, surrendering the generic claims of objective *telos*.

Propounding a possible interpretation of *kakos* and *miasma* cannot take place without a digression on the mechanism of revenge. This mechanism means the reciprocity of evil, the inevitability of righteous, *dikaios* retaliation. In a series of homicide plots joined together in myth we find the continuously recurring structuring principle of revenge, like in the sequence of murders attributed to the Agamemnon-Klutaimnestra-Orestes nomenclature. In tragedy reciprocity continues in an endless flow to dominate plot structure and when the chain is finally interrupted and brought to the impasse of the paradox of divine debt we also feel the impending erasure of the tragic. This structuring principle of returning evil also shows a crucial asymmetry between the deed and its tragic consequences that immeasurably surpass it in magnitude. I may even say that retribution is tragic only as far as it is asymmetric in intensity and weight. It is in this sense that one can claim that tragic retribution is inconceivable in ethical terms, that it is beyond good and evil, a primarily mechanic automation. If divine will is saturated in assisting the subjective *telos* to execute revenge, then retribution is merely a justification of human aspirations, the victory of the human claim for justice, and therefore its suitable genre is melodrama. If, on the other hand, divine will is not, or only apparently, the supporter of subjective *telos* but is primarily the representative of fate and objective *telos* indifferent to human endeavours, retribution becomes tragic fulfilment and the genre pure tragedy.

During the motion of the plot dominated by the mechanism of *kakos* we find an ever increasing spiritual disturbance in the hero, which is the growing sense of defilement, *miasma*. This symbolic pollution for Ricoeur is the most ancient state in the historical consciousness of evil, which he distinguishes from sin and guilt. According to the hermeneutics of the different confessions of evil preceding philosophical reflection, defilement lacks the element of divine imputation, initiative and is the result of the violation of a universal interdict.[33] The transition to the consciousness of sin nevertheless includes the complementary phenomena of reference to a divinity and personal contact.[34] These differentiating features of personal contact and imputation can be maintained only if together with Ricoeur we accept defilement as an all-embracing maid-of-all-work term also for the consciousness of evil in Greek tragedy. This presupposition, as it may be deduced from my investigations so far, fails to consider the extensive semantic variety allotted to *miasma* and also other forms of the tragic, like the already elaborated, most comprehensive and frequent *kakos* or *tolma*, *parabasia, adikema, sfalma, nosema, aitios*, etc. Oedipus' offence lacks the preceding context of personal contact, but following *anagnórisis* the sufferer imputes his misfortunes to the God, "Apollo, friends, Apollo, he it was / that brought these ills to pass" (1330-34). Both personal contact and divine imputation are present in the Oresteia. In the *Eumenides* Orestes reminds the jury of Apollo's personal command and divine incitement is to be the cause of his final acquittal. Here divine imputation and the personal incitement to matricide is involved in the melodramatic debt. Such a debt is to lead to non-tragic reconciliation.

A further distinctive feature of defilement for Ricoeur is its primordial connection with vengeance, "Vengeance and defilement is anterior even to the representation of an avenging God."[35] It is an "objective violation of a universal interdict" through which the violator discerns punishment in that which "falls on man in the guise of misfortune and transforms all possible sufferings, all diseases, all death, all failure into signs of defilement".[36] How are we to apply all this to the tragic hero?[37] The tragic hero is liable to detect signs of allotted retribution in the misfortunes and disasters he suffers, since in a hero's rise and fall nothing happens at random. He may consider his revalued afflictions as righteous and deserved in profound self-reflection, thus complying with human measures, he "with calm strength"[38] subordinates himself. At the same time he may deem them unjust and unde-

---

[33] Paul Ricoeur, *Symbolism of Evil*, 27.
[34] *Ibid.*, 47.
[35] *Ibid.*, 30.
[36] *Ibid.*, 27.
[37] It seems there remains a gap in the phenomenological account of the consciousness of defilement in Riceour's undertaking, namely its essential transformation in tragedy, where the crucial and constant interference of the gods endow it with new dimensions.
[38] Euripides, *Hippolytus*, 207.

served, thus daring beyond human measures, "too high for man / greater than mortal", *meidzó broteias homilias*,[39] he then distances himself from an unreasonable retribution.

The dominant modes of *kakos* and *miasma* thus lead us to a fundamental bifurcation within heroic response: the one self-subordination, the other self-distanciation. Both of these modes will currently recur in the analyses below.

Hamartia

In the process of the foundation on the *Nicomachean Ethics* of what I called the ethical schema, the concept of *hamartia* appeared first as generally embracing all actions of excess and deficiency. Later it has to undergo further qualifications when reconsidered in the classification of injuries. In introducing and differentiating three kinds of injury, Aristotle defines *hamartia* with its relation to concepts like *atychema* and *adikema*. Error committed in ignorance is *hamartema*, when the person affected or the act or the instrument or the result is other than expected. The wider sphere of the application of *hamartema* is then subdivided into the more specified areas of misadventure (or mischance), *atychema*, when the injury occurs contrary to reasonable expectation and culpable error, *hamartema*, this time to be understood in a restricted sense. Though not contrary to reasonable expectation, *hamartema* is committed without evil intent and one is culpable, because in such a case the cause of one's ignorance lies in oneself, in contrast with *atychema*, where the cause is external. The third form of injury does not belong to the category of action committed in ignorance, since it is done knowingly, though not deliberately. It is defined as an act of injustice or wrong, *adikema* (1135b).[40] For the present undertaking, needless to say, the subdivision of actions committed in

---

[39] *Ibid.*, 19.

[40] W. K. Wimsatt is one of the few authors who refers to this conceptual differentiation layed out in the *Ethics* and concludes that there is "a dubious and wavering relation between the term *hamartia* .... and the ideas of volition and responsibility". Though such intertextual cross-references, according to Wimsatt, may run contrary to objections made and inconsistently followed by G. F. Else, they are nonetheless encouraged by Aristotle's own dramatic allusions in the *Ethics*, as in the crucial passage quoted, "those injuries done in ignorance are mistakes (*hamartemata*) when the person acted on, the act, the instrument or the end that will be attained is other than the agent supposed .... The person may be the striker's father and the striker may know that it is a man or one of the persons present, but not know that it is his father" (V.8), cf. W. K. Wimsatt, *Hateful Contraries: Studies in Literature and Criticism*, Lexington: University of Kentucky Press, 1965, 82-83.

ignorance are of primary importance. It may be argued with some credit that when, in another crucial passage of the *Poetics,* Aristotle reintroduces the concept of *hamartia,* it is meant to include the very subdivisions of misadventure and culpable error.

In the *Poetics,* the well-structured plot describes the fall of the hero from prosperity to adversity due to some great error, *hamartia megale* (XIII). The error in tragedy should be great, *megale* enough since its consequences, namely the modes of misfortune, *dustychia,* are ineluctable, irreparable and moderated by no final compensation. Error is tragic inasmuch as it brings about an irredeemable state of affairs, an *Ausweglosigkeit,* to adopt Karl Jaspers' term. On the level of plot government *hamartia* is a principle that sets in motion a causally sequential stream of events labelled *peripeteia, anagnórisis* and last but not least, *katharsis,* the emotional transposition of objective response.

In the diverse scholarly interpretations of *hamartia,* however, there seems to be an apparent ambiguity concerning the possible moralization of the term. It is never clear on what functional basis the term *hamartia* is to be conceived, neither in cases when its moral significance is asserted, nor when it is disclaimed. There is no schematic context outlined, no point of view confirmed. Thus philologists such as Philip Whaley Harsh,[41] Cedric H. Whitman,[42] Lane Cooper[43] and others may claim indisputable moral significance to *hamartia* without foregrounding their schematic viewpoints. Generally speaking, when explained as moral fault, there is no readjustment offered as in the case of *hybris,* where if moralized, it is counterbalanced with moral retribution, *Nemesis. Hamartia* stands in isolation.[44] This isolation may be abridged with its reconsideration as a concept functioning within a larger whole represented by at least two vantage points, that of the hero to whom it is primarily ascribed and that of a metadramatic observation. The latter may be the exclusive prerogative of the audience, the reader, a theorist of drama, like Aristotle. In its ideal form

---

[41] Philip Whaley Harsh, "Hamartia Again", *TPAPA,* 76 (1945), 47-58.
[42] "Scholarship and Hamartia", in Cedric H. Whitman, *Sophocles: A Study in Heroic Humanism,* Cambridge, Massachusetts, 1951.
[43] Lane Cooper, "Hamartia Again and Again", *CJ,* 43 (1947), 39-40.
[44] Naomi Conn Liebler understands *hamartia* as misrecognition and links it to *anagnórisis,* cf. *Shakespeare's Festive Tragedy: The Ritual Foundations of the Genre,* London and New York: Routledge, 1995, 43. This view of tragic error, however, is rather restrictive and fails to account for instances not necessarily involving misrecognition, like the *hamartia* of Creon, Hippolytus, Phaidra, etc. discussed below.

metadramatic observation is the recognition of objective teleology and the mytho-schematic pattern of plot mechanism.

Aristotle's observation is at the same time ambiguous and therefore problematic. Stinton is right to point out the all-pervasive moral schema dominating Aristotle's analysis in the *Poetics*.[45] On the other hand, he also draws attention to a cardinal loss resulting from such an imposition of morals onto tragedy, "to omit the gods is to ignore a vital factor in Greek tragedy and must distort it."[46] This loss is the consequence of the entire lack of an adequate metadramatic observation, which includes myth, fate and the gods. The point of view from which *hamartia* is introduced in *Poetics 13* is restricted to that of the hero and the social dimension, in congruence with its treatment in the *Ethics*.

The hero of the *Nicomachean Ethics* is the moral being whose unmistaken choice of the mean renders him superior and exemplary. The difference is that the moral being is not culpable, he represents the absolute standard against which all culpability is measured, while the tragic hero is claimed to be culpable. What form does this culpability take in the *Poetics*? It is never clear whether the hero's fault is to be understood in the form of a culpable error, *hamartema* or a misadventure, *atychema*. As the two concepts in the *Ethics* represent the subdivisions of faulty deeds committed in ignorance, *hamartia and* as Aristotle in the *Poetics* does include this type of action in his list of the possible constructions of plot,[47] we may conclude that though the hero is liable to fault, yet it is tragic culpability based partly on ignorance. The problem is more important for us than for Aristotle that he is at this point using a concept that is ethically already overburdened in a schematically different context. In the *Ethics* the concept of *hamartia* was defined in relation to issues of responsibility and justice. There it belonged to involuntary actions and specifically stood for those committed in ignorance. *Hamartema*, then, was defined as an action without evil intent, not contrary to reasonable expectation, in case of which the cause of one's ignorance lies in oneself. If the cause lies outside, the action is merely misadventure, *atychema*. As a result of this preliminary distinction two alternatives for the explanation of Aristotle's meaning can be formulated. Either the tragic hero is responsible for his ignorance and consequently falls into adversity due

---

[45] T. C. W. Stinton, "Hamartia in Aristotle and Greek Tragedy", *CQ,* 25 (1975), 222.
[46] *Ibid.*, 254.
[47] *Poetics,* 1453b.

to his moral fault or rather, his error shows tragic culpability that questions his responsibility.[48] Instead of doing away with the equivocation, Aristotle seems content with prescribing the sequence of acts committed in ignorance, and recognition (1453b).

In the *Poetics* tragic error is not explicitly grasped as an ethical phenomenon, a mode of expressing moral culpability. The prescription of a rule and the consistent deduction of judgements from it is the basic structural determinant of both the *Ethics*, where the good is in complying with the rule of the mean *mesotes*, the moral *habitus* and the *Poetics*, where the good dramatist follows the prescribed plot-structuring method.[49] The real sense of *hamartia* is manifest in its role within the larger context of plot structuring rules. Consequently I may say with J. M. Bremer[50] that for Aristotle the significance of tragic error lies primarily in its role played as a component in plot mechanism.

Aristotle is concerned with the construction of the whole genre, the consistent, uninterrupted execution of a sequence of events. It is another question whether this purely technical approach can explain the essence and effect of tragedy. To speak with Svein Osterud, "tragedy has a metaphysical dimension to which Aristotle's psychological and technical study fails to do justice."[51] For the tragic hero, however, his irreparable error with all its consequences presents itself as a monstrous ethical problem, as it is blatantly obvious in most of the tragedies available. A brief architectonic survey of *Hippolytus* may be illuminating by virtue of its complex structure and extreme richness in the basic concepts partly discussed above.

Theseus' curse, *ara* which causes his son's death, is grounded upon a mistake, *hamartia*. The mistake itself is a consequence of another error, *hamartia*, namely that of Phaidra, which is manifest in the love she bears to her own son. The series of errors can be traced back to the original sin, Hippolytus' *hamartia*, since Phaidra's error is also

---

[48] For the problematic status of action and responsibility in Aristotle, see J. L. Ackrill, "Aristotle on Action", in *Essays on Plato and Aristotle*, Oxford: Clarendon, 1997.
[49] Several ambiguities of Aristotle's *Poetics,* as Brian Vickers rightly pointed out in *Towards Greek Tragedy*, London: Longman, 1979, 8, derive from the critical hesitance, whether its rules are to be considered as prescriptive or descriptive.
[50] J. M. Bremer, *Tragic Error in the Poetics of Aristotle and in Greek Tragedy*, Amsterdam: Adolf M. Hakkert, 1969, 61. *Hamartia* is not moral sin for John Jones, either, cf. *On Aristotle and Greek Tragedy*, London: Chatto & Windus, 1962, 15.
[51] Svein Osterud, "Hamartia in Aristotle and Greek Tragedy", *Symbolae Osloenses,* 51 (1976), 77.

a consequence of that crime. This first error, according to Aphrodite's *prologos,* is manifest in the blasphemous behaviour of Hippolytus who is "linked with companionship too high for man", meaning his exclusive adoration of Artemis. This is intolerable for a jealous God, "yet this I grudge not [*phthonó*], what is it to me? But his defiance of me will I avenge [*timoresomai*] upon Hippolytus this day" (18-23). The basic structure of the revenge tragedy is outlined already in the *prologos: hamartia-phthonos-timória,* that is, the hero's fault, the exclusive adoration of one God at the expense of the other brings about the jealousy, *phthonos* of the latter, which in turn will be the cause of all errors, until divine revenge is fulfilled. *Phthonos* is the governing principle that preserves the continuity of the series of errors to finally realize its own will through the mechanism of curse. In the case of Theseus and Phaidra the order of plot-structuring components is reversed, *phthonos* precedes *hamartia,* divine jealousy precedes the woman's love on the one hand, and the error of the falsely motivated curse, on the other. The disproportionate structural presence of *phthonos* and *hamartia* attests to the conspicuous inadequacy of ethical reflection, since for a whole series of tragic errors the jealous deity is responsible. Man finds himself the sufferer rather than the committer of his own fault.[52] In vain he tries to interpret the unfortunate proceedings in ethical terms, when even his own curse transcends his human competence.[53]

With the belated recognition of fault and the experience of its consequences the hero retrospectively assesses the course of events in their relation to divine will, which is also a mode of *anagnórisis.*[54] In the present case the promotor of recognition is Artemis, "well may men transgress when Gods are thrusting on / Thee too I charge, Hippolytus – hate not / Thy father: 'tis by fate, *moira* thou perishest" (1433-36). Here *phthonos* is equivalent to fate, its pre-ordinance is irrevocable even by Artemis. Consolation arriving with *deus ex machina* and the absolution of Theseus does not become melodramatic, since the tragic fulfilment remains intact, the supreme authority of fate introduced in the *prologos,* affirmed.

---

[52] Cf. Sophocles, *Oedipus at Colonus,* 266.

[53] According to the mechanism of curse, the personifier of the subjective *telos* achieves temporal self-transcendence by the short-term capacity to realize the operation of objective teleology. The realization is usually unconscious and temporal.

[54] For an interesting account of *hamartia,* as an act of misrecognition closely linked to *anagnórisis,* see N. C. Liebler, *Shakespeare's Festive Tragedy,* 43.

The manifold and emphasized insertion of the crucial element of *phthonos* in the architectonic construction of *Hippolytus* renders the plot-structuring priority of *hamartia* dubious. This phenomenon, the shift from human to divine responsibility characteristic of Euripides' plays, is the precursor of the mechanism of owing. This is the consequence of the Euripidean anthropomorphization of the gods, when the deity is presented as entangled in human expectations. They appear to be cornered by the human imperative to pay a debt.

Apart from the *phthonos-hamartia* relation discussed above, in what follows I shall consider the similarly important Sophoclean application of the *hybris-hamartia* relation. Antigone's tragic death is the indirect consequence of Creon's *hybris*. Teiresias the *mantis*, seer, the interpreter of divine omens, is also representative of sober judgement, the advocate of compliance with human measures. Due to his gift from Zeus, his exceptional ability to prophesy accurately, he is the embodiment of truth, envisages the fulfilment of fate. From this it follows that non-adherence to his warnings, ignoring his advice is pride, *hybris* in itself, the cause of tragic error, *hamartia*.

Both Oedipus' and Creon's error lies in the fact that they neglect or bagatellize the prophet's predictions and warnings:

> To err [hamartia] is common
> To all men, but the man who having erred
> Hugs not his errors, but repents and seeks
> The cure, is not a wastrel nor unwise

says Teiresias to Creon in *Antigone* (1025-26). The stubbornness implicit in the "hugging of errors", *aboulos*, refers, of course, to Creon's interdict. The obstinate insistence on the unconditional observance of his interdict is Creon's way of keeping to the exclusive programme of his subjective *telos* and simultaneously the categorical renunciation of the explicit imperative of the objective *telos*. This unreflecting adherence to an interdict superimposed upon divine law is Creon's tragic error committed out of *hybris*. Following the discarding of Teiresias, Creon finally recognizes the irredeemable with the assistance of the Chorus, but it is, as always, too late, "fate [*ananke*] is ill to fight" (1106). His retribution is Haimon's death, "evidence he with him bears 'gainst himself .... the guilt [*hamartia*] is his and his alone" (1259-62). However, the unfortunate victims, Antigone, Haimon and Eurudike bear witness to the disproportionate retaliation validating tragic fulfilment.

I have been considering the meaning of tragic error in its close relation with two organizing principles, divine jealousy on the one hand, and human pride, on the other. The respective architectonic descriptions of *Hippolytus* and *Antigone* have been illuminating in the sense that they prove the impossibility of attributing moral significance to tragic error. This is partly due to a surplus of divine initiation, partly to disproportionate retaliation. The consequences of actions triggered by fault are accumulated according to the pre-ordinance of fate and not to human aspirations. On the level of action, therefore concerning the outcome it is more problematic to outline the scope of the hero's responsibilty than it is on the level of pre-action, situation assessment and verbalized disposition. Pride, *hybris* at least partly denotes a pre-action state, a frequently occurring passive, mental-emotional inclination. Such a definition, needless to say, has to be underpinned by a survey of the prevalent interpretations of tragic pride.

Hybris

The identification of the term *hybris* and its comprehensive application for a wide range of inclinations and activities is a much debated issue. Due to the lack of its systematic consideration in the *Poetics*, we have to content ourselves with its non-generic presentations in Aristotle's other works.

In the *Rhetoric* it is included among the triad of slights, for "there are three kinds of slight [*oligória*]: disdain [*kataphronesis*], spitefulness [*epereasmos*] and insult [*hybris*]". Insult is to be understood as a slighting behaviour which "consists in causing injury or annoyance whereby the sufferer is disgraced, not to obtain any other advantage for oneself besides the performance of the act, but for one's own pleasure; for retaliation is not insult [*hybris*], but punishment [*timória*]". The basic characteristic of *hybris* as opposed to *timória* is dishonour, *atimia*, "one who dishonours another slights him."[55] Dishonour is made an explicit concomitant of insult on the one hand, while on the other hand righteous retaliation may be said implicitly to involve the opposite, namely the retaining of honour. According to David Cohen, being dishonoured requires vengeance, which is the only way of "eliminating or diminishing the stain".[56] His version of

---

[55] Aristotle, *Rhetoric* II, 3-6, 1378b. The Loeb Classical Library, trans. J. H. Freese, Cambridge, Mass. and London: Harvard University Press, 1967.
[56] David Cohen, "Sexuality, Violence and the Athenian Law of Hubris", *Greece & Rome*, XXXVI/2 (1991), 174. In the statement that *hybris* activated in the form of

dishonour, however, appears in a thematically restricted analysis focused on the field of sexual violence.

In Aristotle's *Politics hybris* is regarded as insolence and is defined together with malice as being the motive of all wrongdoing, *kakourgia*. In the passage on *hybris*, insolence and grand wickedness are attributed to those, who are "exceedingly beautiful or strong or nobly born or rich", whereas those belonging to the opposite extreme, those "exceedingly poor or weak" are inclined to turn to "malice and petty wickedness".[57] The avoidance of the two extremes for Aristotle is achieved as usual, through the mean. The advised quantity of wealth is the middle amount, *meson*, the possessing of which allows one to obey reason, *logos*.[58] In both works of Aristotle *hybris* is defined as either an insult or an insolence against another person, who as a consequence is dishonoured, slighted, disgraced. This interpretation itself may be interpreted as the taking up of *hybris* into the ethical schema through the mediating concept of dishonour. Remaining faithful to our previous discussions nevertheless, there arises the question of a mytho-schematic recapitulation of *hybris* and especially of its appearance in the tragic schema.

The adumbration of the mitigating term dishonour as a pretext to moralize *hybris* and discard its possible metaphysical interpretations stands in the forefront of an article by N. R. E. Fisher.[59] There the reliance on Aristotle's *Politics* is decisive: *hybris* is given a new meaning. It is elaborated in terms of social injustices, as the cause of civil wars and insulting treatment by those in power against their subjects.[60] The scope of *hybris* is restricted to the sphere of interpersonal relations and the ethico-schematic assessment. The conceptual limitation of the ethical schema prevails in the sphere of metaphysical relations encountered in the tragedies and Fisher ventures to valorize *hybris* within the offence-and-punishment (*hybris-nemesis*) pattern.

In the case of the *Persians*, claimed to be the only Greek tragedy fully founded upon *hybris*, the analysis falls short of grasping the es-

---

dishonour causes stain (*miasma, musos*) which may be eliminated, erased by the counteract of revenge, the conceptual relations between the pairs: *hybris* and *miasma, miasma* and *timoria* remain to be clarified.

[57] Aristotle, *Politics* IV, 5-12, 1295b. The Loeb Classical Library, trans. H. Rackham, Cambridge, Mass. and London: Harvard University Press, 1967.

[58] *Ibid.* The parallel with the rule of the mean, *mesotes* in the *Nicomachean Ethics* is conspicuous.

[59] N. R. E. Fisher, "Hybris and Dishonour I", *Greece & Rome* XXIII (1976), 77-192.

[60] *Ibid.*, 183.

sence of tragedy by recourse to what I may call the historical schema in the stead of the tragic. The offence of the Persians this way will be solely described in a detailed list of the total crimes of Xerxes against the Greeks.[61] Historical evaluation of historical events supersedes the understanding of the dramatic plot in terms of the governing force of myth. History animated in tragic plot is myth or mythicized history one may prefer to call it. There the actual historical events are reflected upon within the tripartite system of relations between man, God and fate. The comparison with Herodotus, regarding the question of *hybris,* lacks differentiation in context, the generic distinction between historiography and tragedy. In the latter the hero's defeat means not merely a lost war: Xerxes can be a tragic hero only because he is the victim of the gods.

The act of inflicting dishonour thus disfavours any allusions to gods as possible objects of disgrace and Fisher even goes so far as to claim that the attribution of moral force to *hybris* is legitimized by an unbroken tradition from Homer to Aristotle.[62] The existence of such a linearity may be doubted already from Homer, to whom the original meaning of *hybris* is ascribed by scholars like J. T. Hooker.[63] Hooker argues that originally *hybris* involved no moral condemnation, but merely meant "exuberant physical strength".[64] In Homer it was never applied as a pejorative term in itself, but only in association with other concepts, like the most frequent *atasthalos* (reckless folly).[65] It is with Hesiod that the concept of *hybris* is said to appear first in conflict with *dike* and in the laws of Solon we find the final objectification of *dike* on the one hand and the condemnation of *hybris* as something inherently wrong, on the other.[66] Solon's laws, however, as Hooker points out, treat *hybris* in the form of offence against an individual and the polis. Nomological registration of the concept therefore remains within the limits of interpersonal and social relations and encourages

---

[61]"Hybris and Dishonour II", 37-38. The concepts of *sophrosyne, ate, nemesis* are interpreted in their relation to *hybris* and thus form the basis of a consistent moral structure designed to explain tragic action.
[62]*Ibid.*, 32.
[63]Cf. J. T. Hooker, "The Original Meaning of Hybris".
[64]*Ibid.*, 125.
[65]*Ibid.*, 126. The absence of pejorative *hybris* was accompanied by the absence of the notion of justice or rather, what was later conceived in the term *dike*. *Dike* and *nomos* in Homer refered to the normally accepted conduct in the world of heroes, 127.
[66]*Ibid.*, 131.

critics like Fisher and MacDowell[67] to conclude that *hybris* is never essentially a religious term.

The general conclusion of disclaiming any religious connotations from *hybris* is the result of handling individual texts ripped from their immediate generic contexts. This lack of distinction in the diverse use of a concept in different genres is further accompanied by statistical reference, the argument that passages including *hybris* with reference to the gods and punishment are few in proportion.[68]

It follows from the above that a metaphysically oriented search for the identification of the concept of *hybris* should limit itself to the latter's generically more consistent presentations. It will consider its wide range of applications within Greek tragedy. The question here remains open whether in dealing with this diversity we may define a form of *hybris* as tragic pride, as a mode of mental-emotional inclination, as a disposition immediately preceding action. Pride defined this way may perhaps be separated from tragic error always already manifest in action. The lack of such a separation would lead us with Richmond Lattimore[69] to the categorical denial of *hybris* as a comprehensive technical term in Greek tragedy. The translation of the verb form of *hybris*, *hubridzó* depends on context and as it is pointed out by Lattimore, is extremely diverse. When not explicitly pride (*Bacchanals*, 247), the committing of *hybris* may refer to teasing or vexing (*Ajax*, 560, *Phoenician Maidens*, 620, E. *Electra*, 266, etc.); insolence (*Antigone*, 480); outrage (*Hippolytus*, 1073); insult, mockery (*Antigone*, 840, S. *Electra*, 881, E. *Orestes*, 1581), etc. The common denominator of these occurrences is the daring beyond human measures, which may either present itself in actions, when it shares the features of error or merely in expressed inclinations, mental dispositions, when it is no more than pride, arrogance, or boastfulness.

Through the partial differentiation between the scope of reference of the two basic concepts one may avoid such extreme conclusions as that of Lattimore. For him men are normally not in a position to commit *hybris* against the gods. The general verdict is based on J. E. Harry's similar but more specific remark, "Prometheus is not in a position to *hubridzein*" (to commit *hybris*).[70] In the case of *Prometheus*

---

[67] Douglas M. MacDowell, "Hybris in Athens", *Greece & Rome* XXIII (1976), 14-31.

[68] Cf. *Ibid.*, 22. MacDowell's concern with proportion in the case of Greek tragedies is hilarious in itself.

[69] Richmond Lattimore, *Story Patterns in Greek Tragedy*, University of London: The Athlone Press, 1964, 23.

[70] *Ibid.*, 24.

Bound it is quite clear that inaction does not also imply refraining from *hybris*. We are informed of the man-god's offence already in the *prologos*, the whole tragedy is nothing but the animation of its due consequences. The hero's afflictions and tortures are the revenge of God for the all-preceding *hybris* manifest in the violation of his will. In suffering this preceding *hybris* remains intact, it is maintained throughout as a dominant organizing principle. Prometheus remains obstinate and unyielding, "such is the proper style for the insolent to offer insult", *outos hubridzein tous hubridzontas khreon* (970).[71] The proper style for insult is in the original the reciprocation of *hybris* or *hybris* for *hybris*. This order of reciprocity expressed in the immovability of Prometheus, evokes the reciprocity of *kakos* discussed as a dominant structural element both in the *Libation-Bearers* and in Euripides' *Electra*. This Promethean immovability is pride in itself, his *khlide* according to Hermes' definition. *Khlide* thus stands for the reciprocity and prolongation of pride, cause of all suffering till the final mercy of Zeus in the second and lost part of the trilogy, *Prometheus Unbound*. A dominant feature of the *hybris*-for-*hybris* programme is also its allotted motive of necessity, *khreon*, which serves as an excuse for statue-rigid inflexibility.

Prometheus prolonged and constantly reaffirmed pride is expressed in the words, "I hate all the gods that received good at my hands and with ill [*kakos*] requite me wrongfully" (975-76). The situation assessment founded on the opposition of good and ill is the persistence of the ethico-schematic reflection based on the polarization of divine will. The distancing silence of Zeus on the other hand, proves the god's inflexible indifference towards the ethical schema and the unfathomable supremacy of his will in the *Prometheus Bound*.

The mode of the tragic in the play is therefore twofold *hybris*, the one preceding and causing suffering, the other maintained, reaffirmed in boastful arrogance, in spite of exposure and humiliation. The recourse to the ethical schema to purge himself clean before the gods also involves divine imputation. Thereby the God is held responsible for the limitless, undeserved pain. The useless insistence on the ethico-schematic reflection and the polarization of divine will brings about the obscuring of the previously clearly understood task, "my allotted doom I needs must bear as lightly as I may, knowing that the might of Necessity brooketh no resistance" (104-106). At this point Prometheus mytho-schematically speaking knows his place and lo-

---

[71] All quotations from Aeschylus' *Prometheus Bound* are taken from the Loeb edition.

cates himself in the hierarchy in self-identifying moderation. This balancing element of sobriety, *sophrosune*,[72] is gradually lost in resurging *hybris*.

From a comprehensive pantragic viewpoint it seems that the faulty deed, error, *hamartia*, is bordered by the preceding disposition of pride from one side and by an immediately following or even simultaneously unfolding sense of defilement on the other. I have discussed these occurrences in different contexts. In such cases the internal formation of *hybris* and *miasma* gives the hero greater freedom and therefore responsibility, than in the actual deed of *hamartia*, which from the moment of realization triggers the consecutive elements of plot structure, *peripeteia* and *anagnórisis*. The complete lack or the removal of pride and defilement, which we find in *Oedipus at Colonus,* at the same time brings about also the absence of tragic error thus shattering the construction of pure tragedy.

Oedipus at Colonus is a drama of consequence, where the recollections of earlier misfortunes and prolonged suffering substitutes the tragic. In other words, the tragic is only represented in memory, the reminiscence of an already experienced, suffered evil. The prolonged story of suffering that leads to glorification is the melodramatic plot structured on endurance instead of pride, which is the capacity of a soul matured in suffering, "for I am taught by suffering to endure, [*stergein*]" (7). The hope of the suppliant, *hiketes*, pleading for mercy on foreign land is to find reconciliation according to Apollo's promise (88). The dominant emotional register of tragedy, that of utter hopelessness is substituted by melodramatic hope, *elpis*. Moderate endurance and hope as non-tragic structural components are further complemented by the appeasable gods, Colonus is the realm of Eumenides (42) and Oedipus may "make atonement to the deities", *katharmos daimonón*, through sacrifice (465). Thus tragic fulfilment is rendered avoidable. Oedipus' defilement, the dominance of which was guaranteed by the wicked God in *Oedipus Tyrannus*, here loses power and significance, and becomes delible before appeasable gods.

In tragedies based on *hybris* nevertheless, the hero enters the scene already proud and immoderate. The *prologos* informs us of the already dominant presence of *hybris* either by reference to the past, to events leading up to the present or by projection into the future.

To conclude, the most significant forms of the tragic in Greek

---

[72]Knowing one's place is the avoidance of haughtiness, cf. M. P. Nilsson, *Greek Piety*, Oxford: Clarendon, 1951, 48.

tragedy crystallize around four modes: reciprocated evil, the (mechanism of *amoibai kakos*), indelible defilement (*miasma*), tragic error (*hamartia megale*) and unyielding pride (*hybris*). The four modes may then be further differentiated into states and actions. The analysis of the various forms of *hybris* led to the distinction between action on the one hand, and mental-emotional inclination or disposition preceding action on the other. The tragic hero's state is therefore characterized by two forms of disposition and consciousness, that of *hybris* and that of *miasma* respectively. The designators of self-consciousness border the sphere of action and remain isolated for the quest for individual responsibility. At the same time the consciousness of the hero also has a prehistory of action necessitated by fate securing the sound totality of myth.[73] What remains is to detect the common denominator of the modes of the tragic belonging to the sphere of action. Through induction we acquire an overwhelming tragic wisdom, something that could be formulated as the necessary failure of actions, where failure or being in the wrong is to be understood on the tragic schema. Individual action appears as incorporated in subjective teleology with no hope to reach beyond. Failure of action in this sense is what is common in reciprocal revenge, where retribution is cyclically predetermined; in committed *hybris,* when pride is manifested in misdeed; and also in a structurally, dramaturgically necessitated flaw, error, which situates the hero as insider in unforeseen extremities. In this decisive failure the hero appears as deprived from the capacity to perform in accordance with his status allotted in myth. The default of performance proves the unacceptability of the mytho-schematic self-location. It is through reflection on this status in tragedy that this insufficiency is dramatized. In drama the intolerability of such an insufficiency is finally elevated to its acknowledgement, when through death, the realization of mortality, the hero is reintegrated in myth in the posthumous reinforcement of proper self-location. This acknowledgement and the identification with the new mortal self is confirmed by the outsider's perspective. Outsider perspective conceives of the lowest level the hero represents within the tripartite hierarchy as the necessary consequence of an insurmountable defect in his being.

---

[73]Oedipus' defilement is preceded by murder and incest in myth, but in tragic temporality the sequence appears the reverse.

II. Modes of the Tragic in Shakespearean Drama

In the following sections I will argue for the dominance of the same concepts of tragedy in the Renaissance. The analysis follows the same route from ethics to drama, through the insertion of myth. The difficulty of attributing uniformity to a heterogeneity of ideas compels us to a selective recourse to some major writings. From this highly restricted selection I shall try to demarcate the prevalent ethical schema, against which theological and dramatic levels will be measured. Needless to say, their indubitable influence on Elizabethan tragedy – either in the sense of containment or subversion – is of crucial importance for the present undertaking.

The Elevation and Depreciation of Man

The Renaissance idea of the dignity of man was posed as unmistakable truth and displaced as untenable deceit in the same historical period. The former took shape due to the pervasive influence of Italian humanism on the Early-Renaissance philosophy of man. Pico della Mirandola's *Oration*[74] contains enthusiastic arguments for human dignity. Man is for him the "most fortunate of creatures", whose "rank which is his lot in the universal chain of Being" is a "rank to be envied by brutes and the stars and by minds beyond this world".[75] Man's position in the hierarchy of Being is a privileged one; he is exalted as the receiver of an exceptional lot. This lot in Pico is engendered by God himself in the majestic act of creation – "thou, constrained by no limits, in accordance with thine own free will, in whose hand We have placed thee, shalt ordain for thyself the limits of nature" – or further, "We have set thee at the world's center". This naively biased alloca-

---

[74] Pico della Mirandola, *Oration on the Dignity of Man,* trans. E. L. Forbes, in *The Renaissance Philosophy of Man*, eds Cassirer-Kristeller-Randall, Jr., Chicago, Illinois: University of Chicago Press, 1948, 223-54.
[75] *Ibid.*, 223.

tion of man in the world is the result of a highly selective reading of Genesis and thus inevitably leads to extreme conclusions. The dignity of man seems to coincide with his divine potential – "thou shalt have the power to degenerate into the lower forms of life, which are brutish" – but at the same time: "thou shalt have the power, out of thy soul's judgement, to be reborn into the higher forms, which are divine."[76] The idea of divine potential in the move from ontology to ethics portrays the exceptional lot as not something merely given, but mainly as something to be achieved, realized, consciously strived after. It becomes an ethical task to "tame the impulses of our passions with moral science by dispelling the darkness of reason with dialectic and by washing away the filth of ignorance and vice, cleanse our soul so that her passions may not rave at random".[77] The standard prescribed as rule for all virtues is the Aristotelian concept of the Mean, the avoidance of excess and deficiency in actions, the compliance with the idea of *meden agan,* nothing too much.[78]

The influence of the *Oration* is conspicuous in *A Fable About Man* written by the Spanish humanist, Juan Luis Vives.[79] The *Fable* expounds its contribution to the idolization of man in an allegorical framework, where the earth is presented as a great stage populated by humans and the gods are the audience sitting in their heavenly stalls and seats. The humans perform tragedies, comedies, satires, mimes and farces directed by Jupiter himself.[80] When Juno inaugurates the divine ceremony the human actors have already started acting and receive great applause from the gods, "the wisest of the gods answered that none was more praiseworthy than man and the father of the gods himself nodded his assent".[81] Through their acting the humans attain divine qualities and are no longer appraised as mortals, but merit the comparison with Jupiter himself. Man's mortality is brushed aside, annihilated through elevation, "man is divine and Jupiter-like, participating in the immortality of Jupiter himself, in his wisdom, prudence,

---

[76] *Ibid.,* 225.
[77] *Ibid.,* 229.
[78] Cf. *Ibid.,* 235. Moral philosophy for Pico is needed to acquire the means of complying with the *meden agan,* in a similar way as *gnothi seauton,* know thyself, is attained by the studying of natural philosophy.
[79] Juan Luis Vives, *A Fable About Man,* trans. Nancy Lenkeith, in *The Renaissance Philosophy of Man,* eds Cassirer-Kristeller-Randall, Jr.
[80] Cf. *Ibid.,* 387.
[81] *Ibid.,* 388.

memory .... "⁸² In fact, man so perfectly mimicks Jupiter that the gods themselves become confused in their desperate attempt to distinguish between them. In other words, man becomes divine by virtue of his unique capacity to imitate.

Vives' short allegorical extolling of man bears no explicit ethical consequences. Human action is good in itself; no standards or rules are needed. The resonance of Pico's exceptional lot seems to leave no place for the consequential moral concomitants, namely the observation of the Mean. Still, Vives' account on man's status opens up a new dimension of human activity, the sole privilege of human beings: mimesis. What this human activity is really about finds its detailed representation in Shakespearean drama, which animates the world itself as a theatre.

The Renaissance idolization of man is reflected on in *Hamlet:*

> What piece of work is a man, how noble in reason, how infinite in faculties, in form and moving how express and admirable, in action how like an angel, in apprehension how like a God: the beauty of the world, the paragon of animals
>
> (II.ii.303-307)[83]

The subversion of this image in the "quintessence of dust" at this point seems yet to be accounted for.

For the illustration of a completely different form of moral behaviour than that expounded in the *Oration* we may consider another influential text, that which combines statecraft with stagecraft, *The Prince* of Machiavelli.[84] *The Prince* as one of the possible readings of Hamlet himself, the Prince of Denmark, seems to merge both the ethical orientation of the *Oration* and the emphasis on acting in the *Fable*. The two planes of human endeavour are discussed in the context of statecraft in general and in the know-how of maintaining power in particular. The standard crystallizes around a restricted application of moral values in terms of various technicalities and strategies, which provide the means for the prince to stay in power. In this sense cruelty is justified if used well, "when employed once for all and one's safety depends on it and not persisted in but as far as possible turned to the

---

[82]*Ibid.*, 389.
[83]William Shakespeare, *Hamlet*, ed. Harold Jenkins, Arden edn., London and New York: Routledge, 1993.
[84]Niccolo Machiavelli, *The Prince*, trans. George Bull, Penguin Books, 1968.

good of one's subjects".[85] Moral philosophy and learning this time does not serve the acquisition of the due Mean, but instead a more pragmatic purpose, "if a prince wants to maintain his rule he must learn how not to be virtuous and to make use of this or not according to need".[86] In such an ethics limited to machinations of statecraft and evaluated solely from the perspective of power and authority, the undertaking of vices appears good if necessary for the defence of the state and justified by historical prognosis.[87] Defiance of good faith, of charity and religion are referred to as necessary dispensations applied in an implicit self-sacrifice on the altar of the state.[88] For the achievement of the latter the prince should develop in himself a character he may adjust to the changing circumstances. This constant need of alteration and adjustment lead to the necessary qualifications of appearance and pretension. For credible performance and behaviour the prince has to be a good actor in the first place, since "to those seeing and hearing him, he should appear a man of compassion, a man of good faith, a man of integrity, a kind and religious man...and there is nothing so important as to seem to have this last quality".[89] The priority of seeming is conceived of in a dialectic of truth and appearance, according to which the prince hides his ability to tell the hawk from the handsaw.[90]

If man was the centre of the world for Pico, we find in Machiavelli a similar treatment of the prince. With his power he should be capable of deciding which virtues bring harm and which vices bring prosperity in the long run. For such an enormous task the prince should also learn from his historical predecessors' failures and make use of those failures in his government. The ability to take advantage of the failures of others for his own interest requires judgement not only cunningly rendered but also irrevocable.[91] This irrevocable judgement elevates the prince to a superhuman status that holds fortune at bay by its capacity to immediately adapt itself to the changing requirements of time and circumstances. Elasticity of character complemented by skilful acting is the crucial factor that make a prince's

---

[85] *Ibid.*, 65.
[86] *Ibid.*, 91.
[87] Cf. *Ibid.*, 92.
[88] Cf. *Ibid.*, 101.
[89] *Ibid.*, 101.
[90] Cf. Hamlet: "I am but mad north-north-west. When the wind is southerly, I know a hawk from a handsaw" (II.ii.374-75).
[91] Cf. *Ibid.*, 102.

power unassailable even by fortune. The ethical preferences of such an idealized prince have been shown to be self-referential, in the sense that he alone decides what is good or evil and does so in sole reference to his power. On the other hand, the prince should preferably employ others in the necessary recourse to "unpopular measures". He needs to undertake only the acts of favour himself. It is the very procedure taken by Claudius in secretly commissioning the King of England to assassinate Hamlet ("Do it, England", IV.iii.68).

Alasdair MacIntyre rightly points out that the allotted place of moral values in Machiavelli is confined to technical rules for achieving political order and stability and regards this conception of ethics as the first representation in which the consequences of actions are prime determinants of moral judgement.[92] A strong ruler should be able to foresee the consequences of all possible actions and judge them in accurate reference to need. This potential superhuman capacity attributed to a prince in terms of judgement and choice, as well as appearance and pretension in credible acting are in line with the apotheosis of man we encountered in the *Oration* and *The Fable*. The exclusive range of potential in individual action takes the form of daring in tragedy, "I dare do all that may become a man, who dares do more, is none" (*Macbeth*, I.vii.46-47). At this point Lear's confusion about the real nature of man seems to be demanding further explanation, "Is man no more than this, consider him well" (III.iv.95).

Inherent deprivation

The frequent affirmations of doubt in Shakespearean tragedy concerning the idolization of man find their source in the dramatic transformation of mytho-schematic thought. The decisive alterations in theological doctrine due to the Reformation can hardly be claimed to be compatible with the localization of the human being in the universe as expounded in the texts considered above. In contemporary Protestant thinking, man's dignity failed to withstand theological scrutiny. It soon appeared dethroned and stripped of its sovereign characteristics by the new dogmatic emphasis on inherent deprivation and corrupt human nature.

In what follows I will look at the formation of inherent deprivation in Calvin's and Luther's teachings on original sin. The new mode of absolute sinfulness appears to substitute *felix culpa*, the fortunate fall, the dominating concept of sin in pre-tragic, medieval thought.

---

[92]Cf. Alasdair MacIntyre, *A Short History of Ethics*, London: Routledge, 1993, 128.

The generic differentiation of the two modes is all the more important, since it will provide us with the means of ascribing the essence of the tragic to Shakespearean tragedy. After the inductive conclusion of the necessary failure of action we arrived at in my brief survey of the basic Greek concepts, I will proceed in a deductive move towards the identification of the Shakespearean counterparts shown to be manifestations of the same.

Felix culpa and absolute sin

In positing inherent deprivation as the basic existential experience of the Shakespearean tragic hero, my analysis moved on to myth. Consequently, it is immediately confronted with the need for a schematic cross-reference, this time in relation to medieval thought. The ethical schema serving as obvious plot-structural basis in medieval moralities manifests itself in didactic representations of life programmes. According to these representations the moral of "how should one act" is confirmed through the plot of the "how one should not". Human frailties and follies are committed by man's free choice with amendable consequences. On this basis we can contest Chaucer's own ascription of the term tragedy to his *Troilus and Criseyde*.[93] Troilus' end is non-tragic, since he survives his own death, enters eternal bliss and condemns all "worldly vanitees". Death here is not fulfilment, but a means to perfection, the transcendence of the subjective teleological bias by the subject himself, who is endowed with such a capacity as a soul redeemed. Death void of finality is also means to convey the moral:

> Such fyn hath, lo, this Troilus for love,
> Such fyn hath all his greate worthinesse,
> Such fyn hath his estate royal above,
> Such fyn his lust, such fyn hath his noblesse,
> Such fyn hath false wordes brotelnesse [fickleness].
>
> (262)

The individuality of death is then extended to the generalized conception of the mortality of everything under the sun, "this world passeth sone as flowers faire" (263). The general moral conclusion thus takes the shape of an instructive warning, the reminder of death,

---

[93] "Go, little book; go, little myn tragedie", Geoffrey Chaucer, *Troilus and Criseyde*, ed. John Warrington, London, 1974, 256.

memento mori. By the representation of human indulgence in worldly vanities the essential futility of human indulgence in worldly vanities is brought to the fore. Such a didactic representation is motivated by the non-tragic preconception of final redemption.

In *Everyman* the conclusion to be arrived at is projected already in the prologue:

> I pray you give your audience,
> And hear this matter with reverence,
> By figure a moral play:
> The Summoning of Everyman called it is,
> That of our lives and ending shows
> How transitory we be all day.

To reach his deserved end Everyman is accompanied by Good Deeds, who in the temporary dominance of despair and hopelessness proves to be the only faithful collaborators in the acquisition of salvation. Temporality of existence in descent is finally transcended by eternity entered through the dramatic countermovement of ascent. Juxtaposition of rise to fall, however, is not a spontaneous form of plot closure. It is rather, the structural crystallisation of an ethically necessitated form of ascent. In moralities it is the ethical schema of the mediaeval Christian worldview that operates as fate in eliminating all uncertainties in a positive conclusion. In this sense Troilus may be said to become Everyman in the final acquisition of deliverance from the temporality of existence. Deliverance from temporality to eternity, from sin and indulgence to salvation is also deliverance from the tragic – to speak with Jaspers and Ricoeur – through the reinforcement of the ethic.

Plot-termination in ascent renders human guiltiness and moral descent fortunate in retrospect, since indulgence and immoderation appear as necessitating factors of human salvation.

The doctrine of the fortunate fall, the happy conscience convinced of redemption pervades Christian thought from Augustine to Karl Jaspers and as we have seen, is the underlying concept of sin in mediaeval moralities. The fall here appears as a necessary prerequisite of redemption, without which no salvation is possible. Karl Jaspers goes so far as to declare the incommensurability of all principal Christian experience with the tragic vision, "alle Grunderfahrungen des Menschen sind als christlich nicht mehr tragisch. Die Schuld wird zur felix culpa, die die Erlösung möglich macht." It is through the moralizing of sin, its integration into the symmetrical structure of descent and ascent, fall and rise, the patterns of crime and punishment that the ethical schema is generically valorized. In this sense Christian tragedy is deemed unthinkable, for tragic irreparability is granted untenable, "die eigene Erlösungmöglichkeit vernichtet die tragische Ausweglosigkeit. Daher gibt es keine eigentlich christliche Tragödie."[94] The Jaspersian treatment of *felix culpa* as a comprehensive formula for the Christian concept of sin nevertheless, has to face the crucial and decisive paradigmatic shift within the Christian worldview, that of the Protestant emphasis on original sin and the inherent corruption of human nature.

For Herbert Weisinger, the paradox of the fortunate fall is not only tenable in tragedy, but represents the key to our response deeply rooted in ancient myths and rituals. Through the fortunate fall of the hero we are enlightened and offered escape, thus tragedy is optimistic in its ultimate effect.[95] In the transposition of effectiveness from plot structure to outsider response the ultimately fortunate consequences of the fall are transferred to the surviving observer. Thus the element of effectual transposition itself proves the inaccessibility of pre-transposed tragic fulfilment.

The identification of tragic sin with *felix culpa* points to the perseverance of the ethical schema as a system of universally applicable formulae for tragedy. This form of retribution means merely punishment in justly allotted proportion. Symmetry and proportion, the basic components of morality are further complemented by the benevolent God of the elect, the bringer of final redemption. It is in a shift of emphasis from the notion of *felix culpa* to the utter corruption of human nature, however, and from the benevolent God of the elect to the incomprehensible,[96] hidden God of the reprobate, that a sense of the tragic disproportion will be recapitulated in the Christian consciousness, "Before we behold the light of the sun we are in God's sight defiled and polluted" says Calvin in his *Institutes*.[97] According to infralapsarian Calvinist doctrine man is predestined after the fall to eternal

---

[94]Karl Jaspers: "Vollendung der Wahrheit", in *Tragik und Tragödie*, herausgegeben von Volkmar Sander, Darmstadt, 1971, 12.
[95]Herbert Weisinger, *Tragedy and the Paradox of the Fortunate Fall*, London: Routledge and Kegan Paul, 1953, 229.
[96]"There is nothing left for us to do but to be amazed at the incomprehesible mind of God", in Calvin, *Commentaries*, trans. & ed. Joseph Haroutunian and Louise Pettibone Smith, London: SCM Press Ltd., 1958, XXIII, 298.
[97]II. i. 5.

perdition if he is not among the elect.[98] The uncertainty of allotment renders the form of judgement asymmetrical in religious consciousness, since man has to face eternal reprobation for one man's sin.[99]

It is the overwhelming determination of human nature by original sin that is emphasized in Calvin's words:

> let it stand therefore, as an indubitable truth, which no engines can shake that the mind of man is so entirely alienated from the righteousness of God that he cannot conceive, desire or design anything but what is wicked, distorted, foul, impure and iniquitous; that his heart is so thoroughly envenomed by sin, that it can breathe out nothing but corruption and rottenness; that if some men occasionally make a show of goodness, their mind is ever interwoven with hypocrisy and deceit, their soul inwardly bound with the fetters of wickedness.[100]

What Jaspers and Ricoeur in their respective analyses of Greek tragedy call the guiltiness of being is strongly highlighted in the paragraphs cited above on inherent deprivation. Inherent deprivation, absolute sinfulness and corrupted nature shatter the grounds of ethical autonomy and create the human predisposition to necessary culpability, the inevitable dominance of immanent evil. Human inclination to evil is necessary from the commitment of original sin according to Calvin,[101] which is also what Luther says of the incapability of man to do good in his works. The impasse of action as such is the point of frustration for a dramatic hero predestined to act in a pre-established situation. It is the case of Hamlet, the victim of necessary though procrastinated action.

The extreme situation of the tragic hero testifies to the untenableness of the concept of *felix culpa* in a paradigmatic shift of theological doctrine. Tragedy describes the plot of reflected confrontation with

---

[98] Calvinism and the notion of an incomprehensible and unappeasable God, the *Deus absconditus* are claimed to dominate religious doctrine in Elizabethan and Jacobean periods by W. R. Elton, *King Lear and the Gods*, California: The Huntington Library, 1966, 9, and John Stachniewsky, *The Persecutory Imagination*, Oxford: Clarendon Press, 1991.

[99] Cf. *Commentaries*, 294, "since in Adam all are sinners, deserving of eternal death, it is obvious that nothing but sin will be found in men."

[100] John Calvin, *Institutes of the Christian Religion*, trans. Henry Beveridge, London: Clarke, 1962, II. v. 19.

[101] *Ibid.*, II. ii. 12.

evil as presented in the new myth of absolute sin, with the possibility of reprobation in the uncertainty of election.[102]

Tragic Ambiguity

Reflected confrontation in Shakespearean tragedy expresses an all-embracing ambiguity concerning the individual awareness of good and evil. Action is necessitated by predestining forces deceiving the hero by the apparent confirmation of subjective *telos*. The despair gradually enveloping the hero is the consequence of an anachronistic application of the ethical schema in the world of the new myth, where the tragic is reaffirmed in the categorical condemnation of man's deeds. What he does cannot lead to any good; failure is encoded in the germ of activity. Through his reflection the ethical impasse of vacillation is adumbrated, thrown into relief. What is more, in the course of the undertaking, this self-paralysing hesitation is confirmed as the only ethically justifiable behaviour. Predestination to fall in drama, in necessitated action, becomes conspicuous in the unpredictable causal chain of events after heroic hesitation.

In *Hamlet* we find the hero triply paralysed: as moral and social being, and as son. However, he is compelled to act in accordance with the requirements of revenge tragedies. These requirements date back to Ovid's apparent justification of human revenge, since Astraea, goddess of justice deserted the earth.[103] It is thus the absence of divine justice that authorizes man to take revenge into his own hands:

> Though on this earth justice will not be found
> I'll down to hell and in this passion
> Knock at the dismal gates of Pluto's court
> Getting by force, as once Alcides did,
> A troop of Furies and tormenting hags
> To torture Don Lorenzo and the rest.

This is Hieronimo in Kyd's *Spanish Tragedy* (III.xiii.106-12).[104]

---

[102]"What proof have you of your election? When once this thought has taken possession of any individual it keeps him perpetually miserable, subjects him to dire torment or throws him into a state of complete stupor", cf. *Institutes*, III. xxiv. 4.

[103]Cf. *Metamorphoses*, trans. Frank Justus Miller, London: Heinemann, 1916, I, 149-150.

[104]See also, "for justice is exiled from the earth", *Spanish tragedy*, London: Methuen, 1969, III.13.140.

The proceedings are constantly interpreted in their subordination to the inexorable completion of human justice by Revenge itself. Revenge as commentator and Chorus presents the drama of just revenge to the victim, Don Andrea.[105]

Kyd's drama is a didactic precursor of *Hamlet*. In the Shakespearean play the personal vocation and scope for retribution is questioned in a complex structure of prolonged self-reflection. The ethical endeavour of "what shall I do" becomes the ontological quest of "who am I" as with Oedipus and the final acknowledgement of cowardice inflicted by a conscience heavily burdened with uncertainty of what is to come. The nature of human will as puzzled and servile appears here as a decisive factor of indecision. The rottenness of Denmark presents itself to the hero as a pre-established situation he is predestined to adjust himself to in necessitated action. The Father is dead and a Freudian-Lacanian reading would extend the precondition to the death of God, which may add to the comprehensive moral confusion, the ambiguity of good and evil. In the void of divine justice Hamlet places the human drives of honour in the execution of revenge. Good becomes incarnate in the self-surrendering obedience to the command, while evil is made explicit in the increasing self-rebuke for verbose idleness, the feminine unpacking of the heart with words. It is again in the final outcome, the restoration of the dominance of objective teleology and disproportionate human retribution, that the pre-action state of hesitation and the tragic ambiguity of good and evil is confirmed.

The self-rebuke for feminine vacillation is present in Macbeth's "I dare do all that may become a man, who dares do more is none". Deed here is not revenge, but murder stimulated by ambition. For Macbeth action takes place in the pre-established amoral context of "fair is foul, foul is fair". He is initiated into a form of speech by chthonic deities, ministers of fate that teach him temporary clairvoyance explicit in his hesitant reflection: "nothing is but what is not". Still, action is a necessary execution of one-dimensional proceedings, where heroic endeavour triggers on the unforeseen events of ultimate recognition and death. In recognition Macbeth experiences the what is not to be, i. e., reality obscured by the "supernatural soliciting" that

---

[105] In revenge tragedies the apparent justification by tradition of human justice and subjective *telos,* however does not necessarily create melodrama, since the execution of revenge in tragedy involves also the death of the executor and an unforeseen massacre of innocent victims. The objective teleology of revenge tragedies present the necessarily disproportionate human retribution.

"cannot be ill, cannot be good" (I.iii.130-31).[106] In death Macbeth learns the necessity of annihilation before the what is not. The "not of woman born" exists and metes out punishment, the fulfilment of objective *telos*.

Hamlet's dead God and Macbeth's deception by preternatural forces are causes of ethical and ontological ambiguities, as is old age in *King Lear*. The confines of Nature in the old king appear as the determinant factor in plot structure. Nature presents itself as fate, generating rashness and folly and bringing about irredeemable consequences. For Gloucester, on the other hand, self-excuse for ageing consciousness is achieved through imputation to the "late eclipses in the sun and moon", when "nature itself finds itself scourged by the sequent effects" (I.ii.96-97). The depiction of Nature as confined and scourged at the same time seems to surpass the actuality of individual imputation. It carries with it a universality exceeding temporality by virtue of pointing to the beyond. What gives credit to Gloucester's apocalyptic vision despite the "excellent foppery" is the already partially realized events it discloses. The blatant parallelisms in Lear's and Gloucester's break in familial and authorial relations give the crisis universal significance, where the beyond transcends subjective orientation and judgement. The disclosure of partially realized unfortunate occurrences is put forward in a threatening generalisation, which in this sense resembles the mechanism of curse by surpassing particularity and actual context.

Nature in Lear is already bursting its seams when the kingdom is divided. The king descends into the realm of "poor naked wretches" by dethroning and profaning himself. This is at the same time the route to self-perfection, the better understanding of his nature. Nature confined descends in rashness to find and master itself in itself, that is, as devoid of roles, imposed authoritative factors. Through scrutinising the "thing itself", a higher understanding of the self veiled by authority is achieved in the ironic "I am the king himself". This new, ripe nature which integrates the self void of borrowed robes is also conscious of the confines of kingship:

> GLOUCESTER: O, let me kiss that hand.
> LEAR: Let me wipe it first; it smells of mortality.
>
> (IV.v.127-28)

---

[106] It is the basic function of Greek oracles to show the future to the applicant without supplying him with the capacity of true understanding.

The acquisition of real nature by the guidance of the Fool and Edgar is also the prerequisite of a better understanding of good and evil. It is the acknowledgement of folly in the plea for forgiveness, "forget and forgive, I am old and foolish" (IV.vi.77). In Nahum Tate's melodramatic version the attained clairvoyance of good and evil would be the ultimate moral of a drama in which suffering is the means to forgiveness. Here, however, belated understanding is attained at the expense of a tragic closure involving disproportionate destruction. Recognition brings only short-term knowledge of ethical importance, whereas the absence of the promised end re-establishes the tragic ambiguity of good and evil.

The placing of the Shakespearean hero in a world he did not choose, and the signs of his inherent deprivation prove the interrelatedness of the new theological myth with dramaturgy. The equivocation of ethical terms discussed above will now be complemented by an outline of the basic tragic modes of sin in Shakespeare.

Tragic folly in King Lear

The basic mode of sin in *King Lear* is the folly mentioned above, which is blunder, mistake or error in the Aristotelian sense.[107] The plot of descent starts "when majesty falls to folly" (I.i.147)[108] and thereby mistakes love for verbose ambition. The narcissistic preference for sycophant rhetoric overlooks the presence of true love in silence. Cordelia's "nothing" articulates this presence in the only available form: negation. This persistent negation represents the authenticity of meaning in contaminated language. Lear's understanding of authenticity nevertheless, is blurred due to his "hideous rashness" (149), the obstacle to sober judgement. Clear-sighted judgement is to be attained through the self-surrendering accomplishment of ripeness. Lear's development[109] is therefore from rashness to ripeness, which incorporates and also surpasses the from-folly-to-forgiveness pattern. The act

---

[107] For a possible distinction between *hamartia* and the Christian concept of original sin, see Dietrich Mack, "Die Schuldtheorie", in *Ansichten zum tragischen und zur Tragödie*, Munich: Wilhelm Fink Verlag, 1970.
[108] William Shakespeare, *King Lear*, ed. Kenneth Muir, Arden edn., London and New York: Routledge, 1975.
[109] Lear's metamorphosis involves the acquisition of authenticity or true identity (to which I shall return to later) and is in this sense development, not decadence as L. L. Schücking would have it in "Character and Action", in *Shakespeare: The Tragedies*, ed. Clifford Leech, Chicago and London: University of Chicago Press, 1965, 66.

of surpassing is granted by Edgar's mediation, "men must endure / Their going hence even as their coming hither" (V.ii.9-10). The subplot gains primacy in inserting the element of surpassing, the going beyond, the exceeding of the moral pattern by that of the mortal. In the metamorphosed state of learned temperance, calm endurance and acquired ripeness, as is the case with Gloucester, we find the final reconciliation with death instead of premature suicide. Reconciliation is rendered through subordination, the ultimate renunciation of suicide, the surrendering of subjective *telos* to the acceptance of finitude. The route from blind nature to purged nature is the subject's personal maturation. Dotage presents itself dramaturgically as the working of fate and as such, brings death to palpable closeness. The death of an old man in itself is not tragic. There is also an additional loss that presents itself as irreparable, as for instance, the premature, unexpected death of an idolized daughter.

Edgar, the mediator of the move of surpassing, is the closest observer of nature, its privileged knower. As minister of fate he evades and metes out deaths, he is a psychiatrist and an assassin, curer and deceiver. He deceives to cure while remaining the impersonal, distanced "thing itself". As initiator into the gnosis of ripeness he also violates the symmetrical pattern of the forgiveness of folly to reinforce tragic fulfilment.

Beside the roles of observer and initiator into *gnosis*, Edgar also has to fulfil the role of the Fool, which is the role of substitution of madness for the Fool's untimely sobriety. Lear's gradually self-engulfing madness is counterpointed with the reverse transformation of the Fool. As co-sufferer, the Fool seems to take on a more definite human shape and a seriousness more adequate to the change of context. The contrasting coexistence of wisdom and folly represented until the hovel scene by the Fool and Lear respectively, would then be annulled without the amending appearance of Poor Tom. Poor Tom is Edgar disguised in nakedness. Lear is further initiated into the recognition of his real (mortal) nature which is then revealed beneath the guise of borrowed robes. Edgar thus takes over the role of the Fool, when the Fool himself succumbs to the afflictions and retreats from the act of initiation to the passive endurance of torments. He reveals his own state of increasing sobriety and disillusion in his situation assessment, "this cold night will turn us all to fools and madmen" (III.iv.73). The statement of becoming a fool is a self-cancelling utterance. As later, in the same way, Lear's statement "I'm old and foolish" testifies to the elimination of foolishness through the understanding of true nature.

The switch of roles in the hovel is therefore fundamental in the transition from descent in rashness to ascent in ripeness. From the point of beholding the "thing itself" Lear can hardly be identified with himself, since identity itself is rendered dubious. It is the dramatic unfolding of a previously impending disintegration of selfhood:

> LEAR: Does anyone here know me? This is not Lear.
> Does Lear walk thus? Speak thus? Where are his eyes? ....
> Who is it that can tell me who I am?
> FOOL: Lear's shadow.
>
> (I.iv.199-204)

At this point, however, Lear's rhetorical questioning seeking support against an unmerited belittling of his authority remains within the constraints of undisturbed self-definition. The shadow-identity projected by the Fool is not yet realized in its fully existential significance. The effects of the previous rash deed penetrate deeper than consciousness, which therefore has to go through a process of violent maturation to achieve better understanding.

Lear's gradually transformed consciousness and lost sense of identity is paralleled by that of Gloucester. Gloucester appears as already learned in ripeness when they meet in Dover. Edgar's presence at the scene is justified by his exceptional role of the initiator-mediator, the privileged knower of self-identity. He is not only a passive observer, since he knows the password, "sweet marjoram". The knowing of the password and its acceptance by Lear ("pass") is the confirmation of a kinship, which explicitly manifests itself in maturity and understanding acquired in madness. The statement of maturity is the revelation and confession of true nature, "they told me I was everything; 'tis a lie, I am not ague-proof" (IV.v.102).

The scenes of forgiveness and recognition are, as it may be concluded from the above, dramaturgically surpassed by the final scenes of tragic fulfilment. The sequence of events proceeding along the passage from folly to forgiveness are, in the outcome, presented as being subsumed, incorporated in a larger context of transformed nature. In Lear's case subsumption is, however, dramaturgical in the sense that it exceeds subjective aspirations to validate objective necessity. In the perspective of objective *telos*, predestined fall, the applicability of the concept of ripeness is questioned. Ripeness is not perfection but the acknowledgement of imperfection and mortality. This interpretation of ripeness as something achieved through learning to accept death renders Gloucester's death non-tragic. Lear's ripeness on the other hand, has to be itself surpassed by another's unripe, premature death, which finally forces him to learn through experience the tragic unacceptability of death.

Defilement and pride in Macbeth

Lady Macbeth's incitement to murder is carried through by masculine decidedness. The plea for *unsexing* is acknowledgement of the limits of female nature impeding homicide, "that no compunctious visitings of Nature / Shake my fell purpose" (I.v.45-46). It is the taking up of the role of a man that guarantees the capability of action. Still, it seems, nature returns to claim her rights after the deed, causing extreme nervous agitation. Repressed nature reactivates itself in somnambulism, which is defined as a "great perturbation in nature" (V.i.9). Perturbation suffered through unsexing is the violation also of the self by the premature undertaking of the role. Here somnambulism is the context for the belated restoration of real nature, in the same way as madness for Lear was the means for clairvoyance and better understanding. In both cases, with regard to action, recognition comes too late and the triggered events are beyond control. The perturbed soul's tortures are expressed in the register of defilement:

> Out, damned spot!, out, I say .... what need we fear who knows it, when none can call our power to accompt? – Yet who would have thought the old man to have had so much blood in him?
> (V.i.33-38)

The stain is indelible, "will these hands ne'er be clean?", "all the perfumes of Arabia will not sweeten this little hand" (41, 48).[110] It is symbolic defilement the physician cannot cure. On the contrary, the

---

[110] The metaphor of pollution and delibility is a recuring element in the sonnets. Cf. *Sonnet 35*: "Clouds and eclipses stain both moon and sun" or *Sonnet 109*: "Like him that travels I return again, / Just to the time, not with the time exchanged, / So that myself bring water for my stain; / Never believe, though in my nature reigned / All frailties that besiege all kinds of blood, / That it could so preposterously be stained, / To leave for nothing all thy sum of good ... " Needless to say, in *Sonnet 35* the pattern is more notably tragic by virtue of an overwhelming, suprahuman determinism (Cf. the last the line of *Sonnet 30*), whereas in *Sonnet 109* delibility offers amends for a regretted stain. William Shakespeare, *Sonnets*, ed. Katherine Duncan-Jones, Arden edn., London: Thomas Nelson and Sons Ltd., 1997.

defilement is the cure, in the same way as Lear's madness is symbolic and self-revealing. The cure itself is not the full recovery of self and real nature for life, but the late recognition of truth before death.[111]

Defilement in *Macbeth* is closely related to pride manifest in the scenes of incitement and confirmation of masculinity, the last and most decisive step to final commitment. Macbeth is daring beyond human measures in his "I dare do all that may become a man". This might be a sequel to the daring of the "unsex me here" beyond human nature. Abandoned womanhood on the one hand, is matched on the other with asserted manhood that appears as the unscrupulous realization of "vaulting ambition", the mode of subjective *telos* motivated by pride. The daring beyond is the tragic necessitation represented by chthonic forces, of transcending the human measures of morality. In the further scenes of the approaching end, already King, Macbeth's daring is reaffirmed in the self-idolizing "I cannot taint with fear". This is the articulation of pride in illusory foreknowledge. The late recognition sheds light on this seeming certainty and restores the dominant tragic key of despair and hopelessness.

If, on the one hand, defilement is contextualized in somnambulism, where true nature activates itself in what seems as its losing, in the disease of the soul and the mind; pride, on the other hand, is to be found in the general discord in nature depicting the post-action period, when nature runs riot and turns against itself. The poetic extension of discord is the simultaneous displacement and transcendence of human evil.[112]

Pride and revenge in Hamlet

"Strange and monstrous are the longings of our pride", says Calvin.[113] For Calvinism pride is the primal sin, as for Augustine, the first disobedience that transformed freedom into necessity.[114] It brings about the necessary coexistence of evil with human works and inclinations. In tragedy nevertheless, the moralizing of the concept of pride is prob-

---

[111] The origins of defilement is made clearer in a more explicitly Christian tragedy. In the torments of his attempt at prayer, Claudius bursts out in the futile pleading of "is there not rain enough in the sweet heavens / To wash it white as snow?" Washing equals repentance, in what follows as futility turns into despair: "try what repentance can. What can it not? / Yet what can it, when one cannot repent?" (III.iii.45-46, 65-66).
[112] Consider the passage: "A falcon, towering in her pride of place", etc. (II.iv.12).
[113] *Institutes*, II.iii.9.
[114] *Ibid.*, II.iii.5.

lematic, since there is also the even more striking coexistence of evil with the ministers of fate. The latter necessitate action before the hero's individual assent inspired by pride. The difference between pride and error, laid down as a decisive feature of the construction of plots in Greek tragedies, seems to be present in the dramatic structure of *Hamlet*, too. There it presents itself in the verbalized mental-emotional disposition preceding assent and the assent itself. Through assent the predestined tragic error triggers the automatism. The former, the actual heroic disposition is made explicit in heroic reflection, in the context of confession.

Hamlet has more self-knowledge than Macbeth.[115] Macbeth is better known by another, Lady Macbeth, who fears her husband's real nature: "too full o' th' milk of human kindness." Hamlet's self-criticism – "I am very proud, revengeful, ambitious" – is problematic in the sense that the very act of the acknowledgement of pride is also its abatement.[116] In the course of events, however, there is pride involved in Hamlet's contempt for everyone apart from Horatio and young Fortinbras. These are exceptions, since they are "not passion's slaves", but representatives of honour. Hamlet's is a pride explicitly denied, implicitly confirmed.

Pride and contempt are in *Hamlet* closely related to the following of the command. Being elected for revenge entails ascent from the crowd and necessitated action as member. Here we find the workings of the mechanism of evil in revenge, the reciprocity of evil for evil:

> Does it not, think thee, stand me now upon –
> He that hath kill'd my king and whor'd my mother,
> Popp'd in between th' election and my hopes,
> Thrown out his angle for my proper life
> And with such coz'nage – is't not perfect conscience
> To quit him with this arm? And is it not to be damn'd
> To let this canker of our nature come
> In further evil?
>
> (V.ii.63-70)[117]

---

[115] The central status of self-knowledge in the tragic experience is confirmed by critics such as Nicholas Grene, see his comments to Lear's self-knowledge (I.i.293) in his *Shakespeare's Tragic Imagination*, London: Macmillan, 1992, 157.
[116] The opposite is asserted in Lear's statement, "I am more sinned against than sinning", which is in itself sin, sin of pride.
[117] The principle of action evoked here bears striking resemblances with Claudius' aspirations: "revenge should have no bounds" (IV.vii.127). The "canker of our nature" refers to Claudius' inherent deprivation, cf. Arden fn. 398.

The originally burdened conscience of uncertainty is modified to what is here presented as perfect conscience, which is not relieved conscience, but rather, the understanding and acknowledging of necessary retribution. Action is also motivated by pride implicit in the premature conviction of being chosen and in the all-embracing contempt maintained even in massacre. The course of events triggered by the murder of Polonius adjusts itself the automatism of evil for evil, which proceeds beyond control and encompasses the act of perfect conscience. Evil here is transcended by the tragic automatism of revenge[118], which involves the death of the revenger, the revenger's tragedy. Hamlet's death itself, the non-distanced death among the crowd proves the ethically indifferent character of the reciprocity of evil.

The interruption of the reciprocal continuity of evil generally speaking, may occur through the insertion of good. In pure tragedy this nevertheless, cannot serve as a substitute for the plot-governing principle. If the good appears it is in disguise,[119] subjected to the teleology of pretence:

> Tell them that God bids us do good for evil:
> And thus I clothe my naked villainy
> With odd old ends stol'n forth of Holy Writ,
> And seem a saint, when most I play the devil
>
> (*Richard the Third*, I.iii.335-38)

Seeming is part of a scheme of destruction, in the shaping of which the transparent mask of goodness serves as the heightening of an effect, namely that of the final reinforcement of evil. At this point revenge loses personal dimension maintained throughout in *Titus Andronicus* and motivating flavour, ascribed to it in *Coriolanus*.[120]

---

[118]"How all occasions inform against me, / And spur my dull revenge" (IV.iv.32-33).

[119]Or too late as in case of Edmund, who might "perchance do good" (V.iii.192), though his orders for assassination in prison have already been partly carried out.

[120]Reinforcement of evil in revenge appears in its highest intensity when revenge itself seems to turn against the executor, cf. *Richard the Third*, "Then fly. What, from myself? Great reason why, Lest I revenge? What, myself upon myself?" (V.iii.186-87, ed. Antony Hammond, Arden edn., London and New York: Routledge, 1981). Revenge is impersonated in *Titus Andronicus*, "I am revenge .... " (V.ii.30, ed. Jonathan Bate, Arden edn., London and New York: Routledge, 1995). In the latter case and in Coriolanus' "sweet revenge", however, there is no explicit split between revenge and revenger (V.iii.45, ed. Philip Brockbank, Arden edn., London and N.Y.: Routledge, 1990).

The generic incompatibility of good and evil is emphasized in the tragic wisdom of Antony in the *Julius Caesar*, "the evil that men do lives after them; / The good is often interred with their bones" (III.ii.77-78). Buried good is resurrected in the crafty rhetoric of the orator who revitalises communal memory to "spur his revenge". The reanimation of good therefore is also its second erasure, this time in its artful subordination to the servile role of effecting revenge. Finally, what we get is the retrospective confirmation of Calpurnia's prophesying dream that locates evil in a metaphysical order of magnitude, "for warnings and portents and evils imminent" (II.ii.81).

Sin in revenge tragedies, as we have seen, cannot be understood as the unscrupulous reciprocating of evil. It is not simply the triggering of the automatism. Evil, on the contrary, appears as already reciprocated, always cyclically returning. The tragic continuity shows the dramatic operation of the doctrine of inherent deprivation contextualized in the new theological myth. The concepts of absolute sinfulness and corrupted nature dominate the plots of reflected confrontation, in ways outlined above. In the new theological myth man is first confronted with primordial evil, as in Greek myths. In a mytho-schematic quest he experiences the emphatic perseverance of original sin, which he measures against the divine will. God's immutable will, however, presents itself in its indifference to human expectations, to the subjective polarization of inscrutable totality. The notion of inscrutable totality of an immutable will attributed to an irresistible Grace reinstates the equivalent of tragic fate in Christianity. To my understanding, Shakespearean tragedy dramatizes the sequence of necessarily evil actions undertaken by the servile will and measured against the hidden God of the reprobate.

It seems that the modes of the tragic are intrinsically bound to the representatives of fate in both Greek and Shakespearean tragedy. I have tried to illustrate in some detail the coexistence of these two elements in tragic drama and to concentrate on their respective manifestations. I have traced their causal relations to dramatic action and considered related questions of heroic disposition and orientation. Such a conceptual analysis necessarily raised the question of genre, the legitimacy of pure Greek and Christian tragedy on the one hand, and that of a possible alternative genre, of melodrama on the other. The ground thus appears to be prepared for the further examination of the element of fate, this time not so much with regard to action, but rather, in its relation to character. The following chapter addresses this problem, which is fundamental for raising the question of tragic identity.

III. Character and Identity

We have seen that the fundamental experiences of the hero of Christian tragedy are characterized by the tragic futility of pursuing subjective goals and by the threat of inescapable reprobation. The inscrutable will of an inscrutably hidden God, the *deus absconditus* prolongs uncertainty for the entire career of the tragic hero. Thus uncertainty assumes the status of a comprehensive existential experience. It prevails even over the transitional feeling of certainty that presents itself in the determinate and stubborn pursuing of a subjective *telos*. It is this prevalence that makes the tragic experience existential, i.e., belonging to being itself. However, according to the golden rule of Aeschylus, *pathei mathos,* tragedy presents man in need of a lesson in the prevalence of uncertainty, to understand it as an existential experience. The road from transitory self-determination or shadow identity to enlightened identity is the road towards accepting the only possible form of certainty in a tragic context: the certainty of uncertainty.

In both manifestations of the genre, in Greek and Shakespearean tragedy, we find an ultimate power indifferent to human aspirations, to subjective *telos* as such. This power represents the totality of action in tragedy, which includes as well as transcends individual-heroic purposes. In the discussions above I called this power, the representative of objective *telos,* fate. Both modes of fate, the *moira* of Greek tragedy or *predestination* in Shakespeare have the common denominator of keeping the hero in temporary certainty. Thus he is made to fulfil his tragic fate instead of his own goals. In Shakespearean tragedy the pre-established context in which the hero is destined to act arouses the justified fears of reprobation, the growing sense of an inevitable failure of actions. To defend my notion of differential teleology as plot-governing force in tragedy I now turn to the somewhat stale but nonetheless important problem of the relation between character and fate.

Character and fate

In his attempt to oppose characters of modern tragedy to those of the Greek, Hegel's arguments seem highly controversial. They reveal a constant struggle to subsume fate into character and to unify blatant incompatibilities. Modern characters are described as either "firm", *Festig* or "inwardly hesitant and discordant" (*inner Schwank und Zerwürfnis*).[121] The latter are defined as liable to vacillation, *Schwank*, understood as internalized collision. Apart from vacillating characters, however, Hegel argues that Shakespeare gives us "firm and consistent characters who come to ruin simply because of this decisive adherence to themselves and their aims .... they allow themselves to be lured to their deed by external circumstances or they plunge blindly on and persevere by the strength of their will".[122] In contrast with the Greek notion of fate, there is more freedom of choice, in Hegel's view, in what he calls romantic or modern tragedy. The latter presents situations where the hero finds himself in "accidental circumstances and conditions within which it is possible to act either in this way or in that".[123]

In order to maintain the idea that action is determined by character, Hegel understandably belittles the tragic phenomenon of vacillation. He seems to lay stress on firm and strong-willed characters instead, attributing great initiative to them in undertaking action. This view nevertheless is in sharp contrast with the notion of internalized collision expounded in the same chapter of the *Aesthetics* and renders the idea of character-fate problematic. The definition of heroic initiative as "allowing themselves, *lassen sich*, to be led by external circumstances" is a euphemistic insistence on an exchanged order of priorities, which immediately poses the obvious question: What can the hero do but allow the guidance of a compelling situation? The Shakespearean tragic experience seems to show that the pre-established situation is of primary importance in the unfolding and the fulfilment of dramatic action. The hero's internal collision presents itself as the consequence of having to allow to be led by such an already given constellation of external circumstances. Let us now recall Schelling's similar views on the issue of character.

For Schelling the absorption of fate by character appears more explicitly in the claim that in Shakespeare's works the "element of character takes the place formerly occupied by fate, *Schicksal*". Yet he

---

[121] G. W. F. Hegel, *Vorlesungen über Aesthetic III*, in *Werke in zwanzig Banden 15*. Theorie Werkausgabe, Suhrkamp Verlag, Frankfurt, 1970, 562. Trans. T. M. Knox, *Aesthetics: Lectures on Fine Art by G. W. F. Hegel*, II, 1228.
[122] Knox, 1229-30.
[123] *Ibid.*, 1226.

posits such a powerful *fatum* into that character that it no longer can be considered free, but stands there rather as insuperable necessity, *Notwendigkeit*. Though Schelling is aware of the significance of the deceiving supernatural forces in the beginning of *Macbeth*, this does not prevent him from disclaiming objective necessity from the deed itself. According to his argument the fact that Banquo does not heed the witches and thus avoids being deluded, *betören*, shows that in Shakespeare it is the character which is decisive.[124] The weakness of this definition is not so much in the anachronistic[125] depiction of events as deluding – at this point Macbeth is not deluded, since he is told the truth about his future – but in the rendering of character-decision a vital difference between Greek and Shakespearean tragedy. To prove the contrary it suffices to recall instances of similar character-decision in Sophocles. The diverse reaction of Oedipus and Creon to the message of the oracle in the *Oedipus Tyrannus* may be assigned to a fundamental difference in character just as Antigone's and Ismene's conflict concerning the burial of Polyneikes.

It may be argued therefore that the Shakespearean notion of fate cannot be conceived of as being incarnate in character anymore than the Greek,[126] though it is a well-worn truism that Shakespearean tragedy is more character-centred. Reflection dominates character-formation to the very limits of rationality. Reflection at the extremes of self-seeking pathos in its turn divides character and calls into doubt all homogenizing attempts at character-drawing. This flexibility and uncertainty revealed through reflection seems incompatible with the rigid, inflexible certainty of fate.

In his systematic account of the tragic experience Robert B. Heilman constantly emphasizes the essential component of the divid-

---

[124] F. W. J. Schelling, *The Philosophy of Art*, trans. & ed. Douglas W. Stott, Minneapolis: University of Minnesota Press, 1989, 269.

[125] Anachronistic in terms of plot-structure, since Macbeth is deluded only in Act IV and by then Banquo had already been assassinated. It may be argued further, that even the two prophecies of the witches are not deluding in themselves, but merely are conceived as such by heroic understanding delimited by subjective *telos*. This distinction appears fundamental in the human deciphering of oracles.

[126] Cf. Gadamer's appertaining statement: "Trotz aller Subjektivität der Verschuldung bleibt selbst in der neuzeitlichen Tragödie noch immer ein Moment jener antiken Übermacht des Schicksals wirksam, die sich gerade in der Ungleichheit von Schuld und Schicksal als das für alle Gleiche offenbart", *Wahrheit und Methode*, Tübingen: J. C. B.Mohr, 1965, 125.

edness of character.[127] Dividedness according to Heilman presents itself already in Aristotle's prescriptive statement in the *Poetics* that the hero is a good man (better than us) who commits a error. Goodness and error characterize the hero from the start, thus necessarily creating internal dividedness. Heilman goes on to distinguish three distinct versions of dividedness or of the more comprehensive form, division. The latter is claimed to be detectable either between two contrasting imperatives or two impulses or further, between an impulse and an imperative. In the first case the hero has to choose between two contrasting orders and this presents him with an insoluble task. In the second case the fall is caused by an internal conflict, while the third indicates an opposition between an internal aspiration and an external higher order regulating action. The concept of the imperative is further complicated by its inclusion of conscience apart from the precepts of tradition. The notion of impulse, on the other hand, is egoism itself according to Heilman, which strives to violate the constraints of the imperative. The incompatibility of these motivations is represented in the irreconcilable oppositions of individuality and community, desire and duty, ambition and law.[128] Heilman's categories in relation to dividedness, needless to say, cannot always be differentiated from each other (as he himself acknowledges). Overlaps are as frequent as isolated occurrences. An imperative may be internalized, become an impulse or vice versa, an impulse may be externalized into an imperative. A Hamlet-like vacillating figure, a character constantly reflecting upon himself and his allotted task may gradually adapt himself to the external imperative by internalizing it and transforming[129] it into a personal vocation. In Shakespeare's first revenge play, *Titus Andronicus*, the hero's impulse for revenge, one may say, is more in harmony with the external imperative of human retribution, the ultimate organizing principle of revenge plays. Consequently, I agree with Heilman in describing the move from the mere personification of human justice to its radical questioning, in Heilman's words, from conflicts between to

---

[127] Robert Bechtold Heilman, *Tragedy and Melodrama: Versions of Experience*, Seattle and London: University of Washington Press, 1968.
[128] *Ibid.*, 12-13.
[129] Internalization and transformation of imperatives go hand in hand: by internalizing the command the hero necessarily transforms it due to the limits of his understanding. This discrepancy of the command and its subjective interpretation (its distortion in favour of subjective *telos*) prove crucial in the unfolding of its dramatic consequences.

conflicts within the character[130] as the generic shift from melodrama to tragedy. Whereas, on Heilman's view, leaving melodrama behind, Shakespeare's middle period is the most tragic; his later plays like *Antony and Cleopatra* or *Coriolanus* represent a return to melodrama. There, the argument goes, the personalities are less challenged by other motives.[131] This statement, though it may hold true of Jacobean drama outside Shakespeare, is hardly tenable with regard to his later work. Antony is deeply challenged by two motives. One keeps him on Cleopatra's side despite the lack of privacy and humiliating publicity. The other draws him home to Rome to take his part in the political aspirations of the triumvirate (love versus honour). Similarly, in the *Coriolanus* what seemed an immovable heroic nature, is finally made to accept the power of family bonds and succumbs to the passion of homoerotic love.[132]

If my argument is correct, the notion of dividedness discredits aspirations to empower character with fate. Moreover, the incompatibility becomes obvious if we think of the hero's death as itself predetermined and enveloped by fate. Before moving on to an alternative delineation of dividedness and taking up the question of identity, we must consider another appointed organizing principle of Shakespearean tragedy: "fortune".

Hamlet's "outrageous fortune" articulates his despair in an unresolvable struggle with a pre-established situation. This form of imputation, however, points to and substitutes the mechanism of fate, in this case the Ghost's command, in individual consciousness. The recourse to fortune as to a form of imputation is made more explicit by the use of adjectives,[133] largely absent in the cases of the respective occurrences of fate or chance. These attributes express much of the hero's state of consciousness, his reaction to the unexpected cluster of events, fortune is chiding, skittish, foolish, wondrous, unhappy, fickle, feign'd, false, etc. Personal disaster is attributed to the "malevolence

---

[130] Heilman, *Tragedy and Melodrama: Versions of Experience*, 164. The author characterizes the earlier works of Shakespeare as largely melodramatic due to the scarcity of character-dividedness.

[131] *Ibid.*, 165. In Jacobean drama the character is cut back to a single motive, says Heilman and the consequence is a melodramatic shaping of personality.

[132] Cf. Ortwin de Graef, "Sweet Dreams, Monstered Nothings: Catachresis in Kant and *Coriolanus*", in *The Ethics in Literature*, eds A. Hadfield, D. Rainsford and T. Woods, London: Macmillan, 1999, 242.

[133] See *New Catholic Encyclopedia*, 1035.

of fortune" (*Macbeth*, III.vi.28),[134] which is reminiscent of the hostile God of Greek tragedy. If the range of attributes applied in the respective evocations of fortune displays a deep human concern and involvement, the occurrences of "chance" seem to indicate the contrary. The word denotes an inversion of the indifference-involvement pattern in relation to current or future events. Man is presented as indifferent as far as his future career is involved, "If Chance will have me King, why, Chance / may crown me, / Without my stir" (*Macbeth*, I.iii.144-45). At this point the recourse to the passive consideration of a possible event of promotion shows merely a delay in understanding the necessity of involvement and the real meaning of the predestining forces. The move from passivity to action is accompanied by the shift of imputation from chance to fate, "... fate and metaphysical aid doth seem / to have thee crown'd withall" (I.v.28-29). The call for action is similarly defined by Hamlet, who in spite of all his ponderous vacillations seems to have a momentary clairvoyance in discerning the unavoidable in the command, "my fate cries out" (I.iv.81).

The representations of fate in Macbeth and Hamlet share the common characteristic of being personal. Fate seems to be selective in allotting personal vocation: revenge for Hamlet, kingship for Macbeth. The personal character of predestination is not contradicted by the general disaster it indirectly causes. The death of innocent or only partially responsible characters may be an indirect consequence of a personal command that seeks to validate itself at all costs. In Shakespearean tragedy personal fate may become universal, for instance through the dramatic adaptation of astrological determinism. Pomponazzi subordinates human freedom to natural and cosmological laws.[135] Cosmology provides the general background for imputation in *King Lear:*

> GLOUCESTER: These late eclipses in the sun and moon portend no good to us. Though the wisdom of Nature can reason it thus and thus, yet nature finds itself scourg'd by the sequent effects. Love cools, friendship falls off, brothers divide
>
> (I.ii.100-104)

Universal determinism in drama may also present itself as a means for averting personal responsibility:

---

[134]William Shakespeare, *Macbeth*, ed. Kenneth Muir, London and New York: Routledge, 1994 (1988).
[135]*The Cambridge History of Renaissance Philosophy*, Cambridge, 1988, 660.

EDMUND: This is the excellent foppery of the world, that when we are sick in fortune, often the surfeits of our own behaviour, we make guilty of our disasters the sun, the moon, and stars; as if we were villains on necessity, fools by heavenly compulsion, knaves, thieves and treachers by spherical predominance; drunkards, liars, and adulterers by an enforc'd obedience of planetary influence; and all that we are evil in, by a divine thrusting on.

(I.ii.115-23)

The bastard Edmund opposes his personal fate to Gloucester's apocalypse, the evocation of universal determinism. This for him is nothing but a crafty aversion of responsibility. Edmund's often quoted footnote to the preceding account of the general state of affairs is widely accepted as a creditable perspective to judge dotage in *King Lear*. It is to the credit of the converging critical assessments that they rightly point to the crucial element of irony in the passages above as regards matters of individual freedom and fate.[136] Imputation as means of self-exemption seems to dominate heroic consciousness also outside the tragic cosmos. It characterizes modes of relations within the hierarchy of myth already in Homer (*Odyssey* I. 32-34).[137] In the face of self-exempting imputation Edmund's stance points to another distinctively tragic element shunned by Gloucester: involvement. Personal involvement in a declining state of affairs is stressed in Edmund in the quoted passage and magnificently versified in *Sonnet 35*:

> No more be grieved at that which thou hast done;
> Roses have thorns, and silver fountains mud;
> Clouds and eclipses stain both moon and sun,[138]
> And loathsome canker lives in sweetest bud.
> All man make faults, and even I, in this,

---

[136] On the other hand, it seems that though Edmund stands opposed to astrological determinism, he in turn betrays another form of determinism, that which defines his character from his birth, cf. Nicholas Grene, *Shakespeare's Tragic Imagination*, 161.

[137] Homer, *Odyssey*, eds J. C. Bruijn and C. Spoelder, Haarlem: H. D. Tjeenk Willink and Zoon N. V., 1959.

[138] Cf. William Shakespeare, *Sonnet 107*, "The mortal moon hath her eclipse endured"; Gloucester's line, "these late eclipses in the sun and moon" (quoted above) and Edmund's "these eclipses do portend these divisions" (126); see also "moon's eclipse" (*Macbeth* IV.i.28); and "Disasters in the sun; and the moist star...Was sick almost to doomsday with eclipse" (*Hamlet* I.i.121-28).

> Authorizing thy trespass with compare,
> Myself corrupting, salving thy amiss,
> Excusing these sins more than these sins are:
> For to thy sensual fault I bring in sense;
> Thy adverse party is thy advocate,
> And 'gainst myself a lawful plea commence:
> Such civil war is in my love and hate
> That I an accessory[139] needs must be
> To that sweet thief which sourly robs from me.

The repeated resort to the first person singular shows a confessed personal involvement, which appears in line 14 as itself determined: I cannot but be involved. In contrast with the "I" of the "even I" of the sonnet Gloucester has yet to learn the truth and the extent of involvement at the expense of losing his sight.

The passages on determinism in *King Lear* on the other hand, have to be considered within the context of the whole plot. Shakespeare doubles the plot of his source and parallels Lear's calamitous descent and learning-through-suffering (the Shakespearean version of *pathei mathos*) with that of Gloucester. This duplication of personal destiny transforms actuality to typicality, the contingent coincidence of particular events into universal necessity.[140] It is by virtue of this extension of dramatic conflict that the fulfilment of Lear's metamorphosis claims universal significance.

Role, nature, identity

In Shakespearean tragedy the gradual deterioration of character is the consequence of the mentioned dividedness. It has been largely ignored, however, that the notion of dividedness runs counter to totalizing assessments of character. It renders attempts at considering tragic character as a whole dubious. This internal division that justifies a pluralistic perspective on character, the contrasting analyses of Hamlets, Macbeths and Lears, will be in the focus of the present chapter.

To specify the two extreme poles of dividedness, the quality acquired and the quality left behind, I offer the concepts of role and nature. R. B. Heilman, in his own account of nature, gives two forms of its dramatic application, one referring to character, the other to physi-

---

[139] I.e., *complicity*, cf. Arden footnote, William Shakespeare, *The Sonnets*, ed. Katherine Duncan-Jones, 1997.
[140] The overwhelming ubiquity of evil, futility and waste in the play is stressed by W. R. Elton, in *King Lear and the Gods*, 113.

cal being and life.[141] It must be noted that here I am not concerned with the latter which dominated my investigations of Shakespearean tragedy in the previous chapter, but rather with the former, the relation between nature and character. Heilman's treatment of the two concepts as synonyms sharply contradicts his notion of dividedness of character.[142] It leaves intact instances of character-formation when character asserts itself in self-distanciation from its own nature.[143] The nature of character, to my understanding, exposes a primary quality that in the sudden surge of unexpected events surrenders itself for the required role. Role in the context of Greek tragedy can be conceived of as the status in myth against which heroic nature, in this sense, the essential quality of the human being rebels through reflection. It appears as such only when reflection unveils this primary quality or nature of character and opposes it to a secondary level of being. Without this element of exposure, an outsider response would fail to ground itself on identification. Taking into account that the identification between insider and outsider perspectives is made possible by the self-manifestation of the character's nature understood in this sense, dramatic performance as a whole would remain ineffectual.[144]

The duplicity of character in Shakespeare is conspicuous in a case like Lady Macbeth's. The route from a self-assumed role to its final surrendering and the succumbing to the demands of repressed nature is a destiny unarguably tragic. It appears as such for the very reason of dividedness. Role, then, in this context seems to indicate a temporary freedom of choice soon to be subdued by a superior power appertaining to being itself. That is when the programme of unsexing in:

> Come you Spirits
> That tend on mortal thoughts, unsex me here, ...
> That no compunctious visitings of Nature
> Shake my fell purpose
>
> (I.v.41-46)

---

[141] Robert Bechtold Heilman, *This Great Stage: Image and Structure in King Lear*, Seattle: University of Washington Press, 1963, 117.
[142] Cf. *Ibid.*, 31.
[143] Cf. Edmund's "some good I mean to do despite of mine own nature" in *King Lear*, V.iii.244 quoted by Heilman himself, 317n.
[144] This failure of performance is made the more apparent in critiques stressing the ritualistic origins of drama.

breaks down in the scene of defilement, the desperate and futile washing of hands, "Out, damned spot!" (V.i.33). In this reflection on being eternally polluted we observe the relentless resurging of nature to claim its rights in indifference to the demands of role-play. The consecutive qualities expressing the stages of character-formation in Lady Macbeth's case are represented by the sequence: nature-role-nature. The difference between the initial and final forms of nature in this construction lies in the seemingly voluntary subordination of the former to the role and the unavertible and unexpected resurgence of the latter indifferent to the subjective preferences of pretence. The restriction implied in "seemingly" refers to the literal understanding of the programme of unsexing, the reference to physical being. Here the two meanings of nature sequestered by Heilman are fused. The application of intention to a question concerning the given factor of Nature is doubtful. One simply cannot choose to abandon one's gender.

Lady Macbeth's determination in the undertaking of the role is preceded by an indeterminacy with regard to her husband's nature. It is through her words that we get the first glimpse into Macbeth's primary nature, "yet do I fear thy nature: It is too full o' th' milk of human kindness" (I.v.15-16).[145] Seen from this preliminary delineation of his character, Macbeth's later regicide seems to be the consequence of a submissive role-play. The constant articulations of reluctance and hesitance concerning murder show that action requires the representatives of external incitement. The hero who is "too full o' th' milk of human kindness" has to be lured and deceived to commit the crime and it is precisely this very inadequacy of personal quality and the necessary external pressure that guarantee the tragic downfall. The original quality of character in both analysed cases is surrendered to an assumed role to be eventually reasserted in accordance with the precepts of tragic experience. It may be argued that we hardly find the counterpart of the final resurgence of Lady Macbeth's nature (the evidence of the indelible stain) in Macbeth's dramatic collapse. The latter on the contrary, seems to keep himself to the laws of the role throughout, to "die as a man" in compliance with the previously acquired self-

---

[145] Most frequently it is the other that holds the key to one's primary nature, see also Edmund on Edgar in *King Lear*, "a brother noble, / Whose nature is so far from doing harms / That he suspects none" (I.ii.184-86). However, the other may be misled by self-disguise and role-play, cf. Cornwall on Kent, "This is some fellow, / Who, having been prais'd for bluntness, doth effect / A saucy roughness and constrains the garb / Quite from his nature" (II.ii.96-99). Similarly, it is doubtful whether we can accept France's depiction of Cordelia, as "tardiness in nature" (I.i.235).

confidence in "I dare do all that may become a man". The absence of repentance and the lack of torturing troubled conscience like that of Claudius shows that reasserted nature is a transformed new nature. A new nature contaminated by role-play. The stages of the character-deterioration of Macbeth could then be represented by the sequence of nature-role-new nature. The difference between role and new nature in this sequence is established in recognition to which I shall turn later.

A similar order of qualities and stages of character-formation is discernable in *Hamlet*. There the role-play is undertaken also with the subordination of nature, though in this case to serve purposes of self-defence, not strategies of offence. Role in *Hamlet* presents itself as the only prerequisite of action. Behind the role of revenger[146] Hamlet's mentally and emotionally aroused and overexcited nature manifests itself in the situation-assessing monologues. This nature is endowed with the capacity of uniting contradictions in one thinking process, with the ability to take opposing standpoints simultaneously (the stances of to be or not to be, etc.). It presents itself as a given quality. Action, however, is by definition one-dimensional and requires the surrendering of the natural tendency of a pluralistic vision. The pressing demands of role-play lead to the gradual subjective revaluation of nature, which is obvious in the increasing contempt for words (the whorish unpacking of the heart with words, II.ii.581). The route from reflection to action is the succumbing of nature to role, of Hamlet's original quality to the following of the Fortinbras' ideal. This personification of the role of revenger cast on him by the fatherly command is unavertible precisely because of what this command represents dramaturgically: the ground rule of traditional revenge plays. It is therefore never a question whether Hamlet takes his revenge or not, but rather, how and when, and at what expense. These latter questions and especially the focus on loss implied in "expense" and expounded here by the concepts of role and nature, form the basis of Shakespearean revenge tragedy. The irremediable loss of a superior quality in Hamlet's role-play is conspicuous in the nihilistically indifferent attitude towards death, including those of his victims. The climax of identification with the role is explicit in the "This is I, Hamlet the Dane",[147] an assertion contradicting all previous reflections on uncertainty. The

---

[146] Cf. Jonathan Bate's understanding of Hamlet's task, which is "to will himself into the very different role of the revenger", cf. *The Genius of Shakespeare,* London: Macmillan, 1997. Different from what, one may ask?

[147] The change in Hamlet is the willing assumption of the title, cf. Arden footnote to V.i.250, ed. Harold Jenkins.

Hamlet returning from exile is an utterly transformed Hamlet. It is a Hamlet exercised in murder and now a passive, unsuspecting participant in the accumulating events.[148] However, under the asserted authority of role-play the subdued voice of nature occasionally seeks to interrupt the continuous flow of events, "Thou wouldst not think how ill all's here about my heart" (V.ii.208). The real significance of this statement is in pointing out the persisting duplicity and dividedness of character.[149] From this point of view role-play may be seen as the prerequisite of the confirmation of real nature. The recognition of the hero's real nature through the intermediation of role-play is the acquisition of identity. The fundamental difference then between nature and identity, according to my use of these terms, would be in the givenness of the one and the acquiredness of the other. Though, as we have seen, the identification of character and its totalizing description is problematic, the recurring phenomenon of nature resurging under the self-assumed role seems to point to a common stage of tragic character-formation in the cases discussed. The reassertion of nature in Lady Macbeth, in Macbeth and in Hamlet follows the stages of trying to surrender one's primary, given quality for the demands of the external expectations of events and tradition (fate). It is by virtue of this prehistory that it becomes acquired. Acquired nature or identity in tragedy involves the confirmation and recognition of the givenness, its challenge and verification.

As I have tried to illustrate above, the relation between role and nature in the delineation of character and the emphasis on dividedness provides a better insight into character-formation than totalizing accounts of character-fate. However, my argument has to account for two extreme examples of impending dividedness, that of Lear and Coriolanus. In the former the role appears as already given and the whole play portrays a forced self-distanciation from the role to discover real nature (identity) in metamorphosis. In the latter, on the con-

---

[148] Harold Rosenberg in his "Character Change and the Drama", *Perspectives on Drama*, ed. J. L. Calderwood, New York: Oxford University Press, 1968, emphasizes that Hamlet's character has to change to make tragedy and cogently describes the new character of the returned Hamlet. For him this dramatic transformation is evident in the graveyard scene, where Hamlet discourses on death as already an insider, i. e., as someone who has found his place in the play. The weakness in Rosenberg's argument, is the ambiguous treatment of the term "identity" in relation to being an insider and the acknowledged process of character development (328-29).

[149] In the transformed language of the returned Hamlet the heart accommodates conflict, fear and bad omen, cf. "Sir, in my heart there was a kind of fighting / That would not let me sleep" (V.ii.4-5).

trary, nature appears as an externally immovable totality until the very end, when it succumbs to the demands of filial obedience. Before this dramatic inversion of character the nature of Coriolanus seems to ward off all compromises with externally imposed roles and appears as statue-rigid persistence in pride, "you are too absolute" (III.ii.39). The ultimate collapse and dividedness becomes the more powerfully dramatic, since something of exceptional magnitude is thus shattered. Such a downfall immediately entails death confirming the maxim that great ones are not divided, they die, "Most dangerously you have with him prevail'd, / If not most mortal to him" says Coriolanus of himself (V.iii.188-89).

Nature of character frequently finds itself in conflict with the precepts of honour. In *Coriolanus* this conflict remains potential:

> I would dissemble with my nature where
> My fortunes and my friends at stake requir'd
> I should do so in honour
>
> (III.ii.62-64)

In *Hamlet,* however, honour is an organizing principle irreconcilably opposed to nature. It stands for the willingness to act and urges deliberation and the abandoning of idle reflection.[150] It is therefore following my argument above, closely related to the problem of role-play, which is to say that it appears to be as questionable as it is necessary in retrospect. It is questionable, because what makes a Hamlet-like intellectual the central figure of discussion and appreciation is precisely his superiority to the military ideal he chooses to honour. It is necessary, because without the role-play based on a (mis)conception of honour Hamlet would never acquire his identity.[151] The duplicity of identity and role-play is explicit in Hamlet's constant struggle to find his own position in the conflicting motivations of his original nature and of the command. The command requires the abandoning, the distanciation of a self paralysed by the impasse of double motivation, "How all occasions do inform against me, / And spur my dull revenge" (IV.iv.32-33). The "troubledness of the heart" of the returned

---

[150] The dichotomy of nature and honour dominates parallel aspirations, too, cf. Laertes' "I am satisfied in nature, / Whose motive in this case should stir me most / To my revenge; but in my terms of honour I stand aloof and will no reconcilement" (V.ii.240-43).
[151] For an illuminating account of honour in relation to *Hamlet*, see Martin Dodsworth, *Hamlet Closely Observed*, London and Dover: New Hampshire, 1985.

Hamlet, textual occurrences of which I mentioned above, may be seen in this light as the natural consequence of such a mode of self-distanciation.

By introducing the concepts of dividedness, character-formation, nature, role and honour I have tried to illustrate the ontological gap that presents itself between character and identity. Following this line of argument I conclude that the identity of a character in tragedy is not a given, preformed, constant quality. It cannot be made compatible with representations of fate. In sharp contrast with the given quality of character I called nature, identity appears as something achieved, acquired in the course of action.[152] In retrospect the secondary status of role-play proves to be a necessary presupposition of this acquisition. Only a nature reaffirmed against and at the same time contaminated by the role can merit its redefinition as identity.

Ripeness versus readiness

The tragic tension between role and nature may be illustrated by two central maxims. One is proposed by Hamlet, "readiness is all", the other by Edgar, "ripeness is all". To understand the real significance of these statements we have to see them as manifestations of the respective stages of character-formation. Both express an advanced state of heroic understanding and represent the main axis around which the plays can be structured. The context in which the "readiness is all" is conceived I have already outlined. The phrase exhibits the possession of something previously claimed to be missing, "I lack advancement" (III.ii.331). As Harry Levin points out[153] this lack refers to the postponement of revenge and not to want of promotion. Hamlet's comprehensive silence with regard to his succession to the throne clearly shows his ambitionless nature. It is being in the possession of the role of revenger that is articulated in the "readiness is all", in the affirmation of being prepared for what is to come, i.e., the final duel. This preparedness is the consequence of the gradual giving up of vacillation and idle self-rebuke. Hamlet is ready to fulfil his role, to act as revenger and nothing more, to leave behind all constraints of uncertainty (the frustrations denoted in allusions to the heart, etc). In this

---

[152] For a different concept of identity and role, their dramatic interrelation and various forms of blending, see Thomas F. van Laan, *Role-playing in Shakespeare*, Toronto, Buffalo, and London: University of Toronto Press, 1978, 21-43.

[153] Harry Levin, *The Question of Hamlet,* New York: Oxford University Press, 1958, 72.

sense Hamlet's often quoted phrase is the culmination of character-deterioration, the contamination of nature by role. The extreme transformation in Hamlet's character is noted by critics like Eleanor Prosser,[154] Harry Levin,[155] A. C. Bradley,[156] G. Wilson Knight,[157] and many others. However, this transformation is nowhere linked to the demands of role-play and the impossibility of living in accordance with a given faculty of nature.[158]

In contrast with the role implicit in readiness, ripeness is expressive of the real nature of character. As we have seen the sequence of qualities in *King Lear* is reverse. The role there appears as the primary, dominating quality, something that is given from the start and which in the course of events will be gradually seen as such from the standpoint of an arduously acquired identity.[159] What in their respective transformations both Lear and Gloucester achieve is the dramatic integration of finitude.[160] The conception of finitude comes along with the state of being bereft of the role and with the recognition, "they told me I was everything; " 'tis a lie, I am not ague-proof" (IV.v.102). The admittance of mortality (IV.v.128) for Lear is contemporaneous with the disillusionment in current manifestations of authority, "the great image of authority: a dog's obeyed in office" (IV.v.151). This ironic self-distanciation from the dubious status of authority, later confirmed

---

[154] In *Hamlet and Revenge* the line "now could I drink hot blood" (III.ii.391) is claimed to evoke the services of the Black Mass. A similar view is expounded by Arthur McGee, "Hamlet has let himself become the tool of the Devil", *The Elizabethan Hamlet*, New Haven & London: Yale University Press, 1987, 103.

[155] Levin stresses the often ignored error in Hamlet's role-play, namely that as a consequence all that the old King fought for has been lost (89).

[156] A. C. Bradley, *Shakespearean Tragedy*, London: Macmillan, 1993, 122.

[157] The author's question, who is closer to Heaven: Claudius at prayer or Hamlet undertaking divine justice draws attention to a crucial scene in the play, which portrays the characters in a different light, cf. *The Wheel of Fire*, London: Methuen, 1949, 36.

[158] With the exception perhaps, of a statement made by Stanley Cavell: "It is the bequest of a beloved father that deprives the son of his identity, of enacting his own existence", cf. *Disowning Knowledge*, New York: Cambridge University Press, 1987, 188. Being deprived of identity suggests an alternative quality of character.

[159] A distinction between initial role and acquired identity in *Lear* exemplifies critical procedures that approach tragedy with regard to the problem of identity, cf. N. C. Liebler, *Shakespeare's Festive Tragedy,* 197, and W. R. Elton, *King Lear and the Gods*, 328.

[160] For the significance of finite consciousness and the limits of human understanding in tragedy, see Stephen Booth, *King Lear, Macbeth, Indefinition and Tragedy*, New Haven and London: Yale University Press, 1983, 85.

as role and the acquisition of the consciousness of mortality and finitude is the final stage of character-transformation. They indicate the achievement of ripeness.[161] Between the recognition of finitude and the achievement of ripeness nevertheless there is a gap that presents itself for heroic consciousness. The absence of a mediating factor between these two poles threatens with an alternative (un)heroic behaviour of realizing finitude in suicide (Gloucester's renouncing of this world, IV.v.24). To bridge the gap and provide the missing link for heroic orientation Edgar introduces the element of endurance, "men must endure their going hence even as their coming hither" (V.ii.9). In *King Lear,* to conclude, the stages of character-development crystallize around three basic modes of behaviour: recognition of finitude, acceptance through endurance, and realization of ripeness.[162] It is this sequence of moves culminating in ripeness that may be subsumed under what I call the acquisition of nature or tragic identity.

The concepts of ripeness and readiness express alternative stages of character-formation, being possible poles of dividedness. They also help to isolate the nature of character from role-play. It was one of my main objectives to present the tensions and conflicts of these faculties in Shakespearean tragedy and deduce what may be called tragic identity. I speak of identity when a preliminarily given faculty of nature is confirmed or acquired. I call this form of identity tragic, because under the given circumstances it can be affirmed only through diverse,

---

[161] Tracing the possible interpretations of "ripeness is all", Elton warns against the decontextualised view which would render the phrase Shakespeare's ultimate wisdom, cf. *King Lear and the Gods*, 107. The argument disclaims the validity of the phrase for general application implied in the "all" and evokes the death of the "most unripe Cordelia" in the final scene. Further, Elton finds justification for his view in a passage where Edgar is claimed to refute his own preferences, "O! our lives' sweetness / That we the pain of death would hourly die / Rather than die at once!" (V.iii.184-86). Elton's assertion that these instances prove that ripeness and endurance are not all implies an attribution of remediability to ripeness, as if ripeness by virtue of its contextualised definition involved a reference to a form of redress, recuperation or even salvation. It is obvious that Edgar's cited articulation of despair does not include an allusion to suicide in contrast with Elton's reading, but rather seems to contain an appeal for the aversion of pain. Elton's treatment of ripeness here runs contrary to his own caveats, since he decontextualises ripeness and neglects the stages of character-formation, through which Edgar's own conception of ripeness evolves.

[162] Cf. Gloucester's learning through suffering, "Henceforth I'll bear / Affliction till it do cry out itself / 'Enough, enough' and die" (IV.v.75-77). This acquired sagacity is further approved by Lear himself, itself suggestive of the self-deposed King's transformed demeanour, "Thou must be patient; we came crying hither" (IV.v.171), ed. René Weis, London and New York: Longman, 1993.

contaminating machinations of role-play. It follows that identity and action belong together and investigations concerning character-formation cannot possibly avoid the encounter with tragic action as such. If there is anything like purpose of character-formation in tragedy, as suggested by the maxim of *pathei mathos*, learning through suffering, it seems inevitable to examine the *telos* of tragic action in general. If so far, I have taken an internal point of view in tracing dividedness and defining tragic identity, it is time to take a step backwards and re-examine dramatic action externally. The significance of a teleological approach to tragedy is elaborated in the following chapter. The concept of *telos* will be reintroduced in its power to isolate two distinct forms of action: the tragic and the melodramatic. It is in this new, generically differentiated dramatic context that the problem of tragic identity will be resumed.

IV. On the Threshold of the Tragic: The Teleological Foundations of Greek and Shakespearean Tragedy

The present chapter does not seek to propose a general definition of tragedy. Such an undertaking would from its inception be discouraged by the general failure of all totalizing critical commitments. Theories of tragedy had to break their way through an intimidating diversity of worldviews inherent in the extant Greek plays. The numerous exceptions, which presented themselves against all attempts at totalization call for the radical questioning of these procedures.

It may be argued that the Greek term *tragoidia* encompassed a wide range of plays dissimilar and incompatible in structure and vision. This argument would like to see all critical investigations about the nature of the tragic secondary to a previously observed primacy of generic totality. At the same time it is tempting to continue along the path of Aristotle's frequent discriminations between tragedies. The *Poetics* seems to encourage fundamental distinctions not only between the various forms of *mimesis*, but also within the most elaborately treated genre: tragedy. Aristotle's use of the superlative "most tragic", *tragicótatos*, itself reveals a tendency for internal diversification. The term occurs in relation to Euripides' plays and betrays Aristotle's exclusively methodological concern. The context, according to G. F. Else, is the defence of Euripides against a groundless public depreciation.[163] Aristotle seeks to abate the general dislike for the dramatist's frequent preference for unhappy endings by applauding his method of plot-construction.[164] The choice of the term, one could say, is exem-

---

[163] Commentary to 1453a30, G. F. Else, *Aristotle's Poetics: The Argument*, Cambridge, Mass.,: Harvard University Press, 1967, 404.

[164] Cf. Bywater's commentary to 1453a30, *Aristotle on the Art of Poetry*, Oxford: Clarendon Press, 1909, 37. See also the commentary of Michael Davis, which stresses that it is precisely what he is reproached for that Euripides should be appreciated, "Euripides is the most tragic of poets because his plays most conform to the rule that

plary of Aristotle's general concern for structural differences he never fails to exhibit in the chapters of the *Poetics*. This partiality for plays and authors singled out for their observance of the particular plot-component discussed, may stimulate the extension of the generic discrimination to its very limits. It is along this route that I hope to reach the threshold indicated in the title. However, this route has to be restricted to avoid the fallacy of unwarranted generalizing, characteristic of critical tendencies.

In what follows the threshold of the tragic will be approached along a teleological itinerary. This takes Aristotle's concept of *telos* in the *Poetics* as its starting point. It will be argued that the concept is not only of outstanding significance in relation to the structure of tragic drama as expounded in the *Poetics*, but may also provide us with the means to isolate the non-Aristotelian genre of melodrama. The foundation of this alternative genre will be seen as more justified when its structural incompatibility with tragedy is revealed by the teleological quest. The threshold of the tragic this way presents itself as bordering melodrama. However, generic classification has to be established on a more elementary understanding of the threshold, involving the beginning of tragic action, which will prove meaningless without the complementary segments of the end and the *telos* itself. What Aristotle has to say about the *mythos* of tragedy therefore will be illuminating, as will Hegel's account of tragic action. I will formulate my teleological conception of the tragic with constant reference to these sources.

The mythos of tragedy

The term *mythos* maintains a privileged status in the descriptive structural analysis of tragedy in Aristotle's *Poetics*. Translated as plot, it is introduced as being more than a mere component among others and claimed rather to represent the essence or soul, *psyche* of tragedy (1450a38). Before attempting to highlight the full significance of this crucial statement of Aristotle in detail, I cannot avoid the preliminary differentiation between plot and myth.

Aristotle makes no distinction in his terminology between the technical term on plot, and the general label for traditional stories, myth. The difference he does insist on, however, is that between poetry and history. Poetry, then, appears superior in being more philoso-

---

tragedies end unhappily", *Aristotle's Poetics, The Poetry of Philosophy*, Lanham: Rowman & Littlefield, 1992.

phical and elevated than history, since it relates more of the universal, while history relates the particulars. The capacity to relate the universal here means the possibility of surpassing the actual by structuring the events according to probability or necessity, *kata to eikos e to anankaion* (1451b5-10).[165] Homer at this point is evoked as exemplary in selecting his material from contingent historical events and creating a sequence of actions based on probability and necessity. Selection therefore appears to be the key to manifest the universal; it is the prescribed method of emplotment.

In the course of selective emplotment there seems to be no explicitly defined preference between history and myth. Both serve the purposes of the poet in the form of raw material for the construction of his plots. At the same time nevertheless, one may add that it is a dominant trait of the tragic hero's reflection on historical events to allude to them in constant mythification.[166] Xerxes in this sense is not primarily a defeated warrior in the *Persians*, but the victim of the gods.[167] His reflection attests to the mechanism of emplotment in that it elevates him to the workings of the universal, in the perspective of which the actuality of historical reality is surpassed. This self-elevating mythification transposes heroic consciousness into a higher form of reality; a reality structured on probability and necessity. Simultaneously, historical time and space are extended to the absolute form of mythological temporality and spatiality.[168] It is the decisive factor of heroic reflection then, to interpret the various forms of conflict and resolution as governed by the gods and fate and assumed to be the consequence of some previous offence. Constant mythification thus carries out the subsumption of identity and action into the tripartite relation of man-God-fate. Man is located on the lowest level in the

---

[165] Aristotle, *Poetics*, ed. & trans. Stephen Halliwell, The Loeb Classical Library, Cambridge, Mass. and London: Harvard University Press, 1995.

[166] Among the numerous critics reducing the mythological plane to social and political conflicts, cf. N. C. Liebler, *Shakespeare's Festive Tragedy*.

[167] H. D. F. Kitto is one of the few critics who stresses the significance of the divine background in tragedies and draws the conclusions. This characteristic, however, is reserved for certain Greek and Shakespearean plays he calls "religious dramas". The divine background holds up a system of coordinates against which we are to evaluate all human deeds and sufferings, cf. *Form and Meaning in Drama*, London: Methuen, 1956, 243.

[168] Which is the same as nontemporality and nonspatiality, cf. Leszek Kolakowski, *The Presence of Myth*, Chicago, 1989, 9.

hierarchy,[169] even despite his occasional elevation among the divine. Peleus in the *Andromache* is elevated finally among the gods, the privilege being due to a divine reward. According to the myth, Peleus's wife is a goddess renounced by Zeus in fear of a threatening prophecy of the Moirai. The apotheosis is, then, the consequence of a chain of events determined by hierarchy. Man's destiny is shaped primarily by the Moirai, secondarily by Zeus and Thetis. This construction of the tripartite hierarchy to which man is exposed, is exemplary in its significance as the ultimate goal of transposition. It is the basis of elevated action, the absolute point of reference. The plot, however, not only manifests, but also dramatizes this transposition. The road leads from the contingency of the particular to the necessitated universal via the causal relation of privileged events presented in emplotment and complemented by heroic reflection.

This understanding of myth comes close to what Northrop Frye says,[170] when he defines the temporality of myth as compressing past and future in the present. The condensation of time and space and action in the plot consequently calls for being conceived of also in terms of myth, with an eye on the past and the future. The plot, in other words, presents the selectively condensed life story of the hero, where condensation itself points to what is condensed, i.e., the totality of myth. This evoked totality on the other hand, should at the same time leave the actuality of representation intact for effective *katharsis*. With all this in mind concerning the differences and congruities of plot and myth, let us now return to what Aristotle has to say about the *mythos* and its role in tragedy.

In contrast with the moral being of the *Nicomachean Ethics*, who may resort to contemplation defined as the perfect activity, the tragic hero is compelled to act. His action is imitated and ordered through selective emplotment, the rules of which are elaborated in different chapters of the *Poetics*. In the famous passage on plot and character, Aristotle subordinates the latter to the former and goes as far as to call the plot, *mythos* the goal, *telos* of tragedy, "without action there could be no tragedy, while without characters there could be" (1450a22-23). This striking preference of *mythos* in the terminology of the *Poetics*

---

[169]Cf. the Sophocles fragment, *anthropos esti pneuma kai skia monon* ("A man is nothing but breath and shadow"), in *Ajax the Locrian*, The Loeb Classical Library, ed. and trans. Hugh Lloyd-Jones, Cambridge, Mass. and London: Harvard University Press, 1996, 13.
[170]"The Koine of Myth", in *Myth and Metaphor: Selected Essays 1974-1988*, ed. Robert O. Denham, Charlottesville: University Press of Virginia, 1990, 8.

led the present undertaking to follow a teleological itinerary in approaching tragedy.

The consistent translation of *telos* as "goal" in the *Poetics* may appear to demand explanation due to its diverse occurrences in the original. Here one has to consider two substantives: *teleute* and *telos*, translated as "end" and "goal" or "purpose", respectively.[171] In prescribing the proper construction of the plot Aristotle defines the stages of beginning, middle and end (1450b25-31). In this passage the end, *teleute* is "that which itself naturally occurs, whether necessarily or usually, after a preceding event, but need not be followed by anything else". The translation of *meta de touto allo ouden* as "need not be followed" is euphemistic and weakens the simple but categorical negation in the original. Both Bywater's[172] and G. F. Else's[173] similar versions, "with nothing else after it" and "not something else after it" respectively, seem closer to preserve the sense of the finality of *teleute*.[174] Later on in the *Poetics*, however, returning to the three parts, the *arche* and *meson* are complemented by *telos* (1459a19). *Telos* in this sequence seems to serve as synonym of *teleute* betraying etymological kinship. In its diverse translations as "end" and "goal" the term appears in the *Poetics* as a decisive segment of plot-structure. It guarantees the completion of *mythos* in its causal relation to the preceding elements and in its finality. The suggestion of Michael Davis that *arche* and *telos* may be grasped not only as temporal units, but as "first principle" and "purpose"[175] seems to support my view in understanding the sequence of components as necessarily following the bias of an underlying authorial intention. The conscious selection and or-

---

[171] Bywater translates *o mythos telos tes tragodias* as "the plot is the *end and purpose* of the tragedy" (1450a22) *Aristotle on the Art of Poetry*, Oxford: Clarendon Press, 1909, 19. This rendering already indicates the inclusive range of *telos*.
[172] *Ibid.*, 22.
[173] *Aristotle's Poetics: The Argument*, 282.
[174] There is a confusing choice of terms Aristotle uses to denote the consecutive parts. For an illuminating analysis of the use of *allo* and *heteron* in reference to "another" in this passage see Michael Davis, *Aristotle's Poetics: the Poetry of Philosophy*, 50. *Teleute* conveys the neutral sense of ending as opposed to the *telos* which also embraces fulfilment, translated *der Endpunkt, das Ende and die Vollendung, der Abschluss*, respectively, in *Synonymik der Griechischen Sprache, IV. Band*, ed. J. H. Heinrich Schmidt, Leipzig: Druck und Verlag von B. G. Teubner, 1886. See also the *Handbook of Greek Synonyms*, where the translations are "conclusion" versus "fulfilment", ed. Th. K. Arnold, London: Francis and J. Rivington, St Paul's Church Yard and Waterloo Place, 1850.
[175] Cf. Davis, 91.

dering of events in emplotment is accomplished through pre-knowledge of the *telos*, the ultimate fulfilment of a dramatic purpose.

But the beginning and end of action are not only structural means of vouchsafing its unity and totality. They are also ontological principles constituting action itself. Rudiger Bittner's question: "by what does an action stand out as an action?"[176] seeks to justify Aristotle's preference for one action. It calls for considering what counts as an action in the first place. His suggestion is that it is the meaningfulness of a totality of activity that qualifies "mere doings" into units of action. This meaningfulness is achieved through the selection of serious (*spoudaios*) doings, as well as their temporal and causal structuring.[177] If this is so and the meaningful totality of action is bordered by its *arche* on one side and its *telos* on the other, it is inviting to examine their essential contents respectively.[178]

According to Bywater's commentary, the concept of beginning in the *Poetics* does not necessarily mean being void of antecedents. It is rather an event, which may be isolated from its antecedents to be applied as the first segment of a new sequence.[179] In this sense the choice of *arche* is determined by the *telos* that elevates an event to the status of a functioning unit in relation to itself. A contingent deed is made the beginning or the opening[180] of a necessitated sequence of actions only by virtue of a preconceived, affirmed *telos*. The *arche* of the plot, however isolated, may incorporate preceding events outside the play, which belong to the traditional myths. The *prologos* introduces a beginning as already effectuating its consequences. The difference between the beginning of a traditional story in myth and the *arche* of the plot, is annihilated through evocation in the *prologos*. There the event is recalled to foster a new form of teleological construction. Evocation of something well-known in mythology and the selective emplotment of its nonetheless famous consequences may reveal an underlying purpose of questioning and subversion. In Euripides this subversive

---

[176]"One Action", in *Essays on Aristotle's Poetics*, ed. A. O. Rorty, Princeton: Princeton University Press, 1992, 99.

[177]For a further account on action in Aristotle including the differentiation between *praxis* and *poiesis*, see J. L. Ackrill, *Essays on Plato and Aristotle*.

[178]For the relation between action, intention and context see Alaisdair MacIntyre, *After Virtue*, London: Duckworth, 1994, 209. A more detailed analysis of action and intention, action and event is to be found included in Paul Ricoeur, *Oneself as Another*, 56-88.

[179]Cf. Bywater, *Aristotle on the Art of Poetry,* the commentary to 1450b27, 178.

[180]Cf. Bywater's commentary to 1451a36, 188.

treatment of myths is extended beyond the framework of tradition and ultimately leads to its excessive mutilation.

So far I have been focusing on the formal characteristics of *arche* and *telos*. In terms of their respective contents, however, we may set them against other sequences of components introduced in the *Poetics*. The similarly triadic division of *hamartia, peripeteia* and *anagnórisis* lends itself to substitution. *Katharsis* in this context, though obviously an ultimate purpose of tragedy, cannot be included in the sequence. It is not a structural element of *mythos*, but rather, the emotional transposition of its hermetic totality.

The substitution of *arche* and *telos* for error and recognition, *hamartia* and *anagnórisis* is illuminating despite the danger of simplifying a complex relation. The conception of *hamartia* as *arche* is dependent on the already mentioned preconception of *anagnórisis* as *telos*. From the hero's point of view, his insider perspective, the conception of *arche* in recognition is inevitably subordinated to a subjective understanding of the teleological totality of action. At this point it is necessary to separate insider and outsider perspectives. The different vantage points of author, reader, audience on one side and the hero, secondary characters and chorus on the other, engender diverse scopes and limits of understanding action. If *telos* is the end and purpose of tragedy, the most important thing of all, *megiston hapantón*,[181] the divergence in its conception may appear to be fundamental in highlighting the tragic in action. Before developing a perspectival understanding of tragedy, an itinerary leading to a teleological classification, the terms in focus need to be further clarified in the light of Hegel's account.

Hegel on action

From the unities described or prescribed[182] for emplotment by Aristotle in the *Poetics* Hegel contests the unity of locale and the unity of time, pointing to their contingent applications. The only inviolable rule for him is the unity of action, which is characterized as the realization of a definite end, *bestimmte Zweck*.[183] This definite end is a dis-

---

[181] *To de telos megiston hapantōn* according to Bywater is modelled on the proverb in Plato's *Republic*: *arche pantos ergou megiston*, cf. the commentary to 1450a22, 167.

[182] It is problematic to define Aristotle's observations on drama as exclusively prescriptive or descriptive, cf. Brian Vickers, *Towards Greek Tragedy*, London: Longman, 1979.

[183] *Aesthetics, Lectures on Fine Art*, trans. T. M. Knox. Oxford: Clarendon, 1975, II, 1166.

tinct object the whole action strives to attain. To understand the nature of this goal as well as of the striving, the beginning of action has to be captured.

The state immediately preceding action is collision for Hegel. Collision is not yet action, but stimulus to action, which characterizes a situation.[184] Collision appears in the act of violation, when a previous harmony is shattered to be later restored in a more advanced form. The opposing elements collide in a situation where the circumstances prove to be untenable. The collision affects the world condition by violating it, and the unity of the Ideal is brought into discord. Hegel sees the main vocation of art precisely in preventing the total destruction of the beauty of the Ideal by representing the discord in a way that harmony may be restored through resolution (205). Action then, starts when the contradiction contained in the situation appears on the scene. This situation which harbours opposing forces like the external world and subjective consciousness, gains shape as a particular situation only through the passion which experiences it as such. The commencement of action is effectuated by the compelling force of untenable circumstances. The "emotional life" reacts in passion against what restricts it, against external constraint and through this confronting action stimulates the countermovement or reaction of the opposing force. Action, then, presupposes circumstances that necessitate collisions, action and reaction (217). When claiming that it is impossible to pinpoint when exactly an action will commence, since the beginning itself may turn out to be the consequence of previous collisions, Hegel refers to the Trojan and the Theban cycle of myths. The lack of differentiation between plot and myth and consequently the means (*prologos*, etc.) of the former to incorporate the latter to the extent of the governing purpose of emplotment, do not prevent Hegel from concluding that the starting point is relative (218). The correct understanding of the beginning is postponed until the end is defined as the concrete reconciliation of actual conflict. If a tragedy is to have one action, it is selected from a series of actions encompassed in myth and actualized in performance.

What Hegel says about action is reaffirmed in the condensed statement by A. O. Rorty, namely that there can be no action without purpose and energy (pathos) to fulfil it.[185] The inherent difficulty con-

---

[184]*Ibid.*, I, 204.
[185]"The Psychology of Aristotelian Tragedy", in *Essays on Aristotle's Poetics*, ed. A. O. Rorty, 7.

cerning the relation between purpose and pathos, however, calls for the justification of their unrestricted juxtaposition. Attributing the same agent to both seems problematic, since as Rorty adds, "an action is only partially identified and directed by the agent's intentions".[186] This seems to make room for alternative purposes that precede alternative intentions of alternative agents. The latter's purpose may be very different, if not contrary to that of the individual, whose passion follows self-made goals. The double purpose of action is qualified more explicitly by Hegel, in the strivings of the individual will against the universal, until the two coalesce in final reconciliation. Definite ends and individuals unite in harmonious action as the contradiction is annihilated: this is Hegel's definition of reconciliation.[187]

To better understand the total effect of reconciliation (*Versöhnung*) as also involving absolution, I must return to Hegel's analysis of action expounded in his *Phenomenology of Spirit*. There the collision is described as the contradiction between two absolute powers: the powers of the ethical order opposed to ethical consciousness, divine opposed to human law.[188] Action in this context necessarily incurs guilt, since it asserts particularity and remains blind in relation to the other, similarly righteous power. These two opposed powers or laws gain shape through the polarization of the ethical substance, *sittliche Wesen* itself. Self-consciousness is the allotted attribute of one of the laws and is countered by the concealed other, as soon as action takes place. Expression or assertion of the particularity of consciousness by the individual through action is, therefore at the same time the negation of the ethical reality and as such inevitably one-sided. The ethical content by definition cannot tolerate one-sidedness and transforms its activity into guilt. Guilt for Hegel then, is the affirmation of this one-sidedness, *Einseitigkeit* through action, which is necessarily contemporaneous with the violation of the opposed pole. It follows from this conception of action that innocence is precisely the want of action, *Nichttun*, which is "a state like the mere being of a stone and one which is not even true of a child" (487). In this negative definition of innocence we find the resonance of Luther's categorical statement

---

[186] Cf. "the ends that direct our actions can be opaque to us, even when we are acting from our clearest and best understanding", *ibid*.
[187] G. W. F. Hegel, *Lectures on Fine Art*, II, 1197.
[188] Trans. J. B. Baillie, London: George Allen & Unwin Ltd.; New York: The Macmillan Company, 1910, 485.

that all human works necessarily incur evil due to the utter corruption of human nature.

The conflict, arising from the individual effectuating his particularity, is tragic. It is tragic, because both of the opposing forces are justified in the struggle to assert themselves and the victory of one necessarily brings about the annihilation of the other. In the final reconciliation of tragedy what is cancelled is the one-sided particularity responsible for the violation of harmony. The action of this one-sidedness is itself the pathos, the real basis of collisions, therefore, since the action is inseparably linked to pathos, the individual has to be sacrificed.[189]

Sacrifice of the individual, however, is not always a necessary culmination in tragedy, according to Hegel. He sees the tragic dominate also in plays like the *Eumenides*, where ultimate downfall is not needed for "obliterating the one-sidedness of both sides" (1218). It seems problematic to subsume under the "tragic" plays like the *Eumenides*, the *Philoctetes* or the *Oedipus at Colonus* on Hegelian grounds. Hegel's own account of these plays is revealing in its aptness to subvert itself. Is the end of the *Oresteia* the removing of the overemphasized one-sidedness of Orestes or, rather, its divine affirmation? Is particularity annihilated in tragic resolution or justified by universality through melodramatic collaboration? Does not fate, defined by Hegel as a power which "drives the personality back upon its limits and shatters it, when it has grown overweening" (1216), find itself shattered? After laying out a conceptually consistent account of tragedy, Hegel's key terms seem to be inapplicable for a systematic, all-encompassing classification.[190]

Tragedy, then, is claimed to accommodate even actions in which the individual surrenders his one-sidedness and appears as void of pathos (*in dem Ablassen von ihrem substantiellen Pathos*) and lacking in character (*characterlos*). Whether such an individual can be made a tragic hero is admittedly questionable, since "this contradicts the masculine solidity [*Gediegenheit*] of the Greek plastic figures" (1218). Destitution of character for Aristotle is to be avoided in tragedy. On the contrary, it should be his foremost aim to be good (1454a16). Furthermore, among Aristotle's criteria for character, we find consis-

---

[189] *Lectures on Fine Art*, II, 217.
[190] A holistic account for all tragedies, Hegelian or other, is inevitably utopian due to the insurmountable diversity that presents itself as defying subsumation under one and the same genre.

tency, *homalon*, "even if the subject represented is someone inconsistent and such character is presupposed, he should still be consistently inconsistent" (1454a25). The individual's surrendering of his self-constituting one-sidedness is at the same time constitutive of a melodramatic closure at the expense of tragic fulfilment. This seems to be the case in Sophocles' *Philoctetes*. It is due to the untimely[191] breakdown of the tragic conflict in *Philoctetes*, a play illustrative of self-surrender, that Hegel's account of tragedy proves once more inapplicable. Philoctetes surrenders himself in submission to Heracles' command. The unresolvable contradiction is abruptly annihilated by a *deus ex machina*.

Similarly, as a further mode of reconciliation, Hegel praises that in *Oedipus at Colonus*, which, being more beautiful than the previous variants of external resolution, takes place in the soul itself (1219). It is highly doubtful whether an action without an irresistible external compulsion for reconciliation can be labelled "tragic". In terms of action Hegel recounts the prehistory of Oedipus in the *Oedipus Tyrannus* and ignores the fact that in the very beginning of the drama of consequence, *Oedipus at Colonus,* the reconciliation has already taken place. The *telos* of action is envisaged before it has started. The pathos emphasizing one-sidedness is replaced by an appeased soul matured in suffering. Where the soul is reconciled with itself and the world before and beyond action, there can be no genuine tragedy. It will be argued that it is the underlying structural principle of melodrama to enable the subject to envisage fulfilment already in the *arche*.

Despite its defects conspicuous in the analysis of the plays above, Hegel's view on the commencement of action and tragic reconciliation is relevant to my present argument, due to its inclusion of perspectival difference. Resolution from the character's point of view is either complete destruction or compelled resignation.[192] Reconciliation viewed internally, however, seems untenable. It may be argued that it makes no sense when taken to be integral to individual aspirations,

---

[191] Untimely and unexpected, in the sense that the two opposing wills, the human will of Philoctetes and the divine will represented by Neoptolemus, coalesce before the fulfilment of tragic reconciliation. In contrast with the immovable determination of Odysseus to mediate divine pre-ordinance, Neoptolemus' plastic character gradually yields to the opposing will. This weakness of antagonism has to be compensated for by the God, whose appearance guarantees a happy ending.

[192] I am following here Osmaston's translation which maintains the original *resignieren, The Philosophy of Fine Art*, trans. F. P. B. Osmaston, London: G. Bell and Sons Ltd., 1920, 297. Cf. Knox, "abandon the accomplishment of its aim" (1197).

for the only reason that the primary cause of individual action was the irreconcilability with circumstances. What in both cases of the internal modalities of reconciliation (destruction and resignation) has to be achieved, is the drastic abatement of the over-emphasized aspects. The abrogation of one-sidedness as reinstatement of harmony on the other hand, is affirmed as such only from a non-one-sided perspective. The abrogation of one-sidedness is therefore concomitant with the confirmed justification of non-one-sidedness that in its turn, as in Hegel's example of the various cycles of myths, proves one-sided in transformed circumstances. The dialectic of one-sidedness and non-one-sidedness in reconciliation thus continues in a dramatic sequence of actions to reveal the ambiguous and temporary character of tragic reconciliation. It seems that for Hegel the over-emphasized aspects inherent in tragic action are overruled by an excess of perspective. Reconciliation can only be cathartically grasped as final and temporary at the same time by the cosmic spirit. In what follows I will attempt to abrogate this excess of perspective and at the same time maintain perspectival difference crucial for a teleological classification.

Dual perspective and teleological classification

Dual perspective, in my use of the term, includes insider and outsider perspectives. The former, as mentioned above, is the prerogative of the hero, other characters and the chorus. The latter is the privilege of the author-reader-audience triad. This sequestering of perspectives is relevant in its mediating role of foreshadowing what will be termed "differential teleology". Differential teleology, characteristic of pure tragedy, harbours the opposition between the subjective *telos* of the hero (immanent and constitutive of his action) and the objective *telos* of plot-structure. It may be argued that the hero's subjective teleological sequence of actions can hardly be isolated and identified without regard to the actions of other characters. Action is always interaction and the interactive potential of the other characters is always already present in its commencement. However, the borders and the procedure of heroic action, similarly to the incurred reaction, are in terms of understanding, subject to an insider projection of subjective *telos*. In other words, interpretation is subjected to a misleading prevalence of delusion.

Delusion here is not merely a contingent attribute of insider perspective. On the contrary, it pertains to its very nature. Deluded perspective becomes enlightened perspective in tragic recognition, when the whole past history of action is illuminated in accordance with the organizing principle of a new *telos* tragically incompatible with its subjective predecessor. The real direction of the action is revealed in retrospect, when the hero discovers at his own expense his identity and fate. This retroactive constitution of the self in the light of the belated understanding of the objective *telos* is also the realization of a new *arche*. The final confirmation of differential teleology is contemporaneous with the final recognition of a new beginning. The acknowledgement and realization of difference is a revelation of identity. Oedipus' act of self-blinding can be seen in this sense, as the only act of learned identity. The *arche* of the action of Oedipus as King in search for the cause of the plague is very different from that of the action undertaken by the Oedipus of recognition. Discovering the real *arche* is made possible only in tragic *anagnórisis*. The subjectively non-envisaged self-affirmation of objective *telos* is a means not only of breaking down insider aspiration, but also a means for informing and constituting identity. Oedipus' self-imposed suffering, following from recognition seen in its double sense of delusion-authentication, is tragic in the *Oedipus Tyrannus* and melodramatic in *Oedipus at Colonus*. In the latter action and identity appear to be more or less independent from differential teleology, which consists in the externality of objective *telos* affirming itself against subjective understanding and authenticating heroic action in recognition. Oedipus appears at Colonus as already authenticated, that is, if we approach the play in isolation, disregarding its mythical prehistory. What remains, then, to be justified is a tragically anachronistic self-validating move in plot-structure. This anachronism in plot-structure is the situating of the acquisition of identity prior to the prescribed plot components of reversal and recognition.

The two Oedipus plays thus reveal the underlying structural discrepancy between tragedy and melodrama. It is relevant, however, to observe that differential teleology perseveres in the face of tragic recognition. The acknowledgement of delusion and the belated (non-anachronistic) constitution of identity in recognition are not contemporaneous with the reconciliation between subjective and objective goals. In this retroactive self-constitution the individual is eventually made to realize the contrary workings of objective *telos*. This individual understanding nevertheless consists in the acknowledgement of these incompatible or parallel tendencies of an alien teleology and not in the full recognition of objective *telos* itself. The division of perspectival goals in tragedy remains irreconcilable. In melodrama on the other hand, as in the *Eumenides*, the tragic discrepancy is substituted for a final justification of human goals. Here the complicity of divine will with human aspirations is the confirmation of the insider-heroic perspective and the self-mitigation of objective *telos*. Orestes' matricide is in this sense, justified by the divine command of Apollo, a process engendering a melodramatic culmination in the reconciliation of goals. This closure is brought about by the cadential moderation of the fate-Erinyes into the appeased Eumenides. It is not by chance that the latter goddesses are the local ruling deities in the *Oedipus at Colonus*.

A similar compatibility of goals presents itself at the end of the *Philoctetes*. The objective *telos* there is announced by the *deus ex machina* and as a consequence, the hierarchical distance is abridged to secure a unification of goals. Heracles brings foreknowledge of and promise for the future. Thereby the hero is willing to surrender his personal struggle for the subjective *telos* and to follow the divine command towards elevation and harmony.

Teleological classification then, enhanced by the perspectival view, as outlined above, asks us to reconsider the Hegelian concept of tragic reconciliation. The absence of generic differentiation within tragedies leads Hegel to merge an extreme diversity into a unified whole. This is carried out at the expense of having to dispense with a pre-established conceptual framework. The problem of reconciliation has to be recuperated under the light of the new findings in relation to differential teleology. For Hegel reconciliation means the final appeasement of conflicting forces through the abrogation of one-sidedness. At the same time, however, reconciliation proved paradoxical in an overruling dialectics attesting to an over-emphasized perspective. From such an endlessly distanced perspective the actuality of performance or reading would fail to achieve its cathartic effects.

A reduced scope of perspectives, in the manner of the proposed differentiation between insider and outsider perspectives, introduced in the present analysis, situates tragic reconciliation on a more focused plane. Following my argument, reconciliation of conflict in tragedy cannot be also the reconciliation of subjective and objective goals. In fact, what the hero is finally made to accept is precisely the irreconcilability of necessarily divergent goals. The conflict is brought to a halt in tragic recognition, the contradiction is apparently resolved, but the open-endedness remains. Resolution in this sense is not concomitant with reconciliation from a teleological standpoint. The irreconcilability of the discrepancy between goals is maintained until death. In death the confirmation of mortality and finitude proves itself to be an integral part of a higher purpose. Finitude dramatized is the performed resignation to the irreconcilability between individual aspirations and the invincible power of tragedy. The objective *telos*, prerogative exclusively of this absolute divine power or fate, subsumes and uses finitude itself in ways insider perspective can never account for. In tragedy nevertheless, the notion of new *arche*, crystallizing in recognition, enables the hero to grasp his finitude as such, that is, as incapable of accounting for itself. The tragic experience framed by delusion-authentication has to be understood in this sense, namely that the miscarrying of deception and its individual recognition are essential preliminaries of an authentic internalization of finitude.[193] The constitution of identity on the level of myth is the proper identification with finitude. It is this representation of a transformed consciousness of finitude that the actuality of performance brings about. The notion of finitude is shared by insider and outsider perspectives and serves as a point of identification, effectuating *katharsis*.[194]

Here we are inevitably confronted with critical attempts at internalizing *katharsis*. The ultimate effect traditionally expected from the spectator is moved into the play itself, like in G. F. Else's innovative commentary.[195] This understanding of recognition as the scene of purification reserves *katharsis* for insider appropriation. Tragedy then, is argued to affect the spectator through the preliminary cleansing of the hero, when outsider response is based not so much on identification but rather, on compassion.[196] We begin to pity Oedipus after he has

---

[193] For the association of the tragic with finitude (*endlichkeit*), see Dietrich Mack's account of an argument by Kurt von Fritz in *Ansichten zum Tragischen und zur Tragödie*, 135-140. Fritz approaches the problem from the question of suffering (Leid) and argues that undeserved tragic suffering is a necessary consequence of a defect in the hero, namely of his finitude. However, my present analysis concentrates on an acquired notion of finitude and not merely finitude *as such*.

[194] The element of finitude, *endliches Sein*, as point of identification between hero and spectator is especially emphasized by Gadamer, *Wahrheit und Methode*, 126.

[195] "The question is how *katharsis* is operated and the answer is that it is operated by the plot .... It is Oedipus's self-blinding, his transport of grief and remorse when he learns the truth, that finally assures us of his purity and releases our tears. Thus recognition is the structural device which makes it possible for the hero to prove that he did indeed act *di' hamartian tina* and so deserves our pity", *Aristotle's Poetics: The Argument*, 438.

[196] This explanation of *katharsis* encourages extreme views on the effects of tragedy, like Lacan's statement that there is no *katharsis* in *Antigone*, since neither Creon, nor Antigone feels fear or pity, cf. *The Ethics of Psychoanalysis*, ed. Jacques-Alain Miller, trans. Dennis Porter, London: Routledge Tavistock, 1992, 258.

been purified. This view of *katharsis*, needless to say, carries us far from Aristotle's own definition which, on the contrary, reserves the application cf the term for the outsider response, the purification of pity and fear, of compassion.[197] Compassion is aroused only to be removed in *katharsis* to engender the identification of insider and outsider perspectives through finitude. A plot structured on probability and necessity asks the reconsideration of the tragic experience from the standpoint of confirmed finitude. The confirmation of finitude then, to my understanding, is contemporaneous with the removal of delusion.

The concept of delusion serves as a structural axis of tragedy, around which the difference of objectives asserts itself.[198] Due to its significance for the present teleological itinerary, it needs further consideration with regard to its manifest forms.

As a general rule, delusion is closely related to one-sidedness characterizing finitude. The finite conception of the *telos* of action is necessarily biased and wayward. This underlying ontological fallacy, a defect in being itself, is expressed in the one-sidedness of action. In Hegel's view, one-sidedness is activated through pathos, when circumstances and conditions are transformed into situation. The situation is established when the circumstances are no longer tenable and harmony is shattered by collision. In tragedy this transformed state of affairs provides the grounds for the pathetic one-sidedness to activate itself. The expressive representation of this waywardness in dramatic action is also the dramatization of finitude and consequently the emplotment of delusion. Delusion appertaining to the nature of pathetic one-sidedness is evident in its inability to see itself as such. This is the tragic blindness of Antigone and Creon alike. Their subjective waywardness in pursuing their respective goals is eliminated only in death. Creon's disproportionate punishment for ignoring the sacred duties of kinship is the irremediable loss of his wife and son. Through this loss the failure of one-sided aspirations and the waywardness of subjective *telos* are revealed and Creon's identity authenticated.

Delusion, however, may be exercised by an external force, when an offended deity descends to mislead the over-confident mortal. The

---

[197] For a defence of the traditional notion of *katharsis* and a criticism of Else's commentary see Wimsatt, *Hateful Contraries*, 87-89.
[198] Elton differentiates between benevolent and malevolent deception and takes the examples of Edgar and Edmund, *King Lear and the Gods*, 86. To my understanding, however, the dramatic function of delusion is not so much characterized by its being benevolent or malevolent, as by its being necessary.

discrepancy between subjective and objective goals in these cases of deceiving divine intervention is most conspicuous. These didactic forms of deception determine action in tragedies like *Ajax*, *Hippolytus*, *The Madness of Heracles*, *Bacchanals*, etc., and elicit the authentication of action and identity. Such extremes of direct interference with human aspirations may seem to be isolated instances of what Ricoeur calls the theology of blinding. Situating these instances in the context of our speculations on delusion, it may be argued that what appears as isolated, is, in fact, a didactic form of representing the manipulative operation of objective teleology. In this sense it is delusion inherent in finitude that is evinced and exposed by the direct external interference.

The respective elicitations of authenticated action prove the inauthenticity of all preceding human endeavours. Both at the same time appear to be indispensable within an encompassing totality of tragic action. By the individual acknowledgement of delusion, inauthenticity becomes a necessary prerequisite for constituting identity. This authentic knowledge of oneself is precisely the integration of inauthenticity as inherent in one's finitude itself. The acquisition of this tragic wisdom takes place in the new *arche* of action, in recognition. Deludedness then, is finally overcome. This stage of overcoming is simultaneously the culmination of tragic action, as in the *Oedipus Tyrannus*, since, as argued above, when made the basis and starting point of action, as in the *Oedipus at Colonus*; appears void of the required preconditions for tragic wisdom and becomes melodramatic. The suicide of Ajax, the self-blinding of Oedipus, the self-sacrifice of Makaria and the various consummations of individual suffering[199] are all instances of authentic action, dictates of tragic wisdom.

The close interdependence of delusion-deception and authentication as illustrated above, has been grasped as such through the preliminary stabilization of what I called dual perspective and differential teleology. The necessary waywardness of the subjective *telos* was claimed to be revealed in the recognition of the contrary workings of the objective *telos*. The stress was laid on the contrary workings, to highlight the persevering irreconcilability of goals. The individual realization of irreconcilability itself was presented as a new understanding of tragic reconciliation. What seemed a substantial precondition for such a conclusion was the immovability and invincibility of the objective *telos* or fate. The identification of the ultimate purpose of

---

[199] For the element of suffering prescribed by Aristotle, cf. *Poetics* 1452b9.

fate is the exclusive privilege of the representatives of outsider perspective versed in mythology.

Fate from a teleological point of view may be equated therefore with the objective *telos*, the preserver of the harmonious totality of myth. It needs to be added at the same time that not all the so-called traditional stories of mythology qualify as raw material for tragedy. According to Aristotle's restrictions, the plot (*mythos*) should recount a transformation from prosperity to adversity, *metabole ex eutychias eis dustychian* (1453a14). It is most tragic, *tragicótatos*, when the plays end in adversity, *eis dustuchian teleutosin* (1453a26). Euripides here is given preference as exemplary dramatist, who despite his other defects, is the most tragic of poets, precisely for his frequent and thorough exploitation of unhappy endings. The role of *mythos* as *telos* of tragedy and the rule of adverse cadence are given prominence in the *Poetics* and linked in this synthetic statement: the end is adversity.

In tragedy therefore action, necessitated by selective emplotment and organized by differential teleology, is also characterized by a pre-subordination to an unfortunate conclusion. The harmonious totality of myth safeguarded by fate and objective *telos* is, consequently, to be understood to contain the necessary pre-subordination to adverse cadence in plot construction.

Melodramatic potential in Shakespeare

The recourse to differential teleology and adverse cadence to secure the isolation of the tragic from the melodramatic proves feasible also in Shakespearean drama. There we find the same mechanism of delusion-authentication expose itself for perspectival scrutiny. We must take into account, however, that it is problematic to label any Shakespearean play a melodrama, with the possible exception of *Titus Andronicus* to which I shall return later. The focus of the following brief survey therefore will be restricted to some indications of melodramatic potential inherent in the tragedies.[200] The pinpointing of this potential may serve to illuminate the architectonics of the genre as a whole.

Instead of the typical commencement of Greek tragedies, which presents a hero predestined to delusion, Shakespearean figures like Richard the Third or Lady Macbeth appear on the stage as endowed with apparently self-assured identity. The self-confidence and com-

---

[200] For a systematic account of the generic regularities of Shakespearean tragedy and melodrama see Robert B. Heilman, *Tragedy and Melodrama: Versions of Experience*.

mitment to individual purpose implies an anachronistically acquired selfhood. This assuredness is made explicit in Richard's prologue, "I am determined to prove a villain / And hate the idle pleasures of these days" (I.ii.30-31).[201] This programmed deliberation is based on a confessed identity, "I am subtle, false and treacherous" (37). Both didactic articulations of aspiration and identity run contrary to Aristotle's appertaining requirements. The hero, according to the *Poetics*, should not fall into adversity through evil and depravity (*dia kakian kai mochterian*), but through some kind of error (*hamartia*) (1453a8-9).

At this point in *Richard the Third* there is nothing to indicate that Richard's self-identity is based on an erroneous judgement of himself. It is only in recognition, enhanced by the ghosts of the murdered victims, that the error of misconception of identity is confirmed in the words of conscience:

> O coward conscience, how dost thou afflict me! [....]
> What do I fear? Myself? There's none else by;
> Richard loves Richard, that is I and I.
> Is there a murderer here? No. Yes, I am!
> Then fly. What, from myself? Great reason why,
> Lest I revenge? What, myself upon myself?
> (V.iii.180-87)

The former self and its misdirected actions are here distanced, "I rather hate myself for the hateful deeds committed by myself" (190-91). The character appears as divided within itself, which in Richard's case is also the surfacing of personal value. In recognition internal division seems to reveal the deludedness of the previously maintained self-identity and authenticates the character through the removal of delusion. This removal of delusion preserving false identity, is constitutive of a new beginning, an authentic identity which sees itself as divided and which as such exposes immanent virtue. Personal excellence and virtue revealed in dividedness cancel an impending melodramatic closure through their final annihilation in death. In other words, one could argue that it is the loss of authentically surfaced value that creates tragic completion.

Misjudgement of personal identity, confirmed in retrospect is an inevitable failure, the acknowledgement of which brings tragic wisdom. Tragic wisdom is authenticated self-knowledge, which accord-

---

[201] All references to Shakespearean plays are from the respective Arden editions.

ing to the generic precepts of tragedy, is concomitant with extensive suffering and death.

We find similar congruence of ceasing delusion and acquired wisdom in *Macbeth*. In her role of proximate instigator, Lady Macbeth appears as a domesticated witch, fully intent on exploiting the rising opportunity of regicide. The fervour of deliberation itself implies an already unsexed or rather sexless[202] nature, which is problematic with regard to effectuating instigation. Lady Macbeth unsexed could not possibly achieve influence on a puzzled husband.

The assumed one-dimensional stabilization of identity is expressly melodramatic in the defiance of human qualities, "no compunctious visitings of Nature / Shake my fell purpose" (I.v.45). It can hardly be doubted that after this determination of identity and purpose, reminiscent of that of Richard's, it is precisely and exclusively the compunctious visitings of Nature, that can secure tragic fulfilment. In other words, this purposive deliberation has to be redefined as a delusion on the tragic schema and proved anachronistic.

It is the scene of recognition in somnambulism that identity is confronted with itself. The futile attempt to eliminate the effects of the deed, "will these hands ne'er be clean?" (V.i.41) shows the unpremeditated delimitation of identity by action. The dividedness of the character is concomitant with the realization of incorrigibility, "what's done cannot be undone" (64). The scene of indelible defilement contextualizes the tragic recognition of identity. The despair foreshadowing the authenticated act of suicide is the unconscious counterpart of Richard's sober conclusion: "I shall despair" (V.iii.201).

A more didactic mode of delusion is, of course, that of Macbeth himself. The prophecy of the witches, which seemingly vouchsafes protection for the hero, engenders overconfidence and pride in him. This pride is manifest in the forgetting of finitude in the supernaturally encouraged mastering of the future.[203] Finitude at the same time asserts itself in the paradox of disbelief: Macbeth cannot conceive of the supernatural mobility of Birnam wood and the possibility of being murdered by a not-of-woman-born, though he never doubts the

---

[202]She will soon confirm her sexlessness in the meticulous arrangement of execution, when she "dares do more than may become a man", and becomes "none". "None" here indicates superhuman or devilish, cf. Arden fn. to I.vii.47, ed. Kenneth Muir, London and New York: Routledge, 1994.

[203]Cf. Macbeth's offhand reaction to the servant's announcement of the approaching English force: "Where gott'st thou that goose look? .... Go, prick thy face and overred thy fear, / Thou lily-liver'd boy. What soldiers, patch?" (V.iii.12,14-15).

prophesying supernatural forces. It is only when the unexpected turns reality, the state of delusion transformed into the state of dividedness, that Macbeth is confronted with the contrary workings of fate, "and be these juggling fiends no more believ'd, / That palter with us in a double sense" (V.viii.19-20). Equivocation presents itself here to reinforce the fair-is-foul-foul-is-fair pattern,[204] and to confirm the nonviable aspirations of self-idolizing finitude. In didactic representations of delusion, however, this inherent double sense is made conspicuous from the very beginning of action, through the duplication of perspectives. The first appearance of the chthonic ministers of fate and their encounter with Macbeth already establish an incompatible divergence of visions, which only outsider perspective can account for. The fair-is-foul-foul-is-fair pattern is the foundation of a superhuman truth, to which the individual can only unconsciously consent, "so foul and fair a day I have not seen" (I.iii.38).[205] This unconscious confirmation of the predominance of a superior organizing principle becomes conscious in recognition through reflection on the double sense.

Apart from Macbeth we hardly find didactic representations of delusion in Shakespeare. Though, it may be argued that the ghost of *Hamlet* predestines with a delusive command. It is not deluding because the ghost "may be a devil" who "abuses me to damn me" (II.ii.595,599), since tragic delusion, as expounded above, cannot tolerate its anachronistic revelation. What never presents itself as an impossibility to Hamlet in his reflecting procrastination is the demand of private revenge. The King is never alone, publicity serves to camouflage privacy in pretence. The only occasion for private revenge is Claudius's attempt at prayer, when considerations of heavenly afterlife prevent the regicide. The scene of prayer then, is significant for at least two reasons.

Firstly, Hamlet's task reveals itself as an impasse, the impossibility of private revenge. The impasse is asserted in the exaggeration of the task on the one hand, and in a mistake on the other.[206] The exaggerated concentration on Claudius's perdition points to the inevitably exaggerated character of the command itself: revenge by definition

---

[204] For the constantly recurring tone of equivocality let us recall Macduff's often neglected though crucial statement following Malcolm's deliberately puzzling self-criticism: "Such welcome and unwelcome things at once, / 'Tis hard to reconcile" (IV.iii.138-39).
[205] The verbal resonance of superhuman truth in Macbeth's first sentence already shows the necessary subordination of heroic aspiration to predicting forces.
[206] Cf. Levin, *The Question of Hamlet*.

transcends privacy. However, at the same time Hamlet is mistaken in postulating salvation for the King, since the prayer is unsuccessful, "words without thoughts never to heaven go" (III.iii.98).

Secondly, the contrition scene averts the melodramatic potential inherent in Claudius's public role-play. The latter involves the Machiavellian machinations of pretence, which characterize Claudius's initial appearance. The speech of the declaration of power presents a rhetorical mingling of public affairs with personal interests. Matters of privacy claim general appreciation and justification through their seemingly casual insertion between the public remembrance of mourning and foreign policy (remembrance of "our dear brother's death" and the territorial claims of young Fortinbras). The stabilization of institutionalized identity is in its inception grounded on role-play and appearance. The apparent perfection of appearance defines the character until recognition, when disguise succumbs to dividedness, intent to guilt, "my stronger guilt defeats my strong intent" (III.iii.40).

The recognition of indelible defilement in the words: "Is there not rain enough in the sweet heavens / To wash it[207] white as snow?" (45-6) reminds of Lady Macbeth's futile washing of her stained hands.[208] The common tone of despair is complemented with an acquired notion of incorrigibility in the experience of an excess of blood stains for Lady Macbeth and of binding present possessions for Claudius, "I am still possess'd / Of those effects for which I did the murder" (54).[209]

Tragic recognition, then, as argued above, involves the transformation of false identity to internal conflict that engenders dividedness and the simultaneous surfacing of human value. Without a proportionate discovery of an object of appreciation in the character, the impending human loss would enhance a melodramatic closure. At the same time proportion needs further consideration as a generic determinant in relation to delusion. The absence of transformation in Iago's character does not make *Othello,* the play, melodramatic, while Aaron's rigid immovability seems to justify the isolation of *Titus Andronicus* as a version of Shakespearean melodrama. The emphasized inflexibility of the deceiver-villain on the tragic schema has to be proportionate with the dividedness produced in the deceived victim. Iago's rigidity,

---

[207] I.e., the "cursed hand" (43).
[208] Cf. "All the perfumes of Arabia will not sweeten this little hand" (V.i.47-48).
[209] See also Lady Macbeth's "What's done cannot be undone" (V.i.64) and Claudius's "My fault is past" (III.iii.51).

in this sense, serves to increase the dividedness in Othello and to prepare a tragic downfall. Aaron's immovability[210] on the contrary, is disproportionately magnified, since there appears to be no counter-movement in Titus's heroic consciousness.

These variations of inter-subjective delusion present a situation, when an opposing aspiration gains predominance temporarily. In such cases these deceivers, observed from outsider perspective, prove merely mediators in the unfolding of a more profound existential experience of delusion, when the deceived seems to enlarge the actuality of delusion to a transformed understanding of Being. The extension of the actuality of delusion can be further illustrated by the examples of *Hamlet* and *King Lear*. Though the forms of delusion in these plays may seem diverse, yet they converge toward the same scope of extension. For Hamlet, the actuality of revenge presents itself as an existential problem from the very start, what is more, this actuality in the course of events proves to be anomalous and consequently delusive, since publicity is throughout implicitly involved. Private revenge under the circumstances is impossible. This existential extension therefore is necessary and, as we have seen, leads to the radical questioning not only of revenge itself, but basically of Being as such:

> What piece of work is a man [....] and yet, to me, what is this quintessence of dust? Man delights not me
> (II.ii.303, 308-309)

In *King Lear* the hero becomes deluded by dotage in the first place and by verbose ambition, which is the natural consequence of the former. The actuality here consists in the dividing of the kingdom and Cordelia's reiterated "nothing" expresses and at the same time subverts this context of commerce. This particular scene of "filial ingratitude" is later to become extended by Lear himself, when in the unforeseen sequence of descending moves he comes to a similar existential experience as Hamlet: "Is man no more than this? Consider him well" (III.iv.95). In these dramatic articulations of extended experience the questioning self as it were, extends his own self-understanding by reflecting on his own finitude. It is along these steps that our initial subject, the threshold of the tragic begins to present

---

[210] Consider: "I am no baby, I, that with base prayers / I should repent the evils I have done; / Ten thousand worse than ever yet I did / Would I perform, if I might have my will. / If one good deed in all my life I did, / I do repent it from my very soul" (V.iii.185-90).

itself. In the following investigations this threshold will take on yet another meaning, namely the severance of self from character.

V. From Character to Self

Heroic stature and dividedness
The tragic hero is a hero by virtue of his high stature. According to Aristotle he is superior to us in contrast to the inferior hero of comedy. He has to be such so as to attract, since without attraction there is no personal involvement and no compassion. Yet exactly because of these necessary forms of outsider response, the hero cannot be of too high a stature. That would isolate him from the human concern for patterns of identification (i.e., has to be a mortal prone to errors and shatterable by his own finitude). His positive features therefore are not unequivocally magnified to the point of apotheosis, nor are his negative inclinations demonized. It needs to be said at the same time that these heroic potentials are not excluded from the delineation of his character. On the contrary, it is precisely the various ways of blending the antagonistic aspirations that constitute heroic stature or heroic character.[211] In this sense can a character like Richard the Third become a hero despite his own self-affirmation: "I'm determined to prove a villain and hate the idle pleasures of these days." His initial devilish presence is later mingled with the godlike power to interfere with and decide the destinies of inferior characters.

At the other extreme we find Timon of Athens, who though determined to prove a Christ-like incarnation of unconditional goodness and generosity, soon proves the opposite, when he becomes *misanthropos*. These alternations of extremities[212] in dramatic action unfold against the intentions and the teleological aspirations of the hero and engender dividedness in him. This accounts for the fact that we do not get to know the "real", actual Timon until he is forced to give up what

---

[211] The difference between hero and character is the difference between two actants, that of myth or history and that of tragedy. The distinguished position or stature of a tragic character, inherited from the mythical hero, explains the use of the term heroic character (later on abbreviated as character).
[212] Cf. Apemantus, "The middle of humanity thou never knewest, but / the extremity of both ends", William Shakespeare, *Timon of Athens*, ed. H. J. Oliver, London and New York: Routledge, 1994, 4.3.301-302.

turns out to be an assumed role and to live the unpremeditated cave-life of a hermit. It is again the retrospective re-evaluation of an apparent identity as mere role and the consequent elimination of the latter that reveals his self-identity. The dramatic pattern of one's finding oneself at the opposite extreme of one's actual position, however, proves melodramatic in Timon's case, since it lacks reflection and regret. He sways from one side to the other unaware of his predilection to extremities. In becoming the detester of mankind, it is to be noted that he never has any regrets concerning his own past delusions.[213] In Greek tragedy we find the same recurrent pattern. Oedipus discovers himself as the object of his own curse in the *Oedipus Tyrannus* and Heracles, the hero of the twelve works, cannot but find himself the assassin of his own children in *The Madness of Heracles*.

The movement from character to self therefore is also a transition from melodrama to tragedy, as I will attempt to demonstrate. However, this transition cannot be but gradual, since it requires an inquiry into characterization as such. The following sections will first of all try to define the basic concepts related to characterization. These stages of argumentation, based on debates with some of the major views held on character, include problems concerning the humanization or personification of character; the question of context; a critique of the emblematic view on character or character understood as sameness; the tensions between narrative and tragic identity; and finally, some dilemmas of outsider – and reader – response theories. It will be only in the last section that, having gone through the preliminary steps and having considered the conceptual paradigm of character, tragic identity – the main concern of this chapter – can be brought under scrutiny.

Character, aspiration, context

The question of whether characters in drama can be regarded as flesh-and-blood people is a troubling and often debated one. When Stanley Cavell addresses the issue he argues for their congruence, since his main purpose is to measure the words of the characters against the reasoning of ordinary language philosophy.[214] This, needless to say,

---

[213] Contrary to Richard's "I rather hate myself for hateful deeds committed by myself" (5.3.189-90); or Macbeth's confession to Macduff: "my soul is too much charged with blood of thine already."
[214] Stanley Cavell, *Disowning Knowledge,* New York: Cambridge University Press, 1987, 42-43.

presupposes that characters use ordinary language, moreover, that the characters are themselves ordinary people. Understanding the behaviour of characters, Cavell argues, is understanding the behaviour of our acquaintances, which we describe with predicates like "is in pain", "is ironic", "is jealous", etc. (40). In mapping out the history of character-centred criticism to introduce his own, Rawdon Wilson aptly summarizes the danger inherent in taking characters for actual persons: "Once characters are accepted as actual persons and not their illusions, it seems that nothing can be off limits: Desdemona may have slept with Cassio, Hamlet with his mother, Falstaff may have been a heroic warrior in past wars ...."[215] Following E. E. Stoll, Wilson points to the recurrent critical behaviour involved in these preferences, namely to projection.[216] We tend to project our emotions, desires, expectations and beliefs onto the characters, thus levelling a positional incongruity and delimiting the surplus of contextualized signification.

If we were to follow the psychologizing characterologists' example in accounting for characters in terms of the reality of everyday life and of our "relations to acquaintances", we would miss one crucial point of discrepancy, namely that characters always and only appear in pre-established contexts. My idea of contextualism goes beyond Wilson's understanding of conventionalism on the one hand, and what he calls "true-to-lifeness" on the other. In my opinion, it is one of the major purposes of dramatic performances, if there are any, to present

---

[215] Rawdon Wilson, *Shakespearean Narrative,* London: Associated University Presses, 1995, 155. At the same time Wilson is alert enough not to discard psychologizing tendencies as a whole: "Frye's proposition that every lifelike character rises upon a stock type suggests the complexity of the actual problem .... if a stock type has not been based upon (someone's) empirical observation and does not abstract actuality, then it would have as much claim upon a reader's attention as do those hybrid creatures of Renaissance romance such as the hippogriffin" (155). It is to Wilson's credit that he argues that characters may be seen not only as actual persons or as "structures of conventions (152), but as both. In delineating Falstaff's character he rightly underscores the weight of conventional types. Falstaff on Wilson's list may consequently be seen as created out of the *senex* or pantaloon (from the *commedia dell'arte*), the buffoon, the parasite, the *miles gloriosus* (a braggart soldier) or even as the medieval Vice-figure, the Riot or the social type of the Lord of Misrule (160). For the transcendence of the latter in the "impersonal pattern" of ritual, as Wilson puts it, see also C. L. Barber's *Shakespeare's Festive Comedy,* Princeton, 1959. Falstaff is, for Wilson, the epitome of both traditions, i.e., of character-centred criticism and conventional typification (270n).
[216] *Shakespearean Narrative,* 156. See also E. E. Stoll's "A Freudian Detective's Shakespeare", *Modern Philology* 48, 122-32.

"true-to-lifeness" as a contextualized mode of being.[217] In doing so they challenge any possible non-contextualized true-to-lifeness. In other words, they point to the ambiguity of the term as it appears in itself. To expose this equivocation is to suggest that true-to-lifeness is problematic as such. It contains two elements of rather ambiguous ontological status, namely "true" and "life". To say that a character at least partly approximates true-to-lifeness presupposes that there exists a prior understanding of these concepts and their relation. We compare our actual life-fragments to the presented episodes of the character's entire career (as it appears in the play). The dramatical context of performance for such an approach will naturally be of lesser importance.

In contrast, context, to my understanding, is not just a secondary attribute or circumstance in the process of characterization, but a determining factor in its creation. Characters for Hegel represent human aspirations (whatever those may be), emphasizing the latter (i.e., human aspirations), which thus seems to precede representation. Changing this order of importance for the present, I place a non-Hegelian emphasis on representation, *mimesis*, distancing contextualization. Making such a distinction is justified all the more when the dramatic context is seen as encompassing possible realities and not merely the current reality of outsiders. The fact that Hamlet's story takes place in Denmark does not impede outsider response in London or elsewhere. The fact that Macbeth's act of murder takes place in the bedchamber of his own castle does not mean we are supposed to be tactfully isolated in our stalls. We are involved because the action presents a quintessentially human aspiration. The actual context is thereby transformed into a primordial human context. Consequently, our secure current reality of the stalls is superseded by the threatening reality of tragic experience, the time and space of dramatic action is extended to an absolute reality. This phenomenon, in other words, is described by many critics and anthropologists as the ritualization of performance.

This conglomeration of possible events in what I called the absolute reality, is what is often understood by myth. In Greek tragedy myth was understood in terms of the tripartite hierarchy of man-God-

---

[217] According to Wilson true-to-lifeness and the unification of scattered psychological traits in the process of characterization is accomplished through self-consciousness, as Bakhtin had argued (269n). An approach to characterization through context, however, would define self-consciousness itself as contextualized, thereby rendering the status of the self of self-consciousness problematic. In Chapter 3 I posed the problem of character-self in relation to role and nature, both determined by context.

fate. It is my conviction that there is no purely tragic experience outside[218] this triadic structure. Extended time and space and the hierarchically framed action are the distinctive features of myth. It is this new form of contextualization that calls for a radical reformulation of the mentioned true-to-lifeness and of the correspondence between insider and outsider perspectives. The main advantage of this reformulation in contrast to character-centred criticism would be in the extra dimension of a contextualized teleological account of characterization. The framework of myth situates the character in the course of a defined teleological orientation, as mentioned earlier in our discussions on subjective and objective goals, the *teloi* of tragic action.

Returning to the problem of true-to-lifeness and correspondence, the question here arises: how are we to consider ourselves and our everyday reality in relation to this abstract composition of possibilities? A possible answer would be: "by way of analogy." It is by virtue of analogy that we allow our contingent actuality to be measured against the necessity ruling the domain of myth; knowing at the same time that a collage of possible realities infinitely exceeds our analogical understanding. It is this excess that renders total identification in the psychologist's sense questionable. Always infinitely more than our noncontextualized (or even decontextualized) acquaintances,[219] characters in tragic drama are closer to the figure of Everyman, though only in this sense and virtually none other.

The ways of analogical understanding and identification are manifold, so here I limit myself to the most conspicuous ones partly as recounted by Wilson. Wilson distinguishes three parallel "conceptual structures" as he calls them: First, the psychological model; second, the intellectual or ideological model; and third, the metahistorical model of split self-awareness (168). On the psychological model Shakespearean characterization is claimed to be based on the contemporary doctrine of humours, according to which the "ruling passion"

---

[218] I.e., without emphatic reference to the gods, fate and predestination or their representatives. In the terminology used above I allude to the blend of the ethical and the mythological schemata in the tragic.

[219] The real scope of this "more" needs some clarification. Wilson argues at one point that characters, when depicted as a cluster of traits are actually less than us, real persons, since the traits recounted are fewer (166). He hastens to add though that "actual human beings do not possess clusters of traits, nor do their traits accumulate in a structural or defining way". The emphasis on structure and definition here refers to the significance of artifice in the accumulation of traits into character (167). The comparative more then refers not so much to the number of traits as to the surplus of meaning generated by contextualization.

of a character is said to correspond to one of the humours, the human counterparts of the four elements, earth, water, air or fire.[220] This view of character combines physical and psychological composition by inferring one from the other. Though Hamlet's character on the psychological model would be explained by reference to the ruling temper of melancholy, it should be noted that this can yield only a partial explanation. For a fuller understanding of Hamlet, the psychological model would need to be complemented or even modified by alternative models or typologies like those of traditional revenge plays. The basic problem of this psychological inquiry is the implication of a continuity of psychological composition between that of Shakespeare's audience and of ourselves. Our knowledge of their actual psychological make-up and its analogical attribution to characters on stage is, of course, itself analogical, proving the lack of continuity[221] on the one hand, as well as the search for possible understanding on the other.

The intellectual model, as understood by Wilson, involves recourse to historical research on what the Renaissance audience had in mind about characters and their relation to these characters (168). Though this model focuses on the characters' intellectual make-up and ideological forms of representation rather than on psychological typification, it has to face similar problems. Critics following the second model would have to rely on a scarce and dubious corpus of textual evidence and engage in a hermeneutical struggle with these texts. Such an undertaking, far from bringing us closer to the patterns of the analogical understanding of the contemporary audience, would yet insert another obstruction to description, this time the deciphering of

---

[220] Cf. *Shakespearean Narrative*, 168. The humours being the four bodily fluids: blood, phlegm, yellow bile and black bile. The corresponding temperaments: sanguine, phlegmatic, choleric and melancholic.

[221] Wilson introduces another category of the psychological model, which may argue for the continuity lacking in the application of humours: psychoanalysis (cf. 169-71). Arguments for and against the psychoanalytical model are numerous and would exceed the scope of the present discussion. Nevertheless, there seems to be at least one factor of discontinuity that presents itself for a psychoanalytical approach. After decades of conceptual application of psychoanalysis to philosophy and literary criticism, as exemplified by Freud and Lacan themselves, it is hard to find an innocent audience who are unbiassed by these tendencies. It is fashionable and widely appreciated to promote psychoanalytical interpretations by turning Gertrude's closet into a bedroom, addressing the question of Hamlet's childhood and explaining King Lear's relation to Cordelia in terms of incest. This pervasion of stage performances and literary criticism by dogmas of psychoanalysis creates an audience well-versed in these theories and apt to consciously apply them in their own schemes of understanding.

historical texts.

The third model, by his own account the most interesting for Wilson, is a "model for the creation of thinking" that so the argument goes, is a distinctively Ovidian convention. This model expresses the split awareness of the character, a hero torn between alternatives, a mind which is in debate with "two antithetical positions and struggles against itself to arrive at a conclusion that supports one at the expense of the other" (174).[222] The critical appropriation of convention at this point brings us back to the issue of contextualism. As I claimed above, contextualism exceeds the scope of Wilson's idea of convention by extending to the "seemingly actual", namely the true-to-lifeness of characters. Considering *both* convention and true-to-lifeness as being necessary schemes for grasping characterization, Wilson is unaware of the blend of the two in tragedy. There one cannot fail to find the the critique of the true-to-lifeness of convention. True-to-lifeness of convention is questioned in tragic reflection, as I argued in Chapter 1, when the hero reflects on his own position allotted to him in myth. In pure tragedies this questioning does not yet shatter the hierarchical structure of myth, as it does in Euripidean tragicomedy and melodrama. It confirms it rather, after and by way of, challenging it.

My understanding of contextualism seeks to incorporate these blends in the structured series of dramatic actions. This series follows a prescribed sequence of plot-components to reach its culmination in *katharsis* and in the crystallization of tragic identity. The question arises whether identification with character apart from analogical is thinkable at all under the premises of a defined plot-structure. In other words: can a character step outside its context into our reality? Is there a point in the almost mechanistic sequence of plot-components where the impact of an event engenders personal (more than analogical) identification? In my view, as I will shortly venture to underscore in some detail, analogy is transcended by personal identification in the ultimate realization of finitude and the acquisition of identity. This moment of identification will be the vantage point from which the learned retrospect transfigures the causal structure of actions into scenes of the trial of finitude. First, however, certain influential views on character need to be addressed.

The concept of character throughout the long history of Shakespeare-criticism has created great confusion. Deviating from Aris-

---

[222] For the *topos* of heroic choice in Ovid's *Metamorphoses* and for the relation between Ovid and Euripides in terms of split awareness, see Wilson, 177.

totle's preference for the plot. A. C. Bradley introduced character-centred criticism in the beginning of the century and inspired a number of critics to follow his example. The term has ever since found its way into the labyrinth of scholarly exegeses rather confused by their own language games. The aporetic struggle to define the concept of character leads to the question: what is, if any, the conceptual paradigm underlying the notion of character?

When Cavell stresses the inseparability of understanding a character from understanding his words, he offers this as an answer to the short-sighted critical convention of dissociating the two. At the same time it also gives him an opportunity to introduce Wittgenstein's theory of language games into the interpretation of dramatic texts. It seems to me that there is yet a lot to be done on the language games of myth and tradition in literature, first and foremost in drama. The immediate (social) context of dramatic dialogues would then be seen in a different light, as a mere segment of the larger context of myth and tradition, which may prescribe other rules of language games. The Ghost's command to revenge may then be understood by Hamlet in diverse ways depending on the context attributed to it: the traditional context of revenge plays, the context of possible reprobation or the context of philosophical scepticism. What is more, one may ask, is not the tragedy of Hamlet the tragic confusion of language games? The impossibility to comply with the rules of tradition? Does not Hamlet's constantly vacillating reflection on this impossibility question the tenability of the myth of cyclic revenge? And his unpremeditated action, his clumsy version of revenge, its ultimate confirmation? It seems here we are discovering the tragic schema again, where myth is questioned by reflection and confirmed through action. The persistent recurrence of the significance of contextualization in tradition or myth brought us back to the alternative schematic ways of approaching dramatic action. It follows from our inferences above that the confusing problematic of characterization calls for the same procedure.

Schemata of characterization

From what has been said in Chapter 1 concerning the fundamental differentiation between alternative schematic modes of thinking, it follows that much of the detailed findings there are to be applied to characterization. There I argued that the tragic schema, being the proper mode of thinking in understanding tragedy, represents a conflict between the ethical schema pursued by the characters and the schema of myth introducing the metaphysics of indifference and hierarchy. The hero's ethico-schematic self-assessment of his allotted place in myth is undertaken through reflection, the exclusive trait of drama. I claimed that it is by and through reflection that the hero's dividedness and transformation is dramatized. Such preliminary diversification of schemata calls for a parallel approach, this time, to characterization itself.

As a continuation of the investigations above I will try to argue for the legitimacy of separating character as agent of moral behaviour from that of tragic action. My guideline in this undertaking will be Ricoeur's *Soi-même comme un autre*,[223] especially his concept of narrative identity in the fifth and sixth studies. It is through a promising confrontation with Ricoeur's ethical stance towards characterization that I hope to underpin my own approach to tragic character.

The fundamental step in constructing the conceptual network of this highly elaborate masterpiece called *Oneself as Another,* is taken in the fifth study, entitled "Personal Identity and Narrative Identity". There two meanings of identity are distinguished, one denoting sameness, *mêmeté,* the other selfhood, *ipséité* (116). The former is sometimes referred to as idem-identity, the latter as ipse-identity. During the entire procedure of grounding the notion of narrative identity, Ricoeur's motto and governing purpose will be the justification of selfhood as different from sameness. The argumentation develops through three points, which indicate the move from sameness to selfhood: Firstly, sameness; secondly, the blend of sameness and selfhood: character; and thirdly, selfhood.

The criteria of sameness for Ricoeur include "numerical identity", first of all, the claim for one thing as "one and the same thing"; "qualitative identity" based on resemblance; "uninterrupted continuity", identifying an individual as the same despite stages of development; and last but not least, "permanence in time", exemplified by reference to structure as opposed to event (116-17). This last criterion, permanence in time provides the link to a further move, namely to ask whether there is a form of permanence in time that cannot be reduced to the question of "what", but which, rather, can be applied to the question "who am I?" In other words, what Ricoeur is in search of is a form of permanence in time belonging to the person, to the "who" of self-interrogation. The two models offered are character, and keeping one's word *(caractère* and *parole tenue,* 118). The essential discrepancy between the two models is claimed to lie in their divergent rela-

---

[223] Paul Ricoeur, *Oneself as Another,* trans. Kathleen Blamey.

tion to the *idem* and the *ipse*, character involving a blend of the two on the one hand, while keeping one's word holding them wide apart, on the other.

In sketching out his "emblematic" notion of character, Ricoeur defines this model as follows: "By character I understand the set of distinctive marks which permit the re-identification of a human individual as being the same" (119). Character would be an emblem for compounding numerical identity, qualitative identity, uninterrupted continuity and permanence in time. However, Ricoeur is well aware of the problematic status of such an emblematic character and is ready to question this immutability with regard to the problem of identity. In opposing the sameness of character to self-constancy implied in the ethical imperative to keep one's word, Ricoeur prepares the grounds for introducing the notion of narrative identity, destined to demonstrate the confusion of *idem* and *ipse* and to illustrate the possible isolation of selfhood from sameness.

A crucial statement beginning the sixth study sets Ricoeur's approach to the question of narrative identity widely apart from alternative, contested versions presented by Louis O. Mink[224] or Alaisdair MacIntyre.[225] It is for Ricoeur the "interconnection of events constituted by emplotment, [*la mise en intrigue*]" that integrate diversity, discontinuity, instability with permanence in time (140). The act of configuration in a narrative renders discordances, like reversals of fortune, concordant by an ordered sequence of events known as plot. This idea, needless to say, finds justification in Aristotle's view of *mythos* outlined already in the previous chapters. Thus the procedure of *poiesis* transforms contingency into necessity and probability by virtue of a preconceived temporal totality (142). In this context character becomes a narrative category as well, which parallels the narrative understanding of the plot itself. Characters are to become plots themselves (143).

It follows, then, that a "person understood as character in a story is not an entity distinct from his or her experiences" or further, "it is the identity of the story that makes the identity of the character" (147-48). This notion of narrative identity for Ricoeur serves to expound the view of "imaginative variations" provided by literature for thought

---

[224] Louis O. Mink, "History and Fiction as Modes of Comprehension," *New Literary History,* I, 1970.
[225] Alasdair MacIntyre, *After Virtue: A Study in Moral Theory,* London: Duckworth, 1994 (1981).

experiments concerning selfhood and sameness. But what, one could ask, do we gain from literary configurations for a person's better self-understanding? It is to Ricoeur's credit that in contrast to MacIntyre's quest he considers the surplus gained from literature in the elaboration of his version of narrative identity. Such a daring, but nonetheless promising step is explained in the statement: "it is in literary fiction that the connection between action and its agent is easiest to perceive" (159). Unlike our life stories, literary fiction provides us with a sequence of events that are ordered according to retrograde necessity, i.e., integrated in a temporal totality, in the literary work as a whole. Being open ended on both sides, our birth and death, our lives cannot possibly be taken as a whole. The story of our birth, as well as the first years of our lives are transmitted to us by others' stories through others' memory, which is to say that we can only be the coauthors of our own narrative identity. Consequently, for Ricoeur literary fiction has all the advantages one needs to make up for the deficiencies of our lives: author-creator, beginning and end and an easily detectable connection between action and agent. Contesting in this manner MacIntyre's notion of the "narrative unity of life", Ricoeur argues that this must be taken as a mixture between fabulation and experience, since the "elusive character of real life" puts us in need of fiction, "to organize life retrospectively". Fiction then, would play a role in what he calls "the apprenticeship of dying" (162). The conclusion reached along this track of thought claims that life histories and literary narratives appear to be complementary despite all their contrasts (163).

Finally, what follows is the reinstitution of the ethical claim in the quest for selfhood. It seems that for Ricoeur narrative identity combines permanence in time of character and that of self-constancy (166). Literature gives numerous instances of the plea for selfhood and loss of identity, which through reading is taken up in real life as a threatening hypothesis.[226] The ethical claim for self-maintenance is

---

[226] For Ricoeur it is the stream-of-consciousness novel and Musil's *Man without Qualities* that best illustrate the loss of identity of character. Calling literature a vast laboratory for carrying out thought experiments the recourse to these literary works seems highly selective. However, Ricoeur substantiates his choice in *Time and Narrative Part 3*. The gradual folding in upon itself of character and the shift from plot to character, that stand in the focus of his interest there, are convincingly exemplified in the stream-of-consciousness novel. This at the same time invokes the problematization of the self also as understood within our conceptual relations. It is by way of reflection, very much like the way I outlined in the case of drama, that this divergence is brought to the surface. An excess of reflection, already in Euripides, we

linked to responsibility, the imperative to keep one's word or in other words, as Ricoeur nicely puts it, that the person recognize himself or herself as the subject of imputation (167). This is the ethical primacy of the other over the self, since it is the call from the other, an ethical imperative that generates self-constancy in the first place.

As I tried to demonstrate in this short reconstruction of Ricoeur's "narrativation" of character and identity, the whole undertaking is governed by an ethical orientation.[227] What finally comes to the surface in the intricate argumentation of these studies is an isolated instance of selfhood generated by the imperative of an ethical demand from the other for self-constancy. This is the point where, eventually, having fulfilled its role, narrative identity is replaced by ethical identity.

It is a basic strategical trait of *Oneself as Another* to subordinate narrativity and literature to an ethical inquiry of self-constitution.[228] Here the tension between ethics and aesthetics comes to the fore. A tension that needs to be dealt with before any combination of the two spheres is elaborated. It is following suit with his own withdrawal from structuralism and l'art pour l'art aestheticization, demonstrated in his analyses in *Time and Narrative,* that Ricoeur seeks to link the two spheres (i.e., ethics and aesthetics) inseparably. In his view it would be the misunderstanding of aesthetics itself, to amputate ethical determinations from narrative configuration (164). For, as the argument goes, our thought experiments carried out in the laboratory of the imaginary are also explorations of the questions of good and evil. But then, one may ask, what is to be taken up in real life, if we already have a preconception of good and evil? What if our notions of good and evil are questioned themselves by the narrative? Under these circumstances how are we to understand the proposition in the ninth study: "instruction of ethics by tragedy", without the imp of the perverse, that what we got so far was the opposite, i.e., the instruction of tragedy and literature by ethics? My questions contesting some of the

---

recall, brought tragic drama to an end, the plot-myth was dismembered and character highlighted in its stead.
[227] Cf. the first paragraph statement in the beginning of the sixth study: "we shall then examine in what way narrative, which is never ethically neutral, proves to be the first *laboratory of moral judgement,* 140.
[228] Consider the statement: " .... there is no ethically neutral narrative. Literature is a vast laboratory in which we experiment with estimations, evaluations and judgements of approval and condemnation through which narrativity serves as a propaedeutic to ethics", 115.

procedures of this inquiry centre around this ethicization of literature, which, problematized by Ricoeur himself, runs into some grave difficulties.

The contradictions that arise in the course of an otherwise fruitful and challenging encounter between "real life" and literature are numerous. Ricoeur's main pursuit throughout these densely argued series of studies is none other than the constitution of selfhood irreducible to sameness. The notion of narrative identity in this procedure served to fill a gap that presented itself between the isolated phenomenon of sameness and that of selfhood, as a field where we find the fusion of the two. The transition from reality to fiction results in their promising coexistence, their complementary roles in the formulation of personal identity. It seems to me nevertheless that the zest for learning from fiction makes this transition too matter-of-fact-like, insufficiently sensitive to the specific features of genres and literary traditions, so that the critical differences (the objects of learning) are avoided. Two major groups of questions come to mind with regard to this transition. Firstly, how are we to transpose ourselves into a world constructed by *poiesis*, the configuring act that transforms all contingency into necessity? Is reading the transition proper? Or is it ritual confined to dramatic performance, what Ricoeur himself calls "the spectacle"?[229] Secondly, how are we to appropriate fictions of discordant concordance governed by a temporal totality in the reality of our everyday lives? Do not the fabulations Ricoeur claims to be woven into our lives contribute to a merely hypothetical unity of life, which would make their compatibility with fiction, structured according to necessity, questionable?[230]

---

[229] Here, it seems reading would stand in sharp contrast with performance. The isolated practice of reading as distinct from the publicity of performance in many cases may serve to avert confrontation. Consider the critical attitude claiming *King Lear* is for the study, not for performance. While reading presents characters in dialogue and interaction, performance of a tragedy brings us face to face with contextualized human suffering and addresses us by the force of ritual. Stress, however, should be laid on contextualization, since, as I argued earlier, it is a distinctive characteristic of drama in particular, literature in general. On the other hand even this distinction fades away if we understand ritual as our initiation into contextualized human suffering. Ricoeur's idea of literature playing a role in "the apprenticeship of dying" is hardly debatable, only that he belittles the ritual side for the sake of the ethical, the weight of performance for the sake of reading.

[230] I am not suggesting that they are incompatible. What my question points to is the lack of a comprehensive analysis of this relation within the large field of reader response theories.

A similar difficulty presents itself in the juxtaposition of the narrative pair, plot and character with the ethical components, action and agent. The argument that "characters are themselves plots" (143) does seem to leave aside instances of non-intersection, cases when character reveals its self in the face of the plot. This phenomenon of discordance between character and plot is brought to the surface in reflected confrontation, where reflection is precisely the questioning of the status of character. Oedipus' self-inquiry is, in this sense, the distancing reflection on his character understood as plot.[231] But what comes to the foreground in these scenes of self-encounter in opposition to character-as-plot? Is it tragic ipseity, a mode of nonpermanence in time defying sameness? A disturbing polarity crystallizes in dramatic situations where intention collides with action. It attests to the dividedness of character I expounded in Chapter 3. Discarding as untenable the phenomenon of character-formation and internal dividedness would lead to such extreme distortions of meaning as defining Hamlet's character as the murderer of Polonius. It would be all too brisk to claim he is not the assassin of the sycophant, since he is, but at the same time with regard to intention, he is not. For a purely ethical approach he is, since the result is the annihilation of the other. For the purely tragic standpoint, however, i.e., with regard to himself, he is not. It seems, then, that scenes of tragic drama may help to isolate self from character (or character from plot) and intention, psychological disposition from action. I would like to propose that these forms of polarity and non-intersection provide the means for transposing ourselves into the world of configured action. The world governed by necessity opens up, since these forms of polarity demonstrate the human conflict with this necessity itself, rather than its confirmation. This way the hypothetical mode of the narrativization of our identity is not so far removed from the contested mode of character-constitution. On one side we have character, plot, action, permanence and necessity, on the other: self, intention, disposition, nonpermanence and challenge of necessity. Naturally, one may argue, these highlighted occurrences of non-intersection and discordance are contextualized together with their polar opposites. Here we should remind ourselves of the premises of the present investigations, namely Ri-

---

[231] By whom? By myth, of course, and the representatives of mythical preknowledge, the *mantis*, the chorus, etc.

coeur's reader-response-based idea of the person's identification with a character in a literary work, in this case, in drama.[232]

What I tried to point out with reference to drama (the field which most blatantly provides illustrations for the discussed phenomena) is that the mentioned disharmonies between the opposite poles on my experimental list allow for more channels of identifications-with.[233] The stream-of-consciousness novel may be seen in this light as not so different from the discussed characteristic of tragic drama. As mentioned above, the increasing doubt concerning the status of character, the phenomena of introversion and the ubiquitous aggrandizement of the self disqualify accepted patterns of identification. Traditional models and myths of characterization are distanced through self-reflection.

A further problem arises with the concept of "keeping one's word", which in Ricoeur's view proves the basis of self-constancy. "Keeping one's word" and "character" were introduced as two models of permanence in time, different in their diverse ways of accommodating *idem* and *ipse* (118). Keeping one's word is said to mark an "extreme gap" between the two, when selfhood frees itself from sameness. This treatment of selfhood in isolation from sameness seems to have a positive and a negative aspect that may, disquietingly annul each other. The positive side is implied in the mentioned self-constancy, the moral *habitus* that I maintain by keeping my word for the other. This permanence of my self would present itself irrespective of the perpetuation of my character. The other side of selfhood, however, points to a form of nothingness documented for Ricoeur in the pleas for selfhood in literary fiction.[234] The readers here are claimed to face their own loss of identity, the "hypothesis of their own nothing-

---

[232]Though it seems that for Ricoeur drama remains excluded from the comprehensive term "literary work", the problems that arise from the inclusion of drama and performance in such an undertaking would call for some readjustments. The tension is brought to the surface finally in the interlude on tragic action, a section of the ninth study (241-49).

[233]The stream-of-consciousness novel, as Ricoeur affirms, inverts the relation of plot and character, which is to give priority to character and kill the narrative. There the identity of character is tried, according to Ricoeur, no definite identity can be attributed to it any more. Finally, the reference to Musil's *The Man without Qualities (Der Mann Ohne Eigenshaften)* portrays the loss of identity altogether, which renders identification dubious. One may say, this yields only temporal and fragmentary ideals for identification.

[234]The example here is the *Ichlosigkeit* confronted by Musil in his *The Man without Qualities*.

ness" (166). Far from reconciling self-constancy with nothingness, this duplicity of selfhood for Ricoeur appears in the transition from narrative identity to ethical identity. It is important to see this transition as one among transitions in Ricoeur's undertaking: the transition from drama in particular to literature in general[235]; the transition from constitutive rules and aesthetics to moral rules and deontology[236]; and finally the transition from sameness without selfhood to selfhood freed from sameness[237] – all accompany the transition from narrative identity to ethical identity. The question, then, becomes "how are we to maintain on the ethical level a self which, on the narrative level, seems to be fading away?" (167).

Instead of tracing further Ricoeur's attempt at answering his own question – this would lead us far from what is at stake at present – let it suffice to question the legitimacy of the question itself. What this questioning brings to the surface is relevant to accentuate my attempt at a criticism of such a transition or, for that matter, of such transitions. It seems to me that what these consecutive transitions thematically and methodologically lack is a parallel transition of worldviews and contexts appertaining to literary works on the one hand and to ethical life, on the other. What I am trying to say to contest these juxtapositions, these ethical presuppositions that make literary theory and criticism the autoreferential resource of an ethical inquiry, can be summed up in the phrase: "the privilege of the how". Ricoeur's arguments centre around the interrogative pronouns of "who" and "what", the former expressing the quest for selfhood, the latter for sameness. It is no wonder that the how is ignored, since it conveys all the difficulties that are to be neglected in an ultimately ethical orientation. Following in the footsteps of a hardly objectionable theory of the stream-of-consciousness novel, we find that the inverse priority of character-plot is precisely the phenomenon introducing the privilege of the "how". If the plot is subordinated to character, as in Ricoeur's view, then, it is not so much action that matters any more, but how the character is to cope with its new vocation. This new vocation is rumination on action instead of acting, the problematization of the very relation between action and agent, the main focus of interest for Ricoeur in the

---

[235] As outlined in Paul Ricoeur, *Time and Narrative 3*, trans. Kathleen Blamey and D. Pellauer, Chicago: University of Chicago Press, 1984.
[236] Cf. *Oneself as Onother*, 155.
[237] Narrative identity forms a link between the two, the permanence in time of character (sameness) and self-constancy, cf. *Ibid.*, 166.

field of literature. Action and plot remain in the distance, the object of hope and desire, symbolized in Virginia Woolf's ever too distant Lighthouse. If, eventually, action is to take place, it is the "why" and the "how" that bias us in our reader response. Likewise, it is the "why" and the "how" that define self opposed to character. This opposition which presents itself in these novels – which portray a character not primarily as agent of action – reveal a self in struggle with its character, a self or agent problematizing its status as being agent of action. Here we witness something very similar to what we underscored earlier as the characteristic of drama, the self exposed by the "how". The self depicted as in conflict with itself or, better, with its character understood in this roundabout way.

For it is in drama that action is the least what counts. Why? Because drama is action *par excellence.* Why action does not really matter is because it is known beforehand. Myth, tradition, conventions bring us foreknowledge which assign the force of necessity to the sequence of plot-components.[238] It is primarily the "how" that differentiates the melodrama of *Titus Andronicus* from the tragedy of *Hamlet* within the horizon of revenge plays. Simultaneously it is the "how" that calls for the reformulation of self in opposition to character, it is the "how" that answers for the discrepancy between Hamlet's self questioning revenge and Hamlet's character as revenger. The self is exposed by the "how" in circumstances of inaction. The same problematization of action characterizes Hamlet and Orestes. In both cases the command of a God (Hamlet's father's ghost, Apollo) is the major motive for action or in Ricoeur's terminology, they seek to keep themselves to the word of God.

The concept of narrative identity, as expounded by Ricoeur and MacIntyre, at this point serves to mediate not ethical identity, but tragic self-formation or tragic identity. For Alasdair MacIntyre the unity of an individual life consists in the unity of a narrative "embodied in a single life".[239] His constant reference to the wholeness of life is to do with the question of a virtuous life, the two being, for him, inseparable, "there is at least one virtue recognized by tradition which cannot be specified except with reference to the wholeness of human life: the virtue of integrity or constancy" (203). Or somewhat later,

---

[238] It may be argued at the same time that tradition may be tempered with by the author, as when Shakespeare alters his source in his version of *King Lear*. However, this modification of material serves to reinforce another tradition, that of the Elizabethan revenge play.
[239] *After Virtue,* 218.

"the unity of a virtue in someone's life is intelligible only as a characteristic of a unitary life, a life that can be conceived and evaluated as a whole" (205). To gather life as a whole together, however, presents a series of difficulties partly acknowledged by both MacIntyre and Ricoeur. My life story is inevitably open ended on both sides, since my birth, the first years of my childhood and my death are all preserved in the memory of others. In this case part of my life belongs to the narrative identity of others. Consequently, as MacIntyre puts it, we are merely the "co-authors" of our own narratives. I can never grasp my life in total since this would require my posthumous stepping outside myself, in the manner of Chaucer's Troilus, to observe my life story in learned retrospect. There is no fixed time within my life put in relief, from where such a totalizing observation can take place. The constant move of life toward death makes only incomplete narratives possible and allows for recounting several stories depending on temporary choices and priorities. It is to the credit to both philosophers to point to the determining influence of the future on a narrative identity constrained to the past. The teleological perspective of MacIntyre (215), as well as Ricoeur's inclusion of anticipations in past-formation – what he calls the "horizon of expectation" (161) – both underpin the ontological instability of narrativized identity.

What tragedy adds to these ideas of narrative identity, it seems to me, is the broadening of the concept of coauthorship to its inclusion in one and the same self. The case of Oedipus is exemplary, as always in dealing with tragic phenomena, in presenting a character at the crossroads of two narratives, of two identities. For it is one thing to be the seeker and another to be the sought. To be redeemer of Thebe and its contaminator. In my view, tragic identity surpasses narrative identity in the totalization of life story and the concomitant stabilization of the self. But how? By tragic recognition, where the weight of the present sheds light on the always already dominating presence of the past and simultaneously bagatellizes possible future influences.[240] Thus the open endedness discussed above appears as secondary to the magnitude of self-formation in the present.

How should we, then, conceive of characterization in tragedy in contrast or at least in tension with the analysed forms of ethical orien-

---

[240] Cf. Hamlet's nihilistic obliteration of the future, "If it be now, 'tis not to / come; if it be not to come, it will be now; if it be not / now, yet it will come. The readiness is all" (V.ii.216-18). This parody of human foreknowledge shows dominance of the present, which is readiness shaped by the past.

tation?

The Hungarian phenomenologist László Tengelyi emphasizes the ambiguous notion of narrative identity – as defined by MacIntyre and Ricoeur – and its contestable applicability to the stabilization of identity.[241] What he calls "spontaneous sense formations" undermines the previously established narrative unity of life. It is these events in life that shatter and disintegrate our self-identity. To illustrate the difference between the homogeneous whole of a life story and these untameable precedents threatening this totality, Tengelyi isolates the notion of fate, pertaining to the former, from what he calls "fate experience", standing for the latter (539). Fate experience signifies a certain incident that brings about a breach of self-identity previously conceived of as the unity of a life story.

According to Tengelyi our self-identity is demonstrated by the frequent urge to re-establish our unity of life under the influence of unexpected occurrences, events that take us by surprise and resist subsumption under the homogeneous whole we thought our lives to be. This aspiration to incorporate the foreign and uncontrollable element of experience in our life story and thus take upon ourselves our fate, finds support in Heidegger's *Sein und Zeit*. It is to this tradition that Tengelyi opposes the idea of fate experience, which expresses the irreconcilable and irreducible difference of the foreign element from our narrative self-portrait. These elements or incidents, Tengelyi argues, demand our stepping outside ourselves (539). In the arguments that these instances of spontaneous sense-formation are not our own initiatives, but are beyond our reach and resist integration into the homogeneous totality of a life story, striking resemblances to tragic identity may be discerned.

In my opinion tragic drama depicts and highlights these very moments of life, the decisive experiences of fate. These subversive elements, however, in my view, simultaneously expose a new agent, a self accommodating these elements and translating them into the determining conditions of an enlightened self-identity. To this I shall shortly return in the next section.

The purely ethical orientations of Ricoeur and MacIntyre and the privileged position of ethical identity here find a tentative alternative, the epiphany of the unmasterable foreign element introduced by Tengelyi. The former quest may be labelled as the ethico-schematic

---

[241] Cf. László Tengelyi, "Élettörténet és önazonosság"[Life History and Self-Identity], *HOLMI*, 1998/4, 525-43.

assessment of character, while the latter leads us towards the schema of tragic characterization. The movement, as shown above, involves also the transition from narrative identity to tragic identity. Similar to the schematization of approaches to the question of evil – carried out in Chapter 1 – tragic characterization embraces both ethico- and mytho-schematic versions of characterization. On the level of myth, character is hero, representing constancy with tradition. The hero and his action, in other words, throw into relief an imposed mythological permanence in time or permanence in mythological time (i.e., transcendental time). In the actuality of performance, however, the weight of the present overwhelms this mythical eternity, reflecting human beings appear questioning their allotted status in myth. Thus Hamlet may be seen as constantly questioning his position as a revenger in the tradition of revenge plays. Thus Sophocles' Oedipus may be seen as a huge question mark to his status in myth. What is it, one may ask, that tragic drama ultimately calls into doubt, if not the priority of action in the assessment of selfhood? Can a human being be fully defined as an actant?

Tragic character-formation is, in turn, characterized by the tension between constancy and inconstancy, permanence and nonpermanence, concordance and discordance. Moreover, by the struggle to remain ethically constant in myth. These are the internal conflicts appertaining to tragic character that explain why I tried to apply and simultaneously to contest the notion of narrative identity. The move towards tragic identity, the ultimate crux of characterization in drama, involved the replacement of open-endedness to the future (determining narrative identity) by the overwhelming present (characteristic of tragic recognition). In the final section I turn to the self freed from character, to tragic identity and to related concepts that form its constructive scaffold.

To pathei mathos, katharsis and tragic identity

The investigated import of context underlying tragic experience and the discussed issues of characterization in tragedy gave us the means to grasp self apart from character. This differentiation followed from the procedure of placing character in the centre of drama, which, paradoxically, did not necessarily run contrary to Aristotle's preference for the plot. As I emphasized above, drama – etymologically as well as structurally – is action *par excellence*. Still, it is precisely this indisputable kinship that calls for considering those elements that problematize action and one's relation to action itself. These instances of questioning shed some light on a self in disharmony with its character and its action. I now hope to further illuminate this split by reference to the related concepts of *pathei mathos* and *katharsis*. From a closer look at the relationship between these forms of experience I also hope to establish what I call the inception and acquisition of tragic identity. I now turn to these concepts in succession.

In Chapter 4 I argued that what the character is made to learn through his sufferings is a learned self-assessment, a non-deluded, that is, correct self-knowledge. This new state of being is, in other words, the result of the acquisition of tragic identity. The way towards this knowledge may be summarized briefly as follows.

In the beginning of the plot we find a character maintaining a dubious state of identity, which for the sake of differentiation I called original nature. This nature from the outset is also an agent of action. The primordial prejudice of associating self with action brings about a mode of understanding of oneself, a self-assessment contextualized in the state of affairs created by the consequences of this same action. In the case of Oedipus, the tyrannical self or nature appears as seeking the cause of plague. He identifies himself with the generous king who seeks to relieve his people from the state of threat. As the necessitated sequence of actions evolve, this state of affairs enters into an unforeseen conflict with an alternative, wholly inconceivable state of affairs. The threat gradually turns against its desperate investigator and envelops him. The latter state of affairs in most cases seems to be an individually unmasterable, deluding anomaly – very much like Tengelyi's "spontaneous sense formations" – which as such has to be overcome and resolved within the scope of the already established and understood state of affairs. The prophecies of the oracle are in this sense only grasped within the limits of the subjective teleological direction and understood in their meaning only when it is too late. In the same way, the moving of Birnam wood and the threat of a "not-of-woman-born" forecast by the witches present themselves as anomalies for Macbeth. Lear and Theseus are similarly deluded in their misjudgement of the behaviour of their respective offsprings. This conflict between the pre-established and the unforeseen state of affairs in its turn brings about an internal collision between the self of original action and the self in conflict with an alternative reality. The alternative reality is the crystallization of the unforeseen, the coming into being of the anomaly, or in other words, the succumbing of the subjective *telos* to fate. A new mode of understanding of oneself emerges and unfolds in the moment of recognition, when all previous assertions of self are reassessed as misconceptions and all interpretations of individual actions as groping in the dark. Oedipus's initial self seems blurred in its contours, since the sequence of actions on which his self-understanding was based turn out to have been very different from its former conception.

The enlightened self looks back on the deluded self with regret, in the same way as Lear, when he asks forgiveness for being old and foolish, a criticism his initial self all but would have endorsed. In more fashionable terms this retrospective self-criticism (self here understood as the initial self) could be defined in the following way: I become an Other to myself. I distance myself from my initial self or character, the selfless actant of a series of actions. The detailed criticism of Ricoeur's stance above may here be summarized by the claim that *Oneself as Another* is also an ultimately tragic experience.

The process is of a double nature, it involves a form a self-distanciation from a previous delusion, but at the same time it also testifies to the indebtedness of the new self to this delusion. This Other has always been me without my knowing it: this is the paradox of tragic alterity. Oedipus's act of self-blinding is the affirmation of a self incompatible with the previous, contaminated self. King Lear's appeal for forgiveness is the affirmation of a matured self detached from the rashness of the Other. The act of detachment presupposes a primordial unity.[242] This unconscious unity is brought to cognition in *anagnórisis*, tragic recognition, when this unconscious unity is eradicated through conscious self-affirmation.

The enlightened self of tragedy is at the same time the agent of a new series of actions, which, according to the rules of pure tragedy, are forms of suffering and death. This is the new context where what I call tragic identity is acquired.

In contrast with the initial self or nature (or character), which appears as a givenness, identity merits its superior status due to its conception as the challenging of this givenness. The agent is finally de-

---

[242] It is important to see another possibility of differentiating between tragic self and its Other besides the mentioned retrospective detachment. The initial self frequently shapes itself according to a prospective projection of the Other. The ways of association with this potential Other are the modes of fear and /or desire. My self – and, consequently, my actions – are partly determined by my fear of or my desire for an actual contingent projection. However, this form of following in the footsteps of an Other in tragedy cannot be separated from following a self-appointed role, whose problematic relation to the original nature and the identity of character was discussed in the previous chapter.

fined as self-identical, when in recognition he realizes the groundlessness of his goals and by virtue of this intelligence becomes a self-identical agent of his later actions. This identity, however, is tragic, because the coincidence of action and self-identical agency comes only too late, on the brink of death, the only domain where this harmony is durable. It is a glimpse into a harmonious, non-deluded being which in itself is the highest form of human existence within the tragic cosmos. Paradoxically, Gloucester has to be deluded by Edgar to be liberated from a delusion that would otherwise fatally persevere. Fatally, because the act of self-annihilation based on delusion would prevent recognition and the emergence of self-identity.

At this point on the other hand, tragic identity may seem to be less acquired than thrust at the character in the form of an external imposition. In this sense any distinction between role and identity as expounded above, would be rendered problematic. The problem asks us to recall our findings concerning certain modes of the tragic, those in particular, which in Chapter 1 I attempted to isolate for the possibility of their insider formation. Tragic identity, then, is acquired through the insider formation of two modes of disposition, *hybris* and *miasma*, pride and defilement. From the frequent occurrences of *hybris* and *miasma* it was those instances that are not necessarily manifested in action, that gained significance for a quest for individual responsibility. These instances were subsumed under what I called "mental-emotional disposition" bordering action. If the series of actions prescribed by the rules of tragedy appear to be structured according to necessity and probability, these forms of disposition seem mostly to allow for individual control.

If our argument in Chapter 1 is correct and the fundamental difference between myth and tragedy is in forms of reflection, it is this phenomenon through which we expect to be informed of these mental-emotional states. Self-reflection is a determinant characteristic of both Greek and Shakespearean tragedy. It verbalizes the character's irreconcilability with himself, with his fate and with predestination. It exposes his inclinations, desires and emotions.

In the final crystallization of tragic identity in recognition, thus there appears to be an additional dimension represented by insider disposition. It is on this complementary, but nonetheless significant internal inclination that the acquisition of identity is grounded. The translation, formulated above, of experiences or incidents of fate into the determining conditions of enlightened self-identity. The informed self has to see his previously deluded character as its inferior and distance itself from it by acknowledging this inferiority.²⁴³ This mode of insider disposition is necessary for the ultimate unfolding of enlightened self-identity. It also enhances the elicitation of the required outsider response. The identification of insider and outsider perspectives takes place together with the affirmation of finitude. What unites the heroic character turned self and his audience is the dramatic realization of finitude in recognition, when finitude becomes identity. Here, this moment of identification coincides with the outsider disposition of compassion. We are made to feel pity and fear to be purged from them, according to Aristotle, release serves liberation. It is through this moment of *katharsis*, the elimination of compassion, that our own *pathei mathos* is realized: we are invited to grasp our own identity through a learned reflection on our finitude. What I called the "trial of finitude", conceived of as such only in learned retrospect, transforms the analogical association between insider and outsider perspectives into their identification. For my relation to death strikes me as undoubtedly unique within the forms of my association with characters, situations and events presented in drama. The more so in performance, where, as I argued, due to the privilege of spectacle, characters appear as human beings. Is it, we may ask, the singularity of death that answers for this singular relation? Is it its mystery and irrevocability that attracts a distinguished alertness? It is at the basis of ritual, as I see it, that we identify with the dying to survive our own death. This survival finds its emotional equivalent in *katharsis*.

Katharsis is both the emotional transposition of a culminated sequence of actions and the expulsion of the same emotions. For its effective unfolding both elements of confirmed finitude and self-distancing insider disposition are necessary. In *katharsis*, one may say, we are invited to recognize finitude as necessity and consequently, to surrender compassion to acceptance.

By this understanding of recognition after a long detour on char-

---

²⁴³The only reason for taking a character in a drama for one and the same is the positional rootedness in a given context. No matter what subversive transformations one may go through, one's determinate position, ranking, status within a microcosm assigns a permanence in time, constituted by a mere label. This is what may be called a nominalistic account of character. It was also to contest this notion of character, that in Chapter 3 I introduced the dichotomy of nature and identity. There identity stood for an achieved quality of character and was opposed to the mere givenness of nature. This time I translate the same dichotomy into the language of identity. Thus the surpassed nature or the inferior self appears as a shadow identity for the learned retrospect of enlightened identity. I adopt the descriptive term "shadow" from the Fool in *King Lear* (cf. I.iv.199-204).

acterization, self-formation and tragic identity we may finally return to the initial task of generic differentiation. The question of genre posed in the beginning of this chapter can now be reformulated in the light of our findings concerning the discussed conceptual basis of characterization. The question becomes: what is the generic significance of the movement from character to self? The isolation of two genres often mingled by tradition – tragedy and melodrama – may now be based on the tragic versus the melodramatic form of recognition. Whenever the initial self is not discarded as in *Oedipus Tyrannus* or *King Lear,* but on the contrary, asserted in its "uninterrupted continuity", to adopt Ricoeur's term, as in the case of Orestes in the *Eumenides* or of Aaron in the *Titus Andronicus,* we feel the generic irreconcilability of the two forms of recognition. However, this is merely one way of laying down a possible generic differentiation and therefore should be seen as complementary with alternative attempts carried out in the preceding chapters.

VI. Forms of Action and Passivity

In the previous chapters the term melodrama was mostly adopted to denote a dramatic structure embracing sequences of actions and forms of heroic behaviour and disposition, which we found incompatible with their genuinely tragic representations. It has been one of my main concerns to justify the reference to an alternative genre when the architectonic survey of tragedies revealed instances of anachronism or omission in plot-structure and the preference for a reverse or deficient succession of plot-components.

The architectonic survey of Greek and Shakespearean tragedy revealed fundamental forms of generic cohesion. The consistent recurrence of certain structural elements discussed expose the contours of a world of experience highlighted for its incompatibility with neighbouring worldviews. By neighbouring I mean the alternative worldview(s) of melodrama in particular, which – as I have tried to point out – frequently accompany instances of critical totalization, the premature subsumption of pure tragedy and melodrama into one and the same genre: tragedy. I was not trying to say that the represented theoretical accounts of drama have no justifiable status in literary scholarship. What interests me rather, is the never too easily resolvable conflict between literary history and what I call the ontological quest of literature. The latter critical stance involves the threat of finding myself implicated in my own interrogation of these texts, which is to say that I become a potential object of my inquiry. This idea of "ontological hermeneutics" follows the lineage of Heidegger, Gadamer and Ricoeur and accentuates what Ricoeur calls the "consciousness of belonging".[244] The notion contests the critical naivety of what may be called the "laboratory-stance", the self-exempting bias of distanciation.

---

[244] For the dialectic of belonging and distanciation, see Paul Ricoeur, "The Task of Hermeneutics" in *From Text to Action: Essays in Hermeneutics II*, trans. Kathleen Blamey and J. B. Thompson, Evanston, Illinois: Northwestern University Press, 1991, 73.

As I will try to point out, the ontological quest eventually problematizes action as such, the premature identification of one with one's actions and the struggle for positing oneself outside action. The question "who am I?" and the question "what is my action?" will be measured against each other by examining not only their frequent conjunctions, but also their recurrent divergences.

However, before such an attempt, it is necessary to consider dramatic action with related concepts like fate, *telos*, direction and then move step by step towards individual cases and ways whereby action itself becomes problematic. The borderline between action and inaction will be found blurred. The aim of the present chapter is finally to point out some instances in drama, which best illustrate these theoretical issues and which exhibit the contrasting paradoxes of active passivity on the one hand, and active paralysis, on the other.

Fate, teleology, irrevocability

The explicit imputation of the causality of events to fate and all its cognates and representatives is what foremost differentiates tragic drama from medieval story patterns, like those presented by the *de casibus* tradition. Henry Ansgar Kelly, in his book *Ideas and Forms of Tragedy from Aristotle to the Middle Ages,* gives a detailed account of the different theoretical approaches to tragedy and concludes: "tragedy was characterized as a poem beginning in prosperity and ending in adversity" (171). Though an Aristotelian prescription, *metabole ex eutychias eis dustychian* (*Poetics 1453a14*), the fall in itself is not tragic. Robert B. Heilman's *Tragedy and Melodrama: Versions of Experience,* points to essential differences between daily used and worn out expressions like catastrophe, disaster, unhappy accident and tragedy. To paraphrase Kelly's cited conclusion in Heilman's terminology, we could say that medieval authors supplanted tragedy by disaster. Action in tragedy does not merely recount a fall from prosperity to adversity, as constantly demonstrated in the *Fall of Princes* by Lydgate and others in the *de casibus* tradition. It is also a fated fall, when a threatening external interference casts doubt on the meaningfulness of human existence.

The concept of irrevocability should be understood within this fated change of circumstances, when culmination in adversity involves an irremediable loss. It is obvious that loss in tragedy is the loss of something of exceptional magnitude, of utmost importance. It is the loss of a highly esteemed human value, like Cordelia, Lear's idol and ultimate consolation. This loss is due to the pursuing of subjective *telos* challenged by the self-affirmation of objective *telos*. What finally happens incorporates and surpasses human endeavours for the sake of the surpassed. For the sake of the surpassed, since what I call differential teleology in tragedy fosters the formation of a self-identical agent from the various aporetic idolizations of roles.[245]

Fate and action

In considering the blend of fate, understood as above and action, we find ourselves before another blend, that of dramaturgy and metaphysics. What the sequence of plot-components in tragedy reveal is an idea of a hermetic totality of action. The adjective *hermetic* describes the impossibility of an alternative unravelling of events or in other words, that things could not have happened otherwise. This fundamentally unalterable[246] material of action is provided by none other than the source itself, tradition, generic conventions or, to use the inclusive term adopted so far, *myth*. "Material" and "action" have to be differentiated, since it is in their divergence that, for Aristotle, the essence of art was to be defined.[247] *Mimesis* in the case of tragedy is the dramaturgical device of representation. It is the imitation of action. Imitation, however, not merely in the sense of a copy, as Ricoeur warns us,[248] but the ordering of the imitated according to probability and necessity.

At this point it would seem that the concept of fate – appertaining to action presented by dramaturgy through *mimesis* – ought to have a primarily dramaturgical role in the structured presentation of events. The dramatist would himself be in the privileged position of fate monitoring a completely controlled and hermetic sequence of events. I would like to suggest that this all-encompassing power of composition totalizes action in order to contest its necessity through reflection. To repeat my earlier proposition, tragedy incorporates the extra phenomenon of reflection understood as the questioning of this necessity inherent in the coincidence of action and character.

---

[245] Cf. the dichotomy of nature and role laid down in Chapter 3.

[246] Unalterable if authorial compliance with conventions is presupposed.

[247] Cf. also the structuralist-semiotic account of the difference between plot and fabula in Keir Elam, *The Semiotics of Theatre and Drama,* London and New York: Routledge, 1990, 119.

[248] "C'est donc par un grave contresens que la *mimesis* aristotélicienne a pu etre confondue avec l'imitation au sense de copie", *La métaphore vive*, Paris: Éditions du Seuil, 1975, 56. Compare also for *Temps et récit 1*, Paris: Éditions du Seuil, 1983, 71-72.

Reflection on self and action adds a parallel understanding of dramatic action to the one based on necessity: the story of self-formation.[249] This latter development exposed through reflection pinpoints a hypothetical mode of self-maintenance as opposed to the enclosed triad of character-action-fate.[250] Dramaturgy in this sense could be seen as the accommodation of necessity in the hypothetical mode of reflection. The road leads from myth to reflection and from reflection to hypothesis.

So far so good, but what is this hypothetical mode? How are we to understand a form of hypothetical self-maintenance? As I argued earlier, the development of the self may be seen in opposition to the character-actant whose career is defined by the workings of fate or the objective *telos*. The hypothetical mode presents itself in the radical questioning of this predestination, of the predisposition that a person can be fully grasped by reference to his character as agent of action (as character-actant). The hypothesis, in other words, is precisely that there remains an essential surplus of meaning in the levelling of self and action. This surplus seems, in terms of action, unmasterable and appears in the isolated domain of inaction or paralysis.

Let us now consider two obvious cases in drama to illustrate this fundamental discrepancy, the case of *Prometheus Bound* and *Hamlet*.

To speak about dramatic action, in the first place, is to speak about a tautology, as I have several times accentuated. A play without action is inconceivable, at least in the two great eras of drama, the Attic and the Elizabethan. It is my presupposition that even in cases of passivity or paralysis[251] – to the illustration of which the two plays in question do lend themselves – action is never completely annihilated, only momentarily frozen to yield in time to necessity. Scenes of passivity in Greek and Shakespearean drama therefore should be seen also as instances of a delayed observance of necessity. This delay itself sheds light on the hypothetical mode of self-maintenance and re-

---

[249]Naturally, this parallel story is also a composed one, thus obedient to another form of necessity, the dramaturgical one, here opposed to the necessity imposed by tradition and source-material.

[250]In Chapter 3 I argued that traditional identifications of character with fate are easily undermined by obvious cases of unforeseen internal dividedness. The inclusion here of character and fate is explained if we take character as the agent cast away in the process of dividedness by the self itself. Our focus on self-formation in the preceding chapter led to seeing self in contrast to character, which here finds its parallel in the dichotomy of necessity (character) and the hypothetical mode of existence (self).

[251]The difference will be defined later in the course of the present chapter.

veals a personal struggle with what one must come to terms with (i.e., necessity). Delay of action or inaction designates a self distancing itself from necessity in this same struggle. How are we to account for a self that is posited in this self-distanciation despite the having-to-come-to-terms-with?

The forced inaction of Prometheus and the self-assumed[252] paralysis of Hamlet are in many ways interesting for an approach to passivity in drama. In the Greek play *Prometheus Bound* which is one part of the trilogy, one may see at least a triple meaning in the being bound. One refers to divine retribution, the other to the becoming mortal (earthbound), and the third to the dramatization of passivity, the focus of my present investigations. The traditional view of the first meaning draws on the notion of a culpable past that explains the sufferings in the present. This understanding of the play would define action as exculpation, purgation, retribution, and thereby freeze the play into an eternally lingering present. The second meaning would bear on the metaphorical understanding of "bound", in the sense of being bound to the human, due to the act of benefaction. One could see in Prometheus' torments the "self-mortalization" of choice, the taking up of humanity on oneself in very much a Christ-like manner. However, it is the third possibility that is of special importance for grasping yet a further idea of action in the play. Since if we take "bound" in a literal way of forced inactivity, which is the dramatization of passivity, how are we then to define the play's action without falling prey to the first alternative? What is action if action is bound?

A close look at the text of *Prometheus Bound* shows that the instances of dramatized passivity are at the same time the precedents of dramatized verbal activities, of speech acts. It is this plane of dramatic dialogue that escapes J. E. Harry and others in his wake who claim that Prometheus is not in a position to commit *hybris*.[253] In my opinion this view could be slightly modified by saying "Prometheus as actant is not in a position to commit *hybris*". Let us recall the crucial statement made by the sufferer in line 970: "such is the proper style for the insolent to offer insult", *outos hubridzein tous hubridzontas khreon*. This dubious self-justification is the speech act of pride manifest in rigid immovability and absence of regret. Hermes in his rebuke calls this persistence in pride *khlide,* which may well be taken as the cause for all further torments. As I claimed before, the word *khreon*, a rhe-

---

[252] Meaning that at least literally, Hamlet is not bound.
[253] Cf. Richmond Lattimore, *Story Patterns in Greek Tragedy*, 23.

torical invocation of necessity, here serves as excuse for individual inflexibility, the point where responsibility truly comes to the fore. What is striking is the double agency of, on the one hand, the benefactor-actant whose action is confined to the past and, on the other, the committer of *hybris* by speech act.[254]

In *Hamlet* we find the phenomenon of double agency operating in a different way. There the recourse to speech acts does not arise as a possible alternative for action; Claudius cannot possibly be killed with a speech act. There is also the need of the venom to do its work. In contrast with the passivity of Prometheus arising from his being bound, Hamlet's inaction is partly self-assumed. One could say he is bound by the impossible command, though in many ways he is free to complete the task of the revenger. Consider the private scene of prayer:

> Now might I do it pat, now a is a-praying ...
> And now I'll do't.   (*Draws his sword*.)
>   And so a goes to heaven;
> And so am I reveng'd. That would be scann'd:
> A villain kills my father, and for that
> I, his sole son, do this same villain send
> To heaven.
> Why, this is hire and salary, not revenge.
>
>   (III.iii.73-79)

At this climactic point, refraining from action is a voluntary decision, which disregards the down-to-earth scope of the command. King Hamlet's call for revenge contains no demand for considerations of afterlife. However, this is merely an episode and as such, cannot account for Hamlet's general delay throughout the plot. In the rest of the scenes Hamlet's inaction appears to follow from inescapable publicity. The privacy of revenge is made impossible by the ubiquitous publicity, the constantly being in the foreground of courtly attention: "madness in great ones must not unwatched go."

Despite being watched and despite the impossibility of the command, Hamlet does have the intention to act. The tension between determinate intention and paralysing reflection dominates the play till the sudden fall into the net, the counter-mousetrap, set this time by the King against the "great one". It is this tension consequent upon the

---

[254] I shall give a brief account of speech act-theory in the section *Speaking and using daggers,* which will make further concretization possible.

call that isolates Hamlet's paralysis from the passivity of Prometheus. It seems that any further clarification of these blending concepts can only take place once dramatic action is approached through its basic elements. This is the task of the following section.

Models of Action

The classification of Shakespearean dramatic action is a task that requires a separate study. In what follows therefore I shall limit my quest to an experimental list of a few major models with the hope nevertheless, that it will suffice to illustrate the variety and complexity of action one has to take into account in Shakespearean dramaturgy. The highlighted models set the context for separating forms of inaction or passivity on the one hand, and of paralysis, on the other.

Let us temporarily accept the presupposition that tradition equals the demarcation of action and drama cannot do away with action altogether without doing away, at the same time with itself. Before the classification of dramatic action we must consider the fundamental differences between the ethics of action and its dramatic counterpart. Or even their counterpoint, as Ricoeur says, since while the former teaches how action leads to happiness through the exercise of virtue, the latter, the tragic *muthos*, turns on reversals of fortune, namely from happiness to unhappiness.[255] This paraphrasing of the contrasting Aristotelian precepts laid down in the *Nicomachean Ethics* and the *Poetics* respectively, points to what might be called the difference of direction. Without even attempting to address the entire problem arising from the dichotomy of *praxis* and *mimesis*, real life and its poetic configuration, as undertaken by Ricoeur in his *Time and Narrative*, I would merely like to look at the basis from which these incompatibly directed actions emerge.

The direction towards happiness and that towards unhappiness cannot be contrasted without the danger of losing an even more radically incompatible element of action: its basis or grounds. It does not occur to Ricoeur that the move towards unhappiness cannot possibly be the counterpoint to the ethical move towards happiness (in the sense of the word counterpoint implied here) due to a substantial discrepancy between the respective bases of action. The two irreconcilable grounds – to the tension of which Ricoeur himself is more sensitive in an earlier work, the *Symbolism of Evil* – expresses the disharmony between two worldviews, the ethical and the tragic. The ethical

---

[255]Cf. *Temps et récit 1*, Paris: Éditions du Seuil, 1983, 94.

worldview presupposes an ethical autonomy whereby the moral agent is capable to decide, deliberate freely and act according to his conscious choice. This view, which takes its source from Aristotle's *Ethics*, a reading of which I proposed in Chapter 1, presupposes the stability of character, the identity of the moral agent and the congruence between choice[256] and the outcome of action. When Ricoeur in his mentioned SE draws attention to the resurgence of the tragic within the ethical worldview, namely in the dominating presence of the serpent in the Garden of Eden, he comes close to what may be called the incompatibility of origins of action. Action with the serpent or without, then, becomes the question of basis, the question of autonomy, the question of context and in turn, the question of action as such. There can be no doubt that the pre-established situation, the already being there of action-regulating factors, casts its shade on autonomy and questions the meaningful exercise of choice and deliberation.

The opposition of worldviews on action crystallizes so far in the incompatibility of directions and bases. Autonomous action on the one side is contested by already given factors of necessity on the other. It needs to be stressed that the tragic plot presents a world in which a pre-established situation transforms the whole of action into *re*action. It is clear, however, that emphasis on reaction does not help much to isolate tragic action from the moral, since the latter may also be a mere reaction to a preceding action in a given situation. Reaction in the field of tragedy therefore has to be further distinguished if we are to keep suit with the opposition of worldviews. However, the reference to the basis of action above does not merely problematize all comparisons of directions, but also comparisons of reactions. Reactions in tragedy stem from an ontologically specific and unique basis. This latter testifies to the overwhelming presence of constraining factors that delimit the scope of exercising choice. This delimitation is, needless to say, also the contesting of the ethical idea of choice. Reaction in tragedy in its germ is characterized by an uncertainty concerning the reality of the preceding action (or reaction). Consider the examples of Oedipus or Hamlet who are anything but certain of events in the past and consequently of their own possible responses. These instances reduce the possibility of moral situation-assessment and resemble more the surrender to the inevitable. It is contribution to the inevitable that defines reaction in tragedy as opposed to ethics, the

---

[256] What is choice if not a conscious deliberation established on the postulation of this outcome, of the *telos* of action?

recognition that choice itself is dubious when it is only capable of realizing extremities. Aristotle's golden mean is unknown in the tragic universe.

Finally, the incompatible forms of direction and basis are complemented by a third element, that of the goal or purpose of action. As I have several times emphasized, the human goals of (re)action in tragedy are never the same as the outcome or the objective *telos*. Individual intention is hardly in harmony with what surprisingly becomes the result or product of the necessitated undertaking. In other words, though the postulated result of my action determines my move, the outcome will never coincide with my postulate. In this sense King Lear's act of exiling Cordelia is undertaken with a postulate hardly reconcilable with receiving her dead in his arms.

Tragic action, then, as I see it, is the form of necessitated reaction characterized by the determinants of basis, direction and goal, the specific pillars of a worldview, as outlined above.

However, one further element of action has to be introduced before the experimental classification of dramatic action, namely the element of the affected recipient.[257] It goes without saying that where the scope of choice is limited to the realization of extremities, the recipient is the more substantially affected. It goes with the radical uncertainty of individual knowledge and evaluation of premises of action that those concerned are more likely to suffer the consequences than in the case of an (ethically presupposed) "controlled" situation.[258] This uncertainty and the delimitation of choice affects the recipient in various ways as I shall try to show, to the extent that he or she may be affected even despite my being unaware of such a possibility.[259]

Action in drama therefore is to be understood as a sequence of inevitable reactions or episodes. The structural role of episodes in tragic drama differs in essence from those of comic plots. In a universe ruled by fate and its representatives the episodes form a continuum, which

---

[257] This triadic constellation of dramatic action differs from but also overlaps with the logical constituents of dramatic action as collected by Keir Elam. His list includes six elements: "agent"; "intention"; "act-type produced"; "modality" (manner and means); "setting" (temporal, spatial and circumstancial); and "purpose", *The Semiotics of Theatre and Drama*, 121.

[258] Controlled in the sense that the agent is conscious of what the real situation is.

[259] Consider the act of my drawing my sword and driving it through the arras thereby not so much disembowelling the king as slaying his lipservant of a councillor. This unfortunate moment deprives me of following suit with the program "to thine own self be true".

guarantees the destined fall and necessitates the particular outcome. Tragic recognition is thereby the consummation of the preceding episodes. In comedy, on the contrary, action is structured according to contingency and chance. In the stead of the tragic continuum we find the accidental cluster of episodes, a comic discontinuity. Consequently, comic recognition is brought about by a chance occurrence hardly explained by the preceding episodes. While a scene of error can easily be left out from the *Comedy of Errors* without weakening the plot-structure, the same cannot equally be said of, say, *Hamlet*. The exclusion of the graveyard scene or the encounters with Rosencrantz and Guildenstern from the play would highly affect the process of character-formation as well as our reader response. Not surprisingly, since these seemingly marginal episodes are all closely linked to the preparation of Hamlet's final disintegration.

We may conclude from the above that the tragic plot is the totality of action or reaction, in which, as Aristotle put it, the consecutive episodes follow one another according to probability and necessity. The reasons for including comedy among the models of action thus appear to be manifold. Not only is Shakespearean tragedy full of comic sub-plots and vice versa, comedy rich in tragic interludes, but it seems to me that, as in the case of the mentioned episodic construction, parallels in comedy help to highlight the general underlying patterns of action characteristic of Shakespearean drama.

The three constituents of the following classification are: the ambiguity of action (whether it has actually taken place or not), forms of response to this ambiguity (distortions, beliefs, camouflages, deceits, manipulations, pretence or their lack),[260] and finally, the ways of affecting the recipient, determined by his or her conscious or unconscious participation. The move from the lack of action through action to paralysis, far from being circular, presents a straight line eventually leading to a better understanding of the tragic phenomenon of active paralysis. In order to posit this phenomenon as an alternative dramatic mode of being, a prior distinction from both inaction and the various forms of action, will be undertaken.

---

[260] It is the possible lack of action that makes adjustments necessary, conveyed by the second element. Where there is no action there should at least be belief that there is, otherwise there would be no drama. This belief may be engendered by the various dramatic devices mentioned.

Model 1: *Lack of action is amended by camouflage of which the recipient is unconscious.*

Lack of action is compensated for by pretence or deceit, which affects the recipient in the same way as if it (i.e., action) had actually taken place. In these cases the absence of action does not freeze the plot, since the effects take shape as if action had taken place. The recipient is unaware of the deceit. Desdemona's adultery did not actually happen, but this does not prevent the plot from moving along scenes of jealousy during which Othello is lured all the way from the stage of incipient fear to that of final conviction and murder. The ultimate resolution is the murder of jealousy, the substitution of action for inaction.

Another example of this model is Edmund's act of forgery in *King Lear*. The fraudulent imitation of Edgar's writing leads Gloucester astray and ultimately leads to his disintegration.

In *Much Ado About Nothing* Hero is slandered by Don Pedro.

Model 2: *Lack of action amended by camouflage, of which the recipient is conscious.*

This model presents obvious cases of refusals of action, when the recipient becomes the victim of passivity. The indifference of Lear's daughters is the more conspicuous after their active verbosity characterizing the scene of flattery. The mere affectedness of the recipient, however, transforms passivity into activity, which is the camouflaging of ingratitude by the excuse of turning down 100 knights.[261]

Timon can be seen as similarly discarded when loss of property and the reversal of fortune puts him in need of the generosity of misjudged friends. This generosity he unconditionally exercised as a benefactor is then returned by ingratitude, the act of renunciation, which is also the act of refusal to act. Becoming a misanthrope is an extreme way of reaction to the extremities of activated passivity.

In comedy this model often takes the form of unrequited love. The neglected lovers in *A Midsummer Night's Dream*, the desperate Silvius in *As You Like It* or Olivia in the *Twelfth Night* all aspire to activate the beloved and engage themselves in a whole series of self-humiliating actions in order to bring about this impossibility. This involves turning the act of rejection into acceptance, which as we know,

---

[261] Compare also for model 5.

is an impossibility inasmuch as their own strivings are concerned. At the same time impossibility can become possible with the help of magic called Puck.

Model 3: *Action takes place camouflaged, of which the recipient is unconscious.*

When Hamlet is wounded by the deadly weapon of Laertes, he is unaware of the real effect and purpose of the hit until he is warned "Hamlet, thou art slain .... / In thee there is not half an hour's life" (V.ii.319, 321).

Angelo's discarded betrothed Mariana is substituted for Isabella in *Measure for Measure* to retain her postmarital rights. The change of sleeping partners takes place in the night and remains unnoticed by the victim, Angelo. Consequently the action following the disguised Duke's manipulations becomes a reunion instead of the desired union.

In *Macbeth* Malcolm tests Macduff's clairvoyance (IV.iii.) and puzzles him by speaking in incompatible ways of himself. What seems a true confession of character is at the same time overturned by self-contradiction. Macduff's desperate struggle with this contradiction is expressed in the line: "Such welcome and unwelcome things at once, / 'Tis hard to reconcile" (138-39). Macduff's dejection is a sign of failing to see the test as a test, which will hardly qualify him for the coming government.

An example from comedy could be Rosalind in *As You Like It,* who, disguised as a shepherd, tries Orlando's love and fidelity.

Model 4: *Action takes place camouflaged, of which the recipient is conscious.*

Claudius's reaction to the mousetrap is the signal that he has grasped the hidden meaning, i.e., he is conscious that the play within the play is Hamlet's inspection of truth. Without Claudius's being aware of this surplus of meaning, the whole strategy would fail, as in fact, it is claimed by W. W. Greg.[262]

When Macbeth is attacked by Macduff, the assault is not dreaded as it is from the "not of woman born".[263] The transformation of

---

[262] Cf. John Dover Wilson, *What Happens in Hamlet*, Cambridge: Cambridge University Press, 1935, 93.
[263] Camouflage here is the being deceived by the double tongue.

Macduff from soldier to one who "was from his mother's womb / Untimely ripp'd" brings Macbeth face to face with his assassin instead of the proclaimed loser.[264]

Apart from its being one of the most obvious models of plot-construction and instead of enumerating further examples, let us bear in mind that in Shakesperean drama the extent of the affectedness of the conscious[265] recipient can hardly ever be prognosticated.

Model 5: *Action takes place non-camouflaged, of which the recipient is unconscious.*

The lack of deceit, pretence to the contrary or other forms of manipulation may not prevent the recipient from suspecting similar distortions of meaning. Examples of modalities of disbelief abound in comedies, most conspicuously in the *Comedy of Errors* where disbelief is grounded on mistaking one character for another. The imputing of action to the wrong person, to Dromio of Syracuse instead of Dromio of Ephesus and vice versa or to Antipholus of Syracuse instead of Antipholus of Ephesus and vice versa, etc. is the recurring source of comic experience.

Model 6: *Action takes place non-camouflaged, of which the recipient is conscious.*

This model is detectable in cases where knowledge of action is gained from non-deceiving revelation. These instances of revelation are closely connected to the dramaturgical means of depicting the past. The function of prologues in this sense is often assigned to a character, like Prospero informing Miranda about the misfortunes of the past to explain the present. Hamlet may well be sceptical at times about the real intentions of the Ghost ("Be thou a spirit of health or goblin damn'd" I.iv.40), but as it turns out, the recounted events of the past did actually take place and Hamlet's lot is the more obviously cast.

Similarly there appears to be no reason to disbelieve Macbeth's thrilling account of his own regicide, the details of which are related to Lady Macbeth who then is ready to administer the necessary corrections, i.e., to act according to the revealed truth of action. It is important to see that access to the truth about action is limited to privacy,

---

[264] Cf. "Thou losest labour .... " (V.viii.8).
[265] Or unconscious, see model 3.

the act of regicide will be camouflaged before the public, which follows model 3.

The following models already present forms of problematizing action itself and the various ways of blends between action and inaction.

Model 7: *Inaction is also action (and vice versa), diverse assessments in accordance with the recipient's affectedness.*

The contrast with model 2, despite overlaps, arises from the difference of points of view. My abstention from acting may be described in terms of passivity when I regard myself in isolation, but as soon as the recipient's viewpoint is considered, my abstention becomes transcribed in the terms of activity. Cordelia's "nothing" can be understood as the avoidance of action and withdrawal to passivity, but also as a speech act of protestation when viewed from diverse perspectives. The lack of hospitality on Lear's daughters' part is also the repeated act of renunciation,[266] as mentioned above. Drama highlights those very precedents of inaction, which undergo reassessments according to shifts of point of view.[267]

Model 8: *Action is problematized by forms of the recipient's unexpected affectedness.*

The very act of revenge is questioned in Hamlet, when the rash and bloody deed is followed by a whole series and the call for revenge is finally obeyed only at the immeasurable expense of six casualties. Hamlet's relation to his mother – to which I shall shortly return in some detail – reflects the impossibility of a command demanding the revenge of the father's death and the sparing of Gertrude at the same time. The unidimensional call for vengeance is dissipated, scattered into numerous side-episodes, the murder of Polonius, the doing away with Rosencrantz and Guildenstern, the slaying of Laertes, the losing

---

[266] Cf. George Orwell's essay "Lear, Tolstoy and the Fool" in *Essays and Journalism*, London: Secker and Warburg/Octopus, 1980.
[267] Those instances of paralysis that bypass the dialectic of passivity and activity will be of concern in a later section of this chapter, where paralysis will be defined as abstention from action as such, from the possibility of action. This phenomenon is accompanied by the displacement of the other and of all concern for the other, when displacement means internalization.

of homeland to Fortinbras, etc. We are left with the puzzling question, what or where is Hamlet's action?[268]

In a similar way the act of regicide affects Lady Macbeth in a way least expected by herself after all the vehemence of the "unsex me here". The futile washing of indelible pollution is also the futile "peeling" of action from character, the obliteration of the past for survival in the present.

Though primarily belonging to tragedy, this pattern of problematization of action by reference to the affectedness of the recepient is not unknown to comedy. Deceiving Malvolio in *Twelfth Night* with a fake love letter is both one of Shakespeare's funniest scenes and a doubtfully laudable act of humiliation. It is the sequence of episodes and their final resolution that determine the play's genre as comedy, though at the same time these disturbing scenes also explain the application of the constraining qualifier: dark.

Examples for each discussed model are numerous, but in my view, even this partial account reveals some recurring patterns in the dramatization of action. Let us now return to tragedy and our main focus, the question of paralysis in tragic drama.

Action and paralysis

Action in drama was approached above in two ways: comparing drama and tragic action to moral behaviour, and investigating models of action within the dramatic plot. The three elements forming the basis of this internal inquiry were the ambiguity of action, the response to this ambiguity and the role of the recipient. The series of models outlined above point to the dominant role of the recipient in constituting action. Regan's and Goneril's indifference and passivity are transformed by Lear's hopes and expectations into (speech) acts of renunciation. It seems, then, that the call from the other may mould our responses into various kinds of action.

In the move from active passivity, in the sense just introduced, to paralysis, we must consider the relation between call and intention. The call from the other and the intention to act in response to or in harmony with that call; to participate in a dialogical relation according to the explicit needs and expectations. It is clear that there is no such intention on Regan's or Goneril's side, nor on Timon's friends' part, to be ready to redress, to support, to activate one's compassion to-

---

[268] Which, as we shall see, will shortly become the no less puzzling question, who is Hamlet?

wards the other in need. Similarly, in Prometheus there is no sign of regret, no response to the fact of being bound, other than perseverance in the speech act of *hybris*.

In cases when there is no intention to answer the call, action is constituted by speech acts of passivity and indifference. The call for revenge in *Hamlet* at the same time seems to posit a new form of inaction, one, which presents itself in the harmony between call and intention. Hamlet wants to take his revenge after he had found confirmation for the Ghost's story. Hamlet is everything but passive and indifferent. His aporetic reflections reveal a constant struggle between alternatives of action, not their avoidance. "I want to confirm the truth and act accordingly" is his reaction to the call. This "I want but I cannot" characterizes Hamlet's lasting delay, his standpoint of active paralysis.

Yet there is much to be said about the borderline between action and inaction crystallizing in paralysis. It seems to me that no other Shakespearean play dramatizes this problematic more penetratingly than *Hamlet*. In the last sections therefore I turn to those vital scenes in *Hamlet*, where recourse to speech acts and the terrors of paralysis are most conspicuously in the foreground.

Doubt, pause, inaction

Hamlet's unrelenting pursuit of the truth starts when the father's Ghost exposes his disturbing version of the past. During the long history of Hamlet-criticism ample evidence has been evoked to underpin his self-displacing doubt following hard upon the revelation. However, doubt was mostly seen merely as the necessary precondition for certifying the truth with the success of which it was annihilated and replaced by belief or conviction. This critical stance takes the transfer from scepticism to conviction as more or less exhaustive in delineating Hamlet's character and thereby fails to account for the nihilist scenes of the post-exile period. Hamlet's unfolding nihilism, I would like to argue, cannot be explained without the reassessment of scepticism as extending to being as such. The burden of doubt cannot be relieved through the act of confirmation, since, pertaining to being itself it is of an all too different magnitude. It is vital to see this gradual expansion of doubt, an early form of which presents itself already in the "or" of Hamlet's first reaction: "Be thou a spirit of health or goblin damn'd" (I.iv.40). This "or" takes on the auxiliary form of "may" later, in the player-inspired self-rebuke for verbose idleness: "The spirit that I have seen / May be a devil .... " (II.ii.595-96). This early form of doubt appertains to the figure, the identity of the Ghost, this strange apparition, which by its own reappearance proves the impossibility of regicide. It is the posthumous return of the king, the haunting omnipresence, the *parousia* of the royal victim. Doubt in this sense may involve the entire problematic of regicide, the self-cancelling command of revenge.

The early form of doubt is extended to being itself in the great monologue. The "or" of identity becomes the "or" of ontological perplexity, "to be, or not to be".

Or so it seems. At closer inspection, however, we find a gradual unfolding of ontological perplexity, which as yet is not conveyed by the first line quoted, not even by the first nine. Let me quote these familiar lines for the sake of convenience:

> To be, or not to be, that is the question:
> Whether 'tis nobler in the mind to suffer
> The slings and arrows of outrageous fortune
> Or to take arms against a sea of troubles
> And by opposing end them. To die – to sleep,
> No more; and by a sleep to say we end
> The heart-ache and the thousand natural shocks
> That flesh is heir to: 'tis a consummation
> Devoutly to be wish'd. To die, to sleep;
> To sleep, perchance to dream – ay, there's the rub ....
>
> (III. i. 56-65)

The difficulty in deciding what the metaphor "take arms against a sea of troubles" stands for – revenge or suicide – should be noted here as one of the causes of critical confusion concerning the import of the whole passage. In my view, Hamlet had ruled out the possibility of suicide as early as the reference to the *deus absconditus* in "that the Everlasting had not fix'd / His cannon 'gainst self-slaughter. O God! God!" (I.ii.131-32). To follow the logic of Hamlet's chiasmic oscillation between alternatives, revenge brings inevitable death[269], the idea of which is immediately countered with oneiric euphemism: "to die – to sleep .... to sleep, perchance to dream". This euphemism is peculiar not only because it is oneiric, that it attributes dreams to dreamless death, but also because it turns against itself in becoming a threat: "ay,

---

[269] The acquired wisdom – revenge equals suicide – may be located somewhere between the original naivity of the "I was born to set it right" and post-exile nihilism, the failure of alternatives.

there's the rub" and an aphorism or truism, as I shall argue later.[270] To quote further:

> For in that sleep of death what dreams may come,
> When we have shuffled off this mortal coil,
> Must give us pause.
>
> (66-68)

Let us take into account the drastic change of auxiliaries, from the "may" in the early form of doubt: "May be a devil" to the "must" of the "Must give us pause". What both "ay, there's the rub" and "must give us pause" signify is not only the mentioned euphemism-turned-threat, but the presence, the actuality of this threat coiling back on the speaker the more drastically, since it seems to mark an uncalled-for and uncontrollable excess of linguistic representation. The pause appears here as a form of paralysis, a necessary consequence of an attempt to grasp the ungraspable through language. Its sudden intervention shows the unavailability of a linguistics of death at the peak point of ontological perplexity. One cannot overestimate the significance of this interval, this break, this rupture in self-expression in the reflective movement towards death.[271] What form of communication is to be expected after this pause? Is there anything to be said that is not conveyed already in the acknowledged impossibility of one's death-sermon over oneself?

What follows after the interval consists in a shift from active to passive voice, an emphatic move towards inaction. Abundance in questions after aphoristic statements include constant echoes of necessitated endurance. The frequent occurrences of "bear" (70, 76, 81) seem to continue along the line of the alternative to action specified

---

[270] See also for contrast the non-euphemistic aphorism of Admetus in the *Alcestis* of Euripides: "One doomed is dead, the dead hath ceased to be", *tethnēk ho mellon, kouket esth' ho katthanon* and Hercules' apathetic response, "Diverse are these – to be and not to be", *khoris to t' einai to me nomidzetai,* trans. Arthur S. Way, The Loeb Classical Library, Cambridge, Mass., and London: Harvard University Press, 1958, 527-8. Euphemism does indeed seem out of place in tragic *pronoia* and when it occurs it only serves to postpone the ultimate recognition of what cannot be shunned, as in *Hamlet*. *Alcestis* up to the quoted lines seems to unfold as a tragedy, but Hercules' redemptive intervention transforms the play into tragicomedy, this characteristically Euripidean genre.

[271] What is Hamlet's most characteristic and persistent mode of being if not this constant pausing in idle rumination?

both in "to be" and the "to suffer the slings and arrows" (57-58).[272] In addition, the idea of endurance as existential precondition is combined with (the burden of) thinking. "Resolution" that may bring about the dreaded dreams – the underlying theme of reflection before the self-silencing pause – "is sicklied o'er with the pale cast of thought, / And enterprises of great pitch and moment / With this regard their currents turn awry / And lose the name of action" (84-88). Inaction then, expressed in the passive voice, is fostered by thought.

At least two important argumentative developments have to be noted here, in relation to the moment of inaction, that immediately qualify its real stake: the interference of the other and a simultaneous shift to the first person singular. The presence of Ophelia brings monological discourse to an abrupt end. A dialogical situation is established in its stead, where things become more concrete. (This is not the only dramatic precedent when accumulated internal conflicts are suddenly unleashed, released in the context of intersubjective scenes of debate, but I shall come back to that in discussing the closet-scene). This becoming concrete seems as abrupt as the appearance of Ophelia and its relevance is the more accentuated in its being an interruption of a chain of generalizations. The entire monologue generalizes its contents by various means, among which we find the use of the pronoun "we" ("we end"; "we have shuffled off"; "give us"; "makes us", etc.); recourse to rhetorical questions ("who would bear the whips and scorns of time"; "who would fardels bear", etc.); to the third person singular ("when he himself might his quietus make"); to infinitives ("to be"; "not to be"; "to suffer"; "to die"; "to sleep"; "to dream"; "to end" etc.); to metaphor ("a sea of troubles"; "to die – to sleep"); to hyperbole ("a thousand natural shocks"); and to aphorism[273] ("The undiscover'd country, from whose bourn / No traveller returns[274], puzzles the will"; "Thus conscience does make cowards of us all").

The first person singular, the ruminating self, hidden behind these forms of rhetorical distanciation is inescapably brought back to recognition by the intervention of the other:

---

[272]Cf. Harold Jenkins' longer notes to the Arden ed., where he claims the initial question to have been decided by the chosen alternative of "to be", "to suffer", "to bear", 487. He specifies this conclusion, however, as paradox, since "we do not so much choose one of the alternatives as passively accept it from fear of embracing the other" 488. One may ask whether the other is embracable at all.
[273]Cf. Jenkins, Ln. 487.
[274]Except our late Father, needless to say.

Soft you, now, the fair Ophelia! Nymph, in thy orisons be all my sins remember'd.

(88-90)

Though there is no explicit verbal link between "lose the name of action" preceding these lines and "my sins", it seems to me that they are, by virtue of their proximity and the overall context of self-rebuke[275], closely related. Hamlet makes concrete the previously generalized inaction[276] as his actual sin. However, this is not the only instance of particularization. The monological universalization of pride in "the proud man's contumely" (71) also undergoes singularization in the confession, "I am very proud, revengeful, ambitious" (124-25). It is crucial to note these occurrences of the particularization of meaning in a dialogical relation, in the context of ethics. What we witness in the move from monological reflection to moral behaviour is the inevitable narrowing down of alternatives of action to more or less definite acts. It is conspicuous that the dialogical involvement with the other brings moral challenges and imperatives into view, the demand to conceive of myself as an actual and concrete first person singular and to leave behind reflection for the sake of action. Correspondingly, the plurality of contemplated alternatives is to be reduced to the singularity of an act, be it a "physical" or "speech" act.

To conclude, my purpose with the brief analysis above was to present a reading of the great monologue, which sees its relevance in the gradual unfolding of Hamlet's ontological perplexity; in the necessary pause presenting itself for a verbal-linguistic appropriation of something beyond language; and in the logically inevitable recourse to endurance, the submission to "to be". Endurance, as I noted above, is posited as coterminous and following from, thinking, which, not for the first time, appears as a burden of being.[277] Besides the importance

---

[275] Cf. the self-irony and the dominant first person singular in "What an ass am I! This is most brave, / That I, the son of a dear father murder'd, / Prompted to my revenge by heaven and hell, / Must like a whore unpack my heart with words" (II.ii.578-81).

[276] Or the "failure of resolution to translate itself into action", as Jenkins puts it, cf. ln. 488.

[277] Cf. "there is nothing / either good or bad but thinking makes it so. To me / it is a prison" (II.ii.49-50). In these cases thinking confines one to dual alternatives, binary oppositions, to the constantly oscillating duplicity of situation-assessments. One may care to examine all the occurences of the conjunct "or" in the play and investigate Hamlet's reflective thought processes and struggles with alternatives. This approach would take the burden of thinking as the main source of Hamlet's lasting delay and paralysis.

of this bond, endurance has to be interpreted also in the light of the general context or the modality of self-rebuke. Though not idleness any more, but an ontologically justified form of inaction, endurance is only one step beyond and one step too short. Its insufficiency is proven by Hamlet's constant self-laceration and his overall dissatisfaction with inaction.

In what follows I turn to the theory of speech act and the philosophy of action together with a vital scene that demonstrates Hamlet's two alternatives to inaction. This further encounter between drama and philosophy serves to bring the question of agency and action into focus.

VII. Forms of Inaction: Speech Acts

Speaking and using daggers

The closet-scene, where accumulated cognitive-psychological tensions find misdirected release, is perhaps the best context for examining physical action and speech act. Before concentrating on this crucial scene in *Hamlet*, however, it is necessary to take a closer look at these alternatives to inaction.

As far as the term physical act is concerned I am aware of its overlaps with verbal utterances or speech acts. Obviously, in trying to separate these two forms of "action", I exclude from the range of "physical act" those movements that are necessarily involved in speech (the movement of the vocal cords, the rhythm of breathing, the movement of lips and tongue, etc.). It is physical as far as it cannot be or is not chosen to be carried out by speech and it is an act as far as it is intentional and purposeful. These latter characteristics of an act present a multitude of problems and I shall shortly come back to them in discussing the killing of Polonius. Let us now move on to the concept of speech act, as it stands opposed to that of the physical.

J. L. Austin's now classic *How to Do Things with Words*[278] pointed to the active potential of speech in a systematic form, unprecedented before. He differentiated between so-called "constatives" and "performatives", the latter defined as not constating, describing anything, as well as not being true or false (5).[279] Quite plainly, saying something is also doing something, performing an act. By saying "I kill you" I achieve something quite different from actually (physically) committing the murder, namely I perform the speech act of threat or warning. This performance does not use a performative verb like "I warn you that", etc., so it is qualified as an implicit performa-

---

[278] John L. Austin, *How to Do Things with Words*, ed. J. O. Urmson, Oxford: Oxford University Press, 1973.

[279] The conclusion prepared by this dichotomy claims that "the truth or falsity of a statement depends not merely on the meanings of words but on what act you were performing in what circumstances", 144.

tive in contrast to the explicit performative which is introduced by a performative verb.[280]

Austin's analysis of performatives necessitates a further distinction between utterances. One can perform an act of saying something, which is to be distinguished from an act performed in saying something. It is the bifurcation of performance into locutionary and illocutionary acts (99). The illocutionary force of an utterance is thereby distinguished from the meaning (or sense and reference) of a locutionary act (100,108). To perform an illocutionary act is also to perform a locutionary act according to Austin (111), and in order to determine the illocutionary act performed we must determine the way we are using the locution (98). This determination of an illocutionary act leads to the isolation of yet a further class of performative, the perlocutionary act. The relation of the illocutionary to the perlocutionary is probably the most troublesome in the whole Austinian enterprise, as he himself admits.[281] The term "perlocution" stands for the effects and consequences something said may produce on the feelings, thoughts or actions of the audience, the speaker or other persons (101). A major difference between illocutionary and perlocutionary acts is, according to the argument, that whereas the former can be made explicit by the performative formula, the latter cannot. I can say "I warn you that", but I cannot say "I alarm you that": "I convince you that" (103). It seems I cannot guarantee the effect on the listener by my intended illocutionary force. Therefore it is not always sufficient to determine the way we are using the locution to determine the illocutionary act. For is the illocutionary force determined by the speaker's intention or by the listener, the recipient? What guarantees the success of the illocutionary act? To speak of success is also to speak of failure. The collective term Austin uses to distinguish the causes of the failure of the performative is "infelicities".

The doctrine of "infelicities" introduced already in Lecture II where it embraces "the things that can be and go wrong". In order that the performative is brought home or with Austin's expression for the "happy" functioning of the performative, there are certain basic conditions to be satisfied. It follows that should any of the conditions remain unsatisfied, the performative is "unhappy" (15). The precondition most central for Austin's understanding of the illocutionary effect is the first on this list of criteria: "there must exist an accepted conven-

---

[280] Cf. Austin, 32.
[281] For it is the use of language that blurs the distinction, cf. 103,109.

tional procedure having a conventional effect, that procedure to include the uttering of certain words by certain persons in certain circumstances" (14). Recourse to convention, necessary to secure the "happy" performative, will also highlight the difference between illocutionary effect and perlocutionary act.

Besides infelicities, however, we must also consider, Austin claims, the distinction between producing effects that are intended or unintended. It is the distinction between attempt and achievement, i.e., when the speaker intends to produce an effect which does not occur (105). Certain effects have to be achieved for securing the "happy" performative, like the so-called "illocutionary uptake" which means bringing about the understanding of the meaning and the force of the locution (116). Apart from uptake Austin gives two more forms of illocutionary effect, the effect of naming a ship by saying "I name this ship the Queen Elizabeth" and the response an illocutionary act may invite by convention. These instances of illocutionary effect are important, because they are characterized as distinct from perlocutionary acts.

Perlocutionary acts are not conventional, according to Austin, but rather employ "inducements" and "personal influence amounting to duress" (117). It seems that the argument opposes convention to personal influence and reserves the possibility of duress for the latter. What is striking, is not only the regrettably missing reflection on the possible duress of convention, but rather, Austin's vague understanding of convention as such and its all too absolute alliance with illocution.[282] It is Strawson who points out this weak point in Austin's undertaking by claiming that "there are many cases in which the illocutionary force of an utterance, though not exhausted by its meaning, is not owed to any conventions other than those which help to give it its meaning".[283] The speech act of warning, for Strawson, in "the ice over there is very thin" does not conform to any established convention (26). Though we may disagree with Austin with regard to the status of convention in differentiating between illocutionary and perlocutionary acts, one has to accept that personal influence and inducements are more obvious in the case of the latter. What else are we told about the perlocutionary act?

---

[282] Convention for Austin extends to non-verbal illocutionary acts as well, cf. 118, 121.
[283] "Intention and convention in speech acts", in *The Philosophy of Language*, ed. J. R. Searle, Oxford: Oxford University Press, 1971, 26.

In his lecture discussing the perlocutionary act Austin makes one further distinction, which will be of utmost importance for us in the analysis of some crucial speech acts in *Hamlet*. Actions having a perlocutionary object, the argument goes, are to be distinguished from those having a sequel (117). In the example "I tried to warn him but only succeeded in alarming him" we find the disturbing discrepancy between attempt and achievement, object and sequel. Further, some perlocutionary acts tend to have sequels rather than objects, namely those that lack appropriate illocutionary formula, Austin argues, like surprising or upsetting someone by the locution itself (there being no illocutionary formula "I surprise you by"; "I upset you by", etc. (117).

There is a highly dramatic potential in this divergence between sequel and object, which I will shortly employ in my interpretation of Gertrude's inconsequential behaviour. The scene in question is rather complex in portraying the various interrelated problems I am dealing with in this chapter and, by applying Austin's terminology I hope to identify a fundamental segment of dramatic action.[284] In what follows I will look at the context of Hamlet's encounter with Gertrude with special regard to effective uses of rhetoric (embedding speech acts); and, subsequently, I will examine the Hamlet-Polonius incident supported by certain guidelines of action-theory.

The encounter with Gertrude parallels the confrontation with Ophelia in many ways. First, as I have already mentioned, a characteristically monological situation is interrupted by having to meet the

---

[284]There is a problem here. Austin would not be too happy with this form of application. Consider the passage "a performative utterance will, for example, be in a peculiar way hollow or void if said by an actor on stage or if introduced in a poem or spoken in soliloquy. This applies in a similar manner to any and every utterance – a sea-change in special circumstances. Language in such circumstances is in special ways – intelligibly – used not seriously, but in ways parasitic upon its normal use – ways which fall under the doctrine of the etiolations of language. All this we are excluding from consideration", 22. This aversion is echoed by Searle in his *Speech Acts: An Essay in the Philosophy of Language*, where he also proposes the differentiation between "normal, real world talk and parasitic forms of discourse such as fiction, play acting, etc.", 78. Austin's and Searle's oversimplifying division of language into its "normal" and "parasitic" use, needless to say, fails to stand poststructural scrutiny. Does not "normal", if there exists such an animal, purloin its meaning from the parasitic? Is it not imbued through and through with the parasitic? What is parasitism, one may ask with Derrida. For his critique of parasitism see "Signature Event Context", in *Limited Inc.*, trans. S. Weber and J. Mehlman, Evanston: Northwestern University Press, 1988. Does not the dream of non-etiolated language etiolate itself on the way to becoming real or normal? For an analytic aversion see Strawson's "Intention and convention in Speech acts" 23.

other, when a dialogical relation demands the forsaking of reflection for the sake of an impending moral challenge. This parallel appears the more emphasized by the verbal resonance in "Soft, now to my mother" (383).[285] Second, Hamlet himself makes the connection explicitly in his confessions to Ophelia: "it were better my mother had not borne me"(124) and "I say we will have no more marriage" (149).

The scene I chose to discuss here in some detail is outstanding for bringing the plurality of the play's conflicts into sudden interference and a climactic explosion. Hamlet is the more enraged since being convinced of his truth and at the same time feeling compelled to spare the praying King's life. The accumulated tensions of frustration verbalized in the great monologue are anabatically intensified in the aftermath of being convinced to the point of discarding premeditated restraint:

> Soft, now to my mother.
> O heart, lose not thy nature. Let not ever
> The soul of Nero enter this firm bosom;
> Let me be cruel, not unnatural.
> I will speak daggers to her, but use none.
> My tongue and soul in this be hypocrites:
> How in my words somever she be shent,
> To give them seals never my soul consent.
>
> (III.ii.383-90)

What we find in the closet-scene is the success of speech acts and the failure of the physical after an unprolongable onslaught of *sticho-mythic* agitation. The exchange of dart-like abuses start *in medias res* underlining the speedy succession of episodes and confrontations where decreasing space is left for reflective situation assessments. This Shakespearean version of *stichomythia* displays a confrontation dramatized by antithesis or *antistoichon,* the symmetrical structuring of contradictory statements:

> GERTRUDE: Hamlet, thou hast thy father much offended.
> HAMLET: Mother, you have my father much offended.
> GERTRUDE: Come, come, you answer with an idle tongue.
> HAMLET: Go, go, you question with a wicked tongue.
> GETRUDE: Why, how now, Hamlet?
> HAMLET: What's the matter now?

---

[285]"Soft" standing for self-silencing, as the Arden fn. tells us, cf. "Soft you now, / The fair Ophelia" (88).

(8-13)

The power of this brief altercatio is achieved by the device of antithesis ("come"–"go"; "answer"–"question"; "idle"–"wicked") and by various forms of repetition: the rhetorical figure of *epistrophe*, the reverberation of the same words in the end of the lines ("offended"; "tongue"); *anaphora,* the recurrence of the same words in successive clauses ("you"; "with"; "now"); and *parison,* the balanced, even structure of clauses. The latter is the more conspicuous where statement follows statement, question question.

Nowhere in the texture of the entire play do we find, I think, the strength of verbal utterances so striking in a dialogical situation. In what follows, the borderline between speech and action appears to be gradually blurred as in the methodical recourse to the antithesis between praise and blame, eulogy and obloquy. For the first time, the late King Hamlet and Claudius are evoked in contrast, Hyperion against the "moor" (55, 67). What is striking in these series of insinuations is the monopolizing of judgement and clairvoyance: "Have you eyes?" (65, repeated in 69): "what judgement would step from this to this?" (71). Hamlet takes it for granted that Gertrude cannot but see and judge as he sees and judges. What may interfere with effectuating such despotic claims is, needless to say, love. That is why love has to be immediately ruled out as a possible self-excuse or self-exemption: "You cannot call it love; for at your age / The heyday in the blood is tame" (68-69). Gertrude thus finds herself cornered by the irresistible absolutism of authoritarian rhetoric. Then follows *chiasmus* and *apostrophe,* to bring the effect home: "Eyes without feeling, feeling without sight, / Ears without hands or eyes, smelling sans all" (78-79), sounds the chiasmic judgement, the speech act of blame or reprimand. In Austin's classification of utterances according to their illocutionary force, Hamlet's implicit performative would qualify as a verdictive which "consist in the delivering of a finding upon evidence or reasons as to value or fact, so far as these are distinguishable".[286]

The subsequent double *apostrophe* of "O shame, where is thy blush? / Rebellious hell" (81-82)[287] exposes Hamlet's main target of

---

[286] Austin, 152. On a different list compiled by Searle and Vanderveken, blame is identified as an assertive. Cf. *Foundations of Illocutionary Logic,* Cambridge: Cambridge University Press, 1985, 183.

[287] A tricky *apostrophe,* since its turning away from the addressee is immediately followed by a return in the blush expected from Gertrude.

insinuation: the elicitation of shame. The speech acts achieve their purpose if shame is elicited successfully:

> QUEEN: O Hamlet, speak no more.
> Thou turn'st my eyes into my very soul,
> And there I see such black and grained spots
> As will not leave their tinct.
>
> (88-91)

Despite the success of speech acts and rhetoric Hamlet does not stop, but secures his perlocutionary object:

> QUEEN: O speak to me no more.
> These words like daggers enter in my ears.
>
> (III.iv.94-95)

The refrain-like reverberation of "speak no more" (88, 94, 102) and the final breakdown: "O Hamlet, thou hast cleft my heart in twain" (158) show that the verdictives attained their goal. It is not before long though, that, to speak with Austin, the perlocutionary act is to lose its object and attain its sequel instead.[288]

To intervene in what may easily become a slow and methodical murder by speech act, there comes the second and last advent of the Ghost: "Speak to her, Hamlet" (115) it commands, as if speaking still maintained the competence to redress. The selective appearance[289] of the Ghost at this climactic point causes confusion instead of settlement.

After the visitation Hamlet needs to cogently defy all traces of real madness, since Gertrude's growing pity may easily stifle her shame. Indeed, I suggest that Gertrude's later behaviour can be understood as the outcome of the victory of pity (the perlocutionary sequel) over her ephemeral shame (the perlocutionary object). The final span

---

[288] Austin, 117. What seemed achieved is soon suspended and the attempt misfires.

[289] Consider the extraordinary emphasis in the four nothings with regard to what Gertrude sees or hears (132, 133, 134, 135). This selective appearance has its Elizabethan predecessors, as well as its versions in popular belief, cf. Jenkins Ln., 519. This case, however, as Jenkins points out, is exceptional in that the Ghost not only appears but speaks to Hamlet. One may consider the double effect of this speech, one enhancing the "almost blunted purpose" of killing the King, the other blunting Hamlet's own, since by provoking verbal response from the "tardy son", he will consequently be taken mad and thereby his main objective, the elicitation of shame will be endangered.

of the dialogue between Hamlet and Gertrude is dominated by imperatives and Gertrude's speech act of promise.

After having been fatefully interrupted by the Ghost, Hamlet strives to retain his authoritarian rhetoric. Instead of abstractions, rhetorical questions, *apostrophes*, his speech abounds in dart-like orders and imperatives, "lay not"; "confess"; "repent"; "do not spread"; "assume"; "refrain". The shift to the concrete is accompanied by a change from past-oriented reprimands to future-oriented demands, from verdictives to exercitives, "the decision that something is to be so, as distinct from a judgement that it is so."[290]

These imperatives aimed at constraining future behaviour fail to hit, as we know, even though, for the present, they do elicit a promise, "be thou assur'd, if words be made of breath, / And breath of life, I have no life to breathe / What thou hast said to me" (199-201). That this is to remain an unfulfilled promise, is obvious from the very first confiding words she exchanges with Claudius:

> QUEEN: Ah, mine own lord, what have I seen tonight!
> KING: What, Gertrude, how does Hamlet?
> QUEEN: Mad as the sea and wind when both contend
> Which is the mightier.
>
> (IV.i.5-8) [291]

Recourse to madness shows that pity had conquered shame and Gertrude's future behaviour will not be constrained by Hamlet's exercitives. Rather, as I see it, Gertrude can only survive those piercing speech acts by taking a step back from heart-cleaving shame and settle on self-defensive pity.

Gertrude's ephemeral contrition shows the temporary but successful offensive of speech acts and as such stands in sharp contrast to the failure of physical action. Daggers are not only spoken but also used.

The *anabasis*, the climax of the scene presents itself as a sudden release, an unpremeditated act of murder. It is through the proceedings just emphasized that Hamlet's deed can be seen as a consequence of a double transfer: first, due to the voluntary though temporary exemption of the praying Claudius, second, to the less voluntary sparing of

---

[290] Austin, 154. On Searle's and Vanderveken's list order is a directive, cf. *Foundations of Illocutionary Logic*, 201.
[291] And somewhat later: "To draw apart the body he hath kill'd, / O'er whom – his very madness, like some ore / Among a mineral of metals base, / Shows itself pure" (24-27).

Gertrude. If the exemption was voluntary, this "rash and bloody deed" can hardly be so defined. Or can it? Is the slaying of Polonius an altogether involuntary act? What is an involuntary act? What is Hamlet's act in the first place?

G. E. M. Anscombe's formula "I *do* what *happens*" was found by many "extremely paradoxical and obscure", as she herself acknowledged.[292] Ricoeur rightly points out that this privileges the objective side of action, i.e., it is characterized by result-centredness.[293] However, I would like to argue that this formula does define the dramatic situation most faithfully in its emphasis on the outcome and the trivializing of agency. But let us quote Anscombe a little further: "I *do* what *happens*. That is to say, when the description of what happens is the very thing which I should say I was doing, then there is no distinction between my doing and the thing's happening" (53). This definition easily substitutes "the thing's happening" for "my doing" and thereby dismisses the significance of agency and a possible severing of action from event. It would hardly serve to differentiate between the statements "Hamlet drove his sword through the arras to kill the King" and "Polonius is dead". The first involves reference to agency, intention and reason; the second merely relates an event. Again, I argue that this is an accurate description of the dramatic situation to blur the difference, but in order to see the significance of such a blend we first have to take the variance of the two statements and of action and event "seriously".

In distinguishing action from event analytic philosophy has often resorted to a parallel differentiation between reason and cause. Action explained by reason and opposed to cause-triggered event, was normally elucidated by reference to forms of intention, wantings or to the comprehensive formula, *pro attitudes*.[294] In Anscombe's so-called

---

[292] G. E. M. Anscombe, *Intention*, Oxford: Basil Blackwell, 1963, 53.
[293] *Oneself as Another*, 70.
[294] Donald Davidson's well-known expression is introduced in his "Actions, Reasons and Causes": "Whenever someone does something for a reason, he can be characterized as having some sort of pro attitude toward actions of a certain kind", which then he qualifies as inluding "desires, wantings, urges, promptings and a great variety of moral views, aesthetic principles, economic prejudicies, social conventions and public and private goals and values in so far these can be interpreted as attitudes of an agent directed toward actions of a certain kind .... Giving the reason why an agent did something is often a matter of naming the pro attitude or the related belief or both .... " The related belief here encompasses knowing, perceiving, noticing, remembering: "that the action is of that kind" claims Davidson and calls this pair the

"piecemeal approach" to the analysis of intention we are confronted with the question: "what distinguishes actions which are intentional from those which are not?" For her the answer is given by reference to the applicability of a certain sense of the question "Why?" The answer, then, would give us the reason for acting.[295] However, there follows immediately a necessary bifurcation in the use of the concept of reason, which shows the constraints such a definition has yet to undergo. In the questions "what was the reason for your starting so violently?" and "What is your reason for excluding so-and-so from your will?" recourse to the interrogative "why?" can hardly account for both occurrences of the concept of reason in the same way. Anscombe warns us against taking for granted that in the case of a sudden start the reason is a cause, due to the great confusion in the field of causality (10).[296]

Can Hamlet's "rash deed" be identified with a "sudden start" and explained away by reference to a confusing form of causality? This seems quite untenable when we think of the murder as the consequence of at least two "sudden starts", the drawing and the thrusting of the rapier.[297] It is important here, I think, to qualify these bodily movements or "primitive actions" as Davidson calls them, in the field of drama. These primitive actions that "we do not do by doing something else, mere movements of the body, these are all the actions there are"; and he concludes: "the rest is up to nature."[298]

"primary reason" for an agent to act, cf. *Essays on Actions and Events*, Oxford: Clarendon, 1985, 3-4.
[295] Anscombe, 9. But consider Anscombe's example, "Why did you kill him?" "He killed my father" (10). What happens with the reason this application of "why" is supposed to supply, when the dialogue is continued, "Who, Polonius?" Will it become cause? Consider further, Anscombe's own exception, "I was not aware I was doing that", where, she claims, the question "why did you do it?" has no application. Actions can have many different descriptions and one may know one description, not another (11-12). Accordingly, "I was not aware that I was thrusting my rapier through the arras" does not hold, whereas "I was not aware I was killing Polonius" does.
[296] Or if we are to except that possibility, it is a strange case of causality, to say the least (*Ibid.*).
[297] It might be opposed that during the brief but heated altercatio with Gertrude, Hamlet has already drawn his weapon to kill her ("You go not until I set you up a glass / Where you may see the inmost part of you" 18-19), but then again, intention and murder at this point, seem to be linked. It would seem that Hamlet is responsible for at least the second " sudden start".
[298] "Agency", 59. On an elementary level of action analysis, it seems undoubtable that "we never do more than move our bodies", to speak with Davidson. For the defence of this statement against possible counterarguments see 49-61.

"Sudden starts" in this sense can be seen as a subset of primitive actions, certain bodily movements that are caused by an external impulse, but not by a preceding movement of the same body. It needs to be added, however, that contingent "sudden starts", as well as mere movements of the body receive their justification in drama by their mediation of significant deeds or actions.[299] They hardly appear in isolation, which in itself attests to the shift from contingency Davidson expresses by nature, to necessity or fate represented by dramaturgy. In other words, those doings that appear to be insignificant turn out to be significant in their insignificance by virtue of contextualization.

Thus Hamlet's "sudden starts" prove to be, under the premises, not so much contingent primitive actions, but reactions that have their explanatory prehistory in the preceding episodes and an ultimate completion in the significant act of murder.[300]

We are still looking for an adequate explanation for Hamlet's physical act which we now see to have been composed by at least two primitive actions, the drawing and the thrusting. Though the former belongs to the Hamlet-Gertrude encounter and the latter to the Hamlet-Polonius incident, I tried to stress the relevance of the transition that made the qualifications to "sudden start" questions necessary. The problem of reason versus cause, nevertheless, persists in relation to the killing of Polonius (the Hamlet-Polonius incident). Before I turn to Davidson's own analysis of the Hamlet-Polonius incident, I would like to recall his famous statement on the issue of reason and cause: "the primary reason for an action is its cause."[301] Giving up the tradi-

---

[299] This, I am aware, may be doubted by pointing out that dramatic performances do include stage settings that appropriate the world of the text to real life situations, where characters appear as ordinary human beings and behave accordingly. In the scene under discussion at present, Gertrude may be combing her hair on Hamlet's entrance or be involved in any other series of primitive actions following the director's ideas about the whole scene. But even then, one may retort, is not a good direction marked by the consistent employment of such doings in the contextualization of significant actions?

[300] It seems then, that Anscombe's question "what was the reason for your starting so violently?" in the Hamlet-Polonius incident has to be answered with an important qualification. The response "the shout behind the arras alarmed me" has to be supplemented by "I was predisposed to act thus by my preceding primitive actions" or "I expected all the time something like that to happen", "I was prepared for such a possibility" which eventually converge in the emphatic past tense. I am not saying that this possibility is absent from ordinary life-situations, but merely that in drama it is difficult to think of sudden starts without these qualifications.

[301] "Actions, Reasons and Causes", 4. Only if, he adds, it consists of a *pro attitude*, which, of course, has to do with intention.

tional contrast between these concepts Davidson considers rationalization of action "a species of causal explanation" (3). The difference between reason and cause, action and event becomes a matter of description for Davidson. We can rationalize an event and thereby attribute agency, though we impute agency only when we imply that the act was intentional, he claims.[302] But how and when do we ascribe intentionality to an event? Let me quote this crucial paragraph in "Agency":

> Hamlet intentionally kills the man behind the arras, but he does not intentionally kill Polonius. Yet Polonius is the man behind the arras and so Hamlet's killing of the man behind the arras is identical with his killing of Polonius. It is a mistake to suppose there is a class of intentional actions: if we took this track, we should be compelled to say that one and the same action was both intentional and not intentional. As a first step toward straightening things out, we may try talking not of actions but of sentences and descriptions of actions instead. In the case of agency my proposal might then be put: a person is the agent of an event if and only if there is a description of what he did that makes true a sentence that says he did it intentionally. (46)

According to Davidson's analysis of the Hamlet-Polonius incident Hamlet's killing of Polonius can be defined as intentional and Hamlet can be defined as agent, since there can be a description of his deed that "makes true a sentence that says he did it intentionally". But any description ascribing intention in this case has to leave the identity of the recipient of the action undecided. As soon as the man behind the arras is named, his identity confirmed, there can hardly be any description assigning agency. Under no description can Hamlet be considered as an intentional executioner of Polonius. And though this may seem too self-evident to be of interest to us, yet it is certainly this very self-evidence that is disregarded in the entire aftermath of the murder. What the reactions of Claudius, Ophelia and Laertes show us is not so much their belief in the intention behind the deed[303], but pri-

---

[302] Which involves a special relation to the beliefs and attitudes of the agent, *Literary Theory After Davidson*, ed. R. W. Dasenbrock, Pennsylvania: Pennsylvania State University Press, 1993.
[303] Except, of course, Gertrude, who is present to see the deed as "rash and bloody". The more conspicuous her later indifference becomes in not even attempting to influence public opinion.

marily, that intention in drama does not count in the reception of action. It is through this roundabout way that we understand the generic significance of Anscombe's "I do what happens".

If naming and action belong inseparably together in the drama, we can say that in the same way as naming confirms action (the man behind the arras is named Polonius), action confirms the name (of the murderer). The naming of the victim provides a name for the assassin, too. That the name "Hamlet" sounds familiar should not be misleading: the person startled by the eavesdropper and the actant slaying Polonius sound the same only by virtue of the illusion of nominal-numerical and positional identity.[304] From the discovery of murder Hamlet will be "the assassin of Polonius", that will be his allotted identity in the aftermath, a development with which he (the neglected person behind the actant) shall have to come to terms with. This leads us to distinguish between two states of affairs in the Hamlet-Polonius incident. One that describes an agent intentionally slaying the man behind the arras and the other, a state of affairs later in time, where the agent is described as having unintentionally killed Polonius. The two agents happen to share the same label "Hamlet".[305] But who or which is Hamlet? Can his identity be fully grasped, exhaustively articulated by this action? Is there a direct passage from action to agent?

What we learn from Davidson for our present purposes is the importance of description in contrasting action and event, reason and cause. He contests Georg Henrik von Wright's definition, that action is not an event, but rather the bringing about of an event, – by examples which describe events regardless whether they were brought about intentionally or not, like "I fall down".[306] However, the problematization of agency and the troubling cohesion between naming (a form of specifying) and action (as non-event), as introduced above, leads us to redescribe agency along with the possible redescription of action as event (or vice versa, event as action). What the Hamlet-

---

[304] Perhaps I should add here, that though this duplication may be dangerous for an ethical orientation, it points to an essentially tragic phenomenon, the split subject.

[305] This duplicity of agency is one way to counter Davidson's quoted observation, since in "Hamlet intentionally kills the man behind the arras, but he does not intentionally kill Polonius" the temporal succession of the two states of affairs is left unnoticed and the concretization of the victim's identity has no parallel modification in the case of the agent's.

[306] The solution for Davidson, again, lies not in isolating actions from events, as von Wright does, but in finding a different logical form for action sentences, cf. "The Logical Form of Action Sentences", in *Essays on Actions and Events*, 113-14.

Polonius incident shows is an agent himself troubled by this crystallization of agency:

> QUEEN: O me, what hast thou done?
> HAMLET: Nay, I know not. Is it the King?
>
> (24-25)

and later:

> HAMLET: For this same lord
> I do repent; but heaven hath pleas'd it so,
> To punish me with this and this with me,
> That I must be their scourge and minister.
> I will bestow him, and will answer well
> The death I gave him.
>
> (174-79)[307]

Whether this reference to heaven convincingly rationalizes event as action or instead, shows the impossibility of any rationalizing description, is difficult to say. Whether Hamlet really accepts the state of affairs as the consequence of his intentional action or rather, succumbs to an unforeseen pressure of a cause-triggered event, is hard to determine.[308]

---

[307] Consider the self-referential first person in each line testifying to the undertaking of a dubious agency and consequently, responsibility. The heavenly punishment may here be take to express the confusion in having to base agency on a failure of action.

[308] For Davidson, of course, mistakes are actions, not events, since as he puts it: "making a mistake must be doing something with the intention of achieving a result that is not forthcoming" ("Agency", 46). Here action equals "doing something with the intention of", following a certain description of that same action. The related alliance between intention and agency, at the same time, is a complex issue for Davidson, the elaboration of which follows two itineraries, one culminating in the conclusion, "we impute agency when we imply that the act was intentional" ("The Logical Form of Action Sentences", 121.), the other outlined in the introduction, "we should try to see if we can find a mark of agency that does not use the concept of intention" ("Agency", 47). The latter itinerary leads to a possible explanation of an action by giving its causes, e.g. one burns down his or her house to collect insurance. In this sense Davidson can claim that although we say that the agent caused the death of the victim, i.e., he killed him, this is an elliptical way of saying that some act of the agent caused the death of the victim (49). What is regrettably missing from Davidson's account, is the question of point of view in establishing agency and describing action. Here I am concerned with what the agent himself has to say about his own agency and with what descriptions he might define his own action.

If there exists a disturbing doubt as to the possible description of his own action, it is vital to see that it evaporates in the reception of the deed. This is not to say, of course, that Hamlet's deed will enter posterity as unquestionably intentional, but, as I argued earlier, whether it was intentional or not ceases to be an issue. The reception of the deed confirms the "I do what happens" pattern introduced in its simplicity as perhaps the best possible description of dramatic action, drastically and ironically. The recipients divide into two groups: those affected directly (Ophelia and Laertes) and those concerned indirectly (Claudius and Gertrude).[309] Though through a diverse and intricate network of relations, these characters share a common trait of reaction, they are in their various ways the sufferers of the result of the deed. Advocates of a result-oriented action-theory. But are they really?

One may glimpse a residue of meaning in madness, madness overwhelming (Ophelia) and madness imputed (Laertes, Gertrude, Claudius all fall back on Hamlet's madness in describing the deed, not to mention Hamlet himself). This madness among its numerous interpretations which I shall not go into here, has a residue of meaning, an excess manifesting itself in the disclaiming of rationality, when rationality inextricably links action to identity. Hamlet's pretended madness, apart from being a device for self-exemption before the public, has this additional role of securing the coexistence of agency and identity. It is a madness with this "method in't" (II.ii.205), the method not only of pretence, but also of irony. For it is seldom noted that Hamlet's reconciliatory speech to Laertes before the duel is ironic through and through. Pretended madness makes such an attempt at reconciliation pretended:

> Was't Hamlet wrong'd Laertes? Never Hamlet.
> If Hamlet from himself be ta'en away,
> And when he's not himself does wrong Laertes,
> Then Hamlet does it not, Hamlet denies it.
> Who does it then? His madness. If't be so,
> Hamlet is of the faction that is wrong'd;
> His madness is poor Hamlet's enemy.

---

[309] That is, emotionally or politically. Though in this qualification Gertrude's status is more uncertain, as her being indirectly concerned has to do with her fears for Hamlet after the murder.

> Sir, in this audience,
> Let my disclaiming from a purpos'd evil
> Free me so far in your most generous thoughts
> That I have shot my arrow o'er the house[310]
> And hurt my brother.
>
> (V.ii.229-39)

In this crucial passage we find the excuses of a split subject disclaiming intentional wrongdoing by imputing it to his own madness. It seems to me that the ironic stance in this otherwise earnest-looking confession serves to convey more than the apology Laertes gleans from it. The line "Hamlet is of the faction[311] that is wrong'd", proclaims the mentioned residue of meaning in the only possible mode of expression under the given circumstances. It is irony directed toward the audience, when all other characters fail to conceive its hidden truth. Hamlet is "wrong'd", but not by his own madness, but by the madness of having to create and realize himself and the future upon the failure of action.[312]

The respective receptions of Hamlet's desperate undertakings, as I have tried to outline above, prove unfavourably influential regarding the aftermath. Unfavourably, because it is the failure that determines the entire plot (Acts IV-V), a mistake that induces a series of no longer controllable events up to the final duel, the parody of action. The closet-scene is linked to the concluding scene as the problematizing of action to its parody. The final scene of *Hamlet*, I believe, can hardly be explained otherwise than a parody of action, a culminating point of failure. What is involved in this drastic defeat, is the death of *ethos*, as I shall argue in the following section.

To sum up, the analysis of the closet-scene exposed two actions

---

[310] Cf. Arden fn.: "the figure of the arrow that, once released, may go farther than one meant is common".

[311] Meaning "party", "the side", "cause followed", cf. Alexander Schmidt, *Shakespeare Lexicon and Quotation Dictionary*, New York: Dover Publications, 1971.

[312] Though indifferent and deaf to irony, Laertes does partially accept Hamlet's explanatory confession, "I am satisfied in nature .... but in my terms of honour I stand aloof" (V.ii.240, 242). His growing sympathy expressed in the heat of the duel in his aside: "And yet it is almost against my conscience" (300) perhaps derives from the common cause (revenge for a father's death), perhaps from the conscience-awakening engagement in dishonour after all the verbal commitments to honour (242, 245) or perhaps from the late understanding of the deceased father's sermon ("To thine own self be true, / And it must follow as the night the day / Thou canst not then be false to any man" I.iii.78-80).

parallel to each other, failed physical action leading up to burlesque-like self-annihilation and mass murder on the one hand and successful speech action, eliciting shame and pity, on the other. The former brings about increasing scepticism, the latter an incident of truth. The point I would like to make is that Hamlet's scepticism turns into nihilism when confidence in this truth is suspended. But what is this incident of truth?

Hamlet's quest for truth, as I pointed out above, begins from the so-called early form of doubt and culminates in ontological perplexity and paralysis,[313] which are the central issues in the great monologue. The encounter in the closet takes place right after this expansion of uncertainty, which explains the two "transfers" and the two "sudden starts", the two "primitive actions" examined. When the truth about Gertrude's self is revealed through her introspection under the pressure of rhetoric,[314] Hamlet finds in her the only one he can confide in[315] (apart from Horatio).[316] The suspension of this confidence comes with the triumph of pity and reaffirms the ontological perplexity. Nihilism thus appears to be partly induced by this disillusionment and partly by other events of the post-exile period.[317]

Nihilism, the parody of action and the death of ethos

The three topics of my argument concerning the final scene of *Hamlet* are closely linked to one another. In the preceding sections I have tried to trace the gradual transformation of scepticism into nihilism, as it

---

[313] Earlier, in a comparison with Prometheus's passivity, Hamlet's paralysis was defined as bearing the distinctive trait of "I want but I cannot". To apply Austin's terminology, Prometheus's speech act of *hybris* is a behabitive which is linked and at the same time contrasted to the verdictive Hamlet issues unscrupulously in the closet scene. Cf. "in one sense of 'blame' which is equivalent to 'hold responsible', the blame is a verdictive, but in another sense it is to adopt an attitude towards a person and is thus a behabitive" (Austin, 154). However, as the exercitives that follow the verdictives in Hamlet's aspiration to elicit Gertrude's shame misfire in the long run and are received with pitying neglect, Hamlet's approach to his own action changes.
[314] Which parallels the certainty obtained by the play within the play which, in the same way, amounts to introspection under the pressure of the reminder (cf. the other incident of truth emerging in the prayer in III.iii.36-72).
[315] Having "created her", i.e., authoritatively extracted such an introspection.
[316] But then, Horatio is not involved in the murder of the late King Hamlet in any way. In fact, he remains a passionless outsider throughout, more like a counterpoint to Hamlet.
[317] I would situate Ophelia's suicide in this period, even though it takes place during Hamlet's exile. Hamlet gets to know about on his return from the exile and his reactions betray an altered consciousness.

followed the irreparable failure of action. It seems that the short-term success of speech act could not eventually counterbalance the impending metamorphosis and could not but enhance the overwhelming ontological perplexity dominating Hamlet's disposition up to and including, the concluding scene. To justify the qualifying term parody with respect to the final duel, some Aristotelian remarks concerning *ethos* must be recalled.

In the *Poetics*, *ethos* is said to manifest (incarnate, impersonate) *prohairesis*, choice (50b10). It is said to appear when speech or action, *logos he praxis*, reveals the nature of moral choice, *prohairesis* (54a17-19). *Logos* stands for thought, *dianoia*, the third most important element of tragedy after *mythos* and *ethos*, "the capacity to say what is pertinent and apt, which in formal speeches is the task of politics and rhetoric" (50b5).

It seems that for this account it hardly matters whether *logos* and *praxis* are in harmony or contradiction, since whatever they signify, they cannot but reveal choice and thereby, *ethos*. However, Aristotle does mention consistency, *homalon*, in delineating the four rules of characterization. Character, *ethos* has to be good; appropriate; involve likeness and consistency. Further, if the subject is represented as inconsistent, he should still be consistently inconsistent" (54a15-29) as we are told, definitely not like Odysseus' dirge in Scylla. It is an example for inappropriate characterization, since masculinity stands in sharp contrast to lamentation. We get two more examples of inconsistency, Menalaus' unnecessary wickedness in the *Orestes* and Iphigeneia at Aulis, whose desperate appeal for life is in disagreement with her later self (54a29-33). These shortcomings of dramatic characterization do not concern *ethos* itself, but merely point out weak forms of representation. Their purpose is not to thematize the question whether the status of *ethos* as such appears to be problematized. The underlying presupposition persists, i.e., that *ethos* exists and exhibits choice, *prohairesis*.

What is missing and can only be missing, from this account of characterization, is precisely this thematization of a shattered *ethos*. The climactic clash between *logos* and *praxis* that defies the totalization of character. The inconsistent inconsistence that goes beyond weak representation and thematizes (ir)representability itself. It is along these lines that action becomes its own parody and *ethos* but its own trace.

In Chapter 1 I have, I hope, made clear my point that Aristotle's ethical orientation can hardly answer for tragic experience in Greek drama. This time, however, I limit myself to the Shakespearean version of shattered *ethos* as it appears in the concluding scene of *Hamlet*.

It is inviting to rethink the final duel as a parody of action that comes in the stead of a long awaited settlement. Action, in the course of the play, gains paramount importance thanks to the long series of delays and hesitations. It stands out as a problem crystal clear due to the light constantly shed on it by its intolerable opposite: inaction. The more we come to expect from it, the less of a settlement it turns out to yield. What we are given is inconsistent inconsistence, failure, disharmony, posthumous retaliation. Hamlet's lack of suspicion concerning the invitation to the duel is inconsistent with his cautious and alert preparations to escape assassination in England. His failure is preempted by the fact that this time he is the one to walk bluntly into the King's mousetrap. What his "readiness is all" regrettably lacks is the effort to pursue his goals, the belief in the effectiveness of choice. Disillusionment is paralleled by a growing disharmony between *logos* and *praxis*, in the manner of complaint: "Thou wouldst not think how ill all's here about my heart" (V.ii.208).

This confession is closely followed by the "we defy augury .... The readiness is all" alternative, the programme of acceptance. Reference to the heart is a moment of internalized truth and its simultaneous defiance betrays an overwhelming indifference towards what may come. It is vital to see that honour as motivating principle has become devoid of meaning for Hamlet. Before the exile honour is accepted as the trigger of action following the example of Fortinbras,[318] it is conceived of as the polar opposite of "unpacking one's heart with words" (II.ii.581). In the post-exile period, however, in my view, honour loses force and promises of greatness and subsides to mere role-play.[319] Accepting the duel therefore involves a split between nature (heart) and honour (role).

The conflict of organizing principles appears to be pretty much the same in the case of Laertes. Hamlet's ironic apology ("Give me

---

[318] Cf. "Rightly to be great / Is not to stir without great argument, / But greatly to find quarrel in a straw / When honour's at the stake" (IV.iv.53-56). Consider the triple emphasis on greatness in relation to honour.

[319] Hamlet's surprisingly changed attitude is expressed in the lines: "I am constant to my purposes, they follow the / King's pleasure. If his fitness speaks, mine is ready. / Now or whensoever, provided I be so able as now" (V.ii.197-99).

your pardon, sir", etc.)[320] is partly accepted, partly dismissed, "I am satisfied in nature, / Whose motive in this case should stir me most / To my revenge; but in my terms of honour / I stand aloof, and will no reconcilement / Till by some elder masters of known honour / I have a voice and precedent of peace / To keep my name ungor'd" (V.ii.240-46). I suggest that unlike Hamlet Laertes is not ironic, which may be confirmed retrospectively, when he confesses the "foul practice" (323) as soon as he is wounded, "Thy mother's poisoned .... the King's to blame" (325-26). It is the dying words of his "satisfied nature" that reveal the workings of dishonour. These words prepare the target of Hamlet's posthumous retaliation.

Many critics intent on redeeming the prince from the deprecating factuality of mass murder try to accentuate the posthumous execution of revenge. It is the ghost of Hamlet rather than he himself (whatever that "himself" may be) who finally accomplishes the deed. This argument of rehabilitation is not as weak as it looks at first sight. It points to the puzzling issue of subjectivity and agency, which I believe, stands in the focus of the final events. Let us carry the idea to the extreme and be informed by the following absurdity. It is the ghost that takes vengeance on the Ghost. The prince revenges the dead father. This turbulence in the family crypt, however, has to give way to yet a third presence, due to the sudden advent of a stranger's ghost. Claudius is killed twice, both by rapier ("The point envenom'd, too") and drink ("Is thy union here?"). Ghost killing ghost to revenge the Ghost: a strange union is here.

What this absurd union reveals is a common attribute, an incapacity, the shared misery of the inability to express themselves in action. For it is quite clear that Hamlet does not intend to kill Laertes anymore than Claudius or the late King Hamlet want the death of Gertrude. The inconsistent inconsistence is ratified and brought to its climax in Hamlet's (ghost's?) final recourse to words. The prolonged oscillation between words and deed, which I think the whole play dramatizes, terminates in ghostly irony: voice is given to the man of deeds: "I do prophesy th'election lights / On Fortinbras. He has my dying voice" (360-61).

This description of the scene may sound exorbitant and quite naturally, one-sided. It rigidly adheres to the perspective indicated in

---

[320] Cf. V.ii.222. I have elsewhere underscored the ironic mode that characterizes Hamlet's behaviour in the entire scene. I may add here that irony gradually envelops his whole split being thus establishing the absurdity of posthumous retaliation.

the title. It seeks to isolate what such a duel can answer for a quest thematizing the threefold problematic of action, agency and selfhood. Action, as I see it, is delayed until the very end and when it is accomplished, it is not "itself" anymore, but its own burlesque, its own parody. What we get is absence (delayed action) and, finally, something that is not itself, but its own caricature. But how could one narrate, describe such an unfolding? How can one account for a void in the language of what it is the void of? Was action undertaken at all? Or it just "came about", as Horatio claims? Consider the difficulty in laying a narrative grasp on the past:

> And let me speak to th' yet unknowing world
> How these things came about. So shall you hear
> Of carnal, bloody and unnatural acts,
> Of accidental judgements, casual slaughters,
> Of deaths put on by cunning and forc'd cause,
> And, in this upshot, purposes mistook
> Fall'n on th'inventors' heads.
>
> (384-90)

The word "unnatural" must give us pause. Harold Jenkins may be right to add in the footnote that this refers to the fratricide.[321] Still, it seems to me that the recurrent conflict between nature and honour is too recent to be forgotten. Hamlet and Laertes, as I argued above, both admit to this discordance of motives. When action eventually "comes about" it is destined to follow the prescripts of honour at the expense of nature. Thus "unnatural acts" signifies at least two things besides fratricide. It alludes to the sacrificed human nature and also conveys, I think, the failure of honour-centric behaviour.

What the conflict of the organizing principles in *Hamlet* shows, is the inaccessibility of identity through *ethos*. The parody of action is also the caricature of *ethos,* which presents subjects alienated from themselves, agents severed from their identity. Parody and caricature display distorted patterns of heroic behaviour, which epitomize a characteristically Shakespearean radicalization of the problem inherent also in Greek drama: what is left behind in tragedy that is irreducible to this form of subjectivity? Or, to return from where we started: where is the self apart from action?

---

[321] Cf. Arden *Hamlet*, fn. to 386-88, 417.

Epilogue

It has been characteristic of these investigations of dramatic structure and its components to be informed by constant polemics between drama and philosophy. The interdisciplinary formulation of the basic questions of genre on the one hand and identity, on the other, led to the concentration on their possible convergences. It is due to the interpretative wealth of these polemics that the generic conceptions of identity could be thematized. However, the recurrent defect of similar procedures in hermeneutics or moral philosophy is, in my view, the reluctance or refusal to take tragedy "seriously". Instruction of ethics by tragedy for Paul Ricoeur and Martha C. Nussbaum is viable only by subordinating tragedy to ethics, tragic insight to ethical criteria. In other words, ethical presuppositions designed to uphold and support philosophical maxims can survive the encounter with drama only by its radical subordination and abatement.

    Throughout these analyses I have tried to emphasize the overwhelming presence of these abated elements in human experience and their relevance to the particular forms of self-constitution. To be a tragic character is to be divided, as I argued, to be split drastically and irreparably. This coexistence of tragic selfhood and moral being in one and the same character is expressed in tragedy by the contrast of monological and dialogical self-maintenance, as, I hope, my analysis of *Hamlet* has shown. The fundamental difference between these two alternatives of self-maintenance, as drama informs us, has also to do with two distinct forms of alterity. In *Macbeth* the internal other is symbolized by the alienated hand. Macbeth, having committed the regicide distances himself from his own hand that did the deed:

> What hands are here? Ha! they pluck out mine eyes.
> Will all great Neptune's ocean wash this blood
> Clean from my hand?
>
>   (II.ii.58-60)

I have traced the phenomenon of indelible defilement especially peculiar to *Macbeth* in discussing the modes of the tragic in Chapter 2. Both Macbeth's and Lady Macbeth's hands need washing and the rhetorical device used to express the impossibility of this cleansing redress is *hyperbole*, compare "all great Neptune's ocean" with the somnambulist Lady's "all the perfumes of Arabia will not sweeten this little hand" (V.i.48).

This alienated hand in Macbeth's case is observed by the eye, symbol of truth or factuality.[322] To escape from bitter truth either the eyes have to be plucked out or thinking avoided: "I am afraid to think what I have done; / Look on't again I dare not" (II.ii.50-51).

The threat of visual truth is thus paralleled by reference to menacing thought, which echoes an earlier premonition:

> Present fears
> Are less than horrible imaginings.
> My thought, whose murther yet is but fantastical,
> Shakes so my single state of man,
> That function is smother'd in surmise,
> And nothing is, but what is not.
>
> (I.iii.137-42)

The symbolism of the eye recalls the tragedy of Oedipus, of course, who also becomes another for himself as soon as the truth is revealed. There the eyes are plucked for not being able to see the truth. The reference to menacing thought, as well as to surmise, recalls Hamlet to whom thinking contrasts good and evil and fuels all the aporetic reflections on being.

The external other in tragedy is hardly ever external enough. It is, rather, so palpably close that it is often internalized in some way or other. The representatives of fate, the gods, Macbeth's weird sisters, Hamlet's ghost or the more immediate others like Lady Macbeth, Ophelia, Gertrude, Iago, all embody different levels of proximity. The externality of the other diminishes as his or her influence increases and the mind becomes a storehouse of conflicting voices. However, it is this dialogical encounter with the external other, which seems to me the proper sphere of ethics. In contrast, what tragedy voices apart from this confrontation, is an internal form of alterity, inaccessible to ethics, a self, grasping itself as other in monological self-reflection. To conclude, let me quote the probably most powerful Shakespearean soliloquy of internal alterity, taken from *Richard the Third:*

---

[322] For more about the hand-eye opposition in *Macbeth*, see Kenneth Muir's introduction to the Arden edition, xxix-xxx.

EPILOGUE

Have mercy, Jesu! – Soft, I did but dream.
O coward conscience, how dost thou afflict me!
The lights burn blue; it is now dead midnight.
Cold fearful drops stand on my trembling flesh.
What do I fear? Myself? There's none else by;
Richard loves Richard, that is, I and I.
Is there a murderer here? No. Yes, I am!
Then fly. What, from myself? Great reason why,
Lest I revenge? What, myself upon myself?
Alack, I love myself. Wherefore? For any good
That I myself have done unto myself?
O no, alas, I rather hate myself
For hateful deeds committed by myself.
I am a villain! – yet I lie, I am not!
Fool, of thyself speak well! Fool, do not flatter.
My conscience hath a thousand several tongues,
And every tongue brings in a several tale,
And every tale condemns me for a villain:
Perjury, perjury, in the highest degree;
Murder, stern murder, in the direst degree,
All several sins, all us'd in each degree,
Throng to the bar, crying all, 'Guilty, guilty!'
I shall despair. There is no creature loves me,
And if I die, no soul will pity me –
And wherefore should they, since that I myself
Find in myself no pity to myself?

(V.iii.179-204)

Appendix: History Aside in *Richard the Third*: mimesis or poiesis?

An intimidating corpus of critical literature on Shakespearean drama today stresses the embeddedness of the genre in history. Cultural materialist and new historicist critics have discredited essentialist readings. It is to their credit, that we tend to see a historically uprooted, autotelic text as an impossibility. If deconstruction had made us suspicious of the dividing line between literature and philosophy, in the twilight of an unavertably overwhelming textuality; that much can be said of materialist and historicist modelling of critical reading: they have made us suspicious of the dividing line between literature and history. In what follows I will present a suspicion of this suspicion and address the issue of a possible impossibility. Richard's own self-cancelling suspicion of history expressed in an Aside brings the matter into textual focus.

Shakespeare's *Richard the Third* can be the test case due to the confusion its generic classification has always caused. Should the source decide the genre (history or tragedy), or the drama itself? Is there any such thing, a drama in itself? It is well-known that, similar to the history plays, the main sources of *Richard the Third* are the chronicles. Consequently, the discrediting of the source by the characters adopted from it is a sheer impossibility. However, this is precisely what takes place in the following dialogue between the young Prince Edward, Buckingham and Richard:

> RICHARD: If I may counsel you, some day or two
> Your Highness shall repose you at the Tower,
> Then where you please and shall be thought most fit
> For your best health and recreation.
>
> PRINCE: I do not like the Tower, of any place.
> Did Julius Caesar build that place, my lord?
>
> BUCKINGHAM: He did, my gracious lord, begin that place,
> Which since, succeeding ages have re-edified.
>
> PRINCE: Is it upon record, or else reported
> Successively from age to age, he built it?

> BUCKINGHAM: Upon record, my gracious lord.
>
> PRINCE: But say, my lord, it were not register'd,
> Methinks the truth should live from age to age,
> As 'twere retail'd to all posterity,
> Even to the general all-ending day.
>
> RICHARD [ASIDE]: So wise so young, they say, do never live long.
>
> PRINCE: What say you uncle?
>
> RICHARD: I say, without characters fame lives long.
> [ASIDE] Thus, like the formal Vice, Iniquity,
> I moralize two meanings in one word.
>
> (III.i.64-83)

As one of the obstacles to the throne, Prince Edward has to be isolated and later killed in the Tower, according to Richard's plan. The young but wise prince at this point, is not that willing to inhabit the Tower for his "best health and recreation", and tries to find excuses. This is the immediate context of this strange rumination on the history of the Tower. Who built it, has it been "re-edified", what historical record is there to rely on, etc. It is important that the untrustworthiness of the historical origin of the Tower is thematized in the modality of excuse, regret, distancing.

The dialogue has no precedent in the sources.[323] Shakespeare's inclusion is of interest, because a crucial qualification of historical reference is made thereby. The Prince's sudden interest in the history of the Tower under the premises is strange, not to say, ridiculous. He is demonstrating his wit, his competence, that he is fit to become king. The irony of this is, that by such behaviour he is just giving more reason to be killed. Self-promotion becomes a step towards self-annihilation. Annihilation in the Tower: annihilation in history. For the contextualized reference to the history of the Tower makes the Tower the symbol, the metonymy of history, makes the Tower History itself. History becomes the site where people find themselves locked up and killed. The only means of survival then, is to avoid History, avoid being historicized, and discredit historical records:

> PRINCE: But say, my lord, it were not register'd,

---

[323] Cf. the Arden fn. by Antony Hammond.

Methinks the truth should live from age to age,
As 'twere retail'd to all posterity,
Even to the general all-ending day.

It seems that the Prince may be wise, but nevertheless, he is doomed. He is destined to be immersed in History. His wisdom likewise, may diminish into the prattling of a child was it not to be confirmed in Richard's first Aside: "So wise so young, they say, do never live long." The Aside is to present an alternative truth-claim to that of history. As such, it is hardly a surprise that it has been widely ignored by historicists.

PRINCE: What say you uncle?

RICHARD: I say, without characters fame lives long.
[ASIDE] Thus, like the formal Vice, Iniquity,
I moralize two meanings in one word.

What is the truth-claim of Richard's response? Where is it? What say you Richard? What we get is an ambiguity in the first place, and an interpretation of this ambiguity in a sequence of normal-audible talk, and an Aside inaudible to the Prince. Richard's response to the Prince's witty remarks is the retort of ambiguity to wisdom. The ambiguity in question lies in the word "character": the character standing for historical record on the one hand, and the character of the Prince shortly to become the record, on the other.[324] The wisdom of pointing to the unreliability of the historical record is now to face the rival wisdom: the wisdom of ambiguity. It is the truth behind the seemingly obvious, the truth behind the apparently self-evident. Richard here is equivocating, allowing two truths inhabit one word, making one victorious over the other.[325] Analogous to Richard's killing the Prince, the character (history) is to kill the character (person). The ambiguity, then, is followed by the Aside that explains Richard's meaning. It explains, interprets the ambiguity as intended ambiguity. It transforms the dialogue into an allegorical confrontation between History and Interpretation. The only way to avoid History is to interpret it. That is, if we think of History in terms of factuality. There are no facts in

---

[324] Cf. the Arden fn.

[325] The equivocation reminds of the double tongue of the oracle, cf. Macbeth's "And be these juggling fiends no more believ'd, / That palter with us in a double sense" (V.viii.19-20).

themselves, but only interpretations, as Nietzsche often reminds us in *The Will to Power*.[326] What is more, interpretation is not just all we have, but it is also a form of the will to power, as a fragment tells us.[327] Richard's allusion to the Vice-figure therefore becomes one of the rhetorical manifestations of the will to power. The Tower is in the hands of the Vice. On the textual level metonymy (of History) is supplanted by allegory (of interpretation).

The convention of the Aside (French "L'aparté", German "Beiseitessprache") is of utmost importance in such a confrontation.[328] It introduces a "different modality" into the dialogue, and expresses the character's "true intention or opinion" in a turn towards the audience, as Patrice Pavis tells us.[329] It is a turning away and a turning toward at the same time. Among the numerous variants of Asides this version is never heard by the actual interlocutors, it is audible only to the spectators.[330] If it is overheard, as in the present case, when the Prince asks "what say you uncle?", this merely gives an opportunity to Richard to verbalize his ambiguity, which he does with clever rhyming to avert suspicion ("do never live long" and "fame lives long"). Strangely enough, it requires the audience's willing suspension of disbelief that the other characters standing nearer to the speaker cannot hear the crucial words. What is interesting in this turning toward the audience, in this involvement of the spectators in a dialogue is precisely its differ-

---

[326] Friedrich Nietzsche, *The Will to Power*, trans. Walter Kaufmann and R. J. Hollingdale, New York: Vintage Books, 1968, fragments 70, 477, 481, 604.
[327] Fragment 556.
[328] A systematic treatment of this stage convention is regrettably missing from much of the pioneering works of theatre semiotics. It is not even mentioned in Petr Bogatyrev's "Les signes du theâtre", trans. from the Czeck by Marguereite Derrida, in POÉTIQUE, 8, 1971, nor in Tadeusz Kowzan's *Littérature et Spectacle*, Paris: Mouton, 1975. For a comprehensive study of the Asides in Greek drama see David Bain, *Actors and Audience, a Study of Asides and Related Conventions in Greek Drama*, Oxford: Oxford University Press, 1977. For Shakespeare's use of the Asides see Anne Righter, *Shakespeare and the Idea of the Play*, New York: Barnes and Noble, 1962, and Keir Elam, *Shakespeare's Universe of Discourse: Language-Games in the Comedies*, Cambridge, London: Cambridge University Press, 1984.
[329] "L'aparté est une forme de monologue, mais il devient au théâtre un dialogue direct avec le public. Sa qualité essentielle est d'introduire une modalité différente de celle du dialogue.... Il signale la "vraie intention ou opinion du caractere", *Dictionnaire du Theâtre*, Éditions Sociales, 1980.
[330] For *Beiseite ad spectatores*, or *Publikumsanrede* cf. Manfred Pfister, *Das Drama*, Munich: Wilhelm Fink Verlag, 1997, 194-95.

ent modality of self-expression.[331] We are provoked by the explicit challenge to truly interpret the scene. The Aside becomes the guideline of true interpretation, it reveals a (kind of) truth. It not only subordinates history to interpretation, but, by the same move, I would like to say, it undermines mimesis:

> [ASIDE] Thus, like the formal Vice, Iniquity,
> I moralize two meanings in one word.

There is an obvious contradiction here. Having discredited written records Richard resorts to written records in his comparison. After the oracular equivocation the ambiguity of the medieval Vice-figure is invoked. Thus through the simile Richard places himself in a peculiar tradition: the tradition of duplicity. Its distinctive feature, however, is in being a duplicity avowed, confessed, at least, to the audience. Comparing himself to the Vice-figure is relevant also in another sense: the conventional idea of mimesis is undermined, or as one may prefer to put it, a new form of mimesis is promoted. The imitation of previous imitators sheds light on the eternal regression underlying all *poiesis* of duplicity. It shows the impossibility of any exit from this mimetic sphere. It shows that a non-mimetic representation is an anomaly, a contradiction in terms.

The *poiesis* of ambiguity deconstructs its source. It offers parallel versions of referentiality, and thereby uproots all authoritative truth-claims and representations. Theories of intertextuality have radically questioned the homogeneity of a text, and, consequently, the exhaustibility of its mimetic potential. Elizabeth Freund emphasizes the necessary citationality of writing and reading.[332] Her essay exemplifies deconstruction's hostility against mimetic strategies of reading. What both intertextuality and citationality then bring about is the constant interruption of this mode of reading by what Freund calls the experience of *déja lu*.

We encounter another methodical dethroning of mimesis in Michael Riffaterre's semiotics. Riffaterre explicitly restricts his investigations to poetry, and the analyses of a selection of poems, but his innovative conceptualizations, I believe, reach far beyond. In fact,

---

[331] The *modus operandi* of the Aside is *parenthesis*, cf. Keir Elam, *Shakespeare's Universe of Discourse: Language-Games in the Comedies,* 252.
[332] Cf. "Ariachne's broken woof: the rhetoric of citation in Troilus and Cressida" *Shakespeare and the Question of Theory*, eds Geoffrey Hartman and Patricia Parker, New York and London: Methuen, 1985.

those reservations he makes in order to isolate poetry within the wider realm of literature constitute the weak points of an otherwise magnificient book.[333]

In poetry mimesis is destabilized by what he calls "semantic indirections". The three forms of indirections are displacing, distorting and creating. Displacing takes place when a sign shifts from one meaning to another; distorting, when there is ambiguity, contradiction, nonsense; creating, when new signs are made out of linguistic items following a principle of organization.[334] The basic characteristic of mimesis, according to Riffaterre, is its being linked to representation and the referentiality of language, the direct relationship of words to things.[335] This claim recalls the mentioned hostility of deconstruction to mimesis which it sees as constructed upon the one-to-one relationship of the signifier to signified. However, Riffaterre discards mimesis only to introduce his daring claim about the poem's unity. Here semiotics and deconstruction cease to proceed hand in hand. The unity of a poem for Riffaterre, is both formal and semantic, and "includes all the indices of indirection". It is what he terms "significance", and opposes to "meaning" informed by mimesis.

These differentiated steps in the process of reading poetic texts help us reformulate our findings in *Richard the Third*, and help to re-lexicalize the poetics of ambiguity outlined above. The meaning of "character" in Richard's statement, "without characters fame lives long" is both displaced and distorted. It contains a shift from one meaning to another (from historical record to person), and it is therefore ambiguous (historical record or person). These two forms of indirection produce the significance of the utterance.

At the same time the dethronement of mimesis does not mean its total elimination from the sphere of poetics for Riffaterre. It is rather restricted to a preliminary level of reading, "the reader's acceptance of the mimesis sets up the grammar as the background from which the ungrammaticalities (deviant grammar or lexicon) will thrust themselves forward as stumbling blocks, to be understood eventually on a second level." This second, perfected level of understanding is the

---

[333]"Within the wider realm of literature it seems to me that poetry is peculiarly inseparable from the concept of text: if we do not regard the poem as a closed entity, we cannot always differentiate poetic discourse from literary language", Michael Riffaterre, *Semiotics of Poetry*, Bloomington and London: Indiana University Press, 1978, 2.
[334]Riffaterre, 2.
[335]*Ibid*.

manifestation of *semiosis*.[336] Semiotics thus is linked to mimesis through grammar, while *semiosis* links to significance through ungrammaticality. It is clear from this charting of a step-by-step reading process that semiosis remains parasitic on mimesis:

> The poem's significance, both as a principle of unity and as the agent of semantic indirection, is produced by the *detour* the text makes as it runs the gauntlet of mimesis, moving from representation to representation .... The harder it is to force the reader to notice the indirection and to lead him step by step through distortion, away from mimesis, the longer the detour must be and the more developed the text[337]

Mimesis is presupposed, its role made temporary and subordinated to distortion. But what if mimesis turns out to be a distortion in itself? What if Riffaterre's notion of "referential fallacy" itself becomes distorted? The fallacy of the reader to stick to the referentiality of the poetic sign at the second level of interpreting significance becomes the semiotic fallacy to stick to the referentiality of the poetic sign at the first level of interpreting meaning. Interpretation, as we saw in Nietzsche, extends to factuality underlying the claim of referentiality.

As mentioned above, the only way to avoid History is to interpret it. Let me go further than that: Interpretation avoids History by making it, by creating it. This is the inevitable defeat of mimesis: *poiesis*, creation with the abuse of language, *catachresis*. Richard avoids being locked up in the Tower by locking up others there. Instead of suffering History he makes History.

Let us finally return to the Aside and its truth-claim. As I mentioned above the Aside is a turning away, an *apostrophe*, a parenthesized revelation. As such it refers us to a similar convention: the *parabasis*. The Greek word etymologically means "going aside", "stepping forward". In Greek Old Comedy the Chorus came forward unmasked and addressed the audience directly in a speech that expressed the personal view of the author.[338] Elaborated by Friedrich Schlegel and adopted by Paul de Man, *parabasis* figures for both thinkers in relation to irony and rhetoric. Schlegel stresses its role in the mediation of the author's views: " .... in der Mitte des Stücks vom Chor im Namen

---

[336]*Ibid.*, 6.
[337]Riffaterre, 19.
[338]J. A. Cuddon, *Dictionary of Literary Terms*, London: Penguin Books, 1976.

des Dichters an das Volk gehalten wurde."[339] Correspondingly, irony is defined as "eine permanente Parekbase".[340]

For de Man it is the "interruption of a discourse by a shift in the rhetorical register".[341] He places parabasis into the long tradition of the disruption of illusion: the term is related to the *buffo* Schlegel takes from the commedia dell'arte. Furthermore, de Man finds its equivalent in the "aparté", the Aside, and gives their common denominator in the German "aus der Rolle fallen", dropping out of one's role.[342] It seems, however, that what was possible for Schlegel remains an impossibility for de Man. Schlegel could conceive of a narrative that can be interrupted any time, to bring about the disruption of an illusion. Parabasis and irony thus appear under the control of an authorial intention. De Man's allusion to the text machine, the play of the signifier reflects deconstruction's scepticism about this control, "Words have a way of saying things which are not at all what you want them to say."[343] There is an uncontrollably overwhelming irony determining and undoing narration. Dropping out of a role is as impossible as reaching beyond a signifier. The conventional idea of irony is therefore questioned in the same way as that of mimesis. What truth-claim then, can we expect from the Aside? Is it merely the falling into another role?

Richard's self-reflexive commentary in the Aside gives us the key to understand the ambiguity in the word "character". On the one hand, it explains the ambiguity as ambiguity, states the irony as irony. It also presents the role as role, the mimesis as mimesis. The great dissem-

---

[339] Friedrich Schlegel's definition of *parekbasis* (as he calls it) can be found in *Fragmente zur Poesie und Literatur. Kritische Ausgabe* 16Bd. Kommentar V/137, IX/952, ed. Hans Echner, Paderborn, Vienna, and Munich: Verlag F. Schöningh, 1981.

[340] "Zur Philosophie", Fragment 668. in Friedrich Schlegel, *Philosophische Lehrjahre 1, 1796-1806*, ed. Ernst Behler, in *Kritische Ausgabe,* Paderborn, Vienna, and Munich: Verlag F. Schöningh, 1963.

[341] Paul de Man, *Aesthetic Ideology*, ed. Andrzey Warminski, Minneapolis, London: University of Minnesota Press, 1997, 179. We find a similar formulation in his *Allegories of Reading*, New Haven and London: Yale University Press, 1979, where *parabasis* is "a sudden revelation of the discontinuity between two rhetorical codes", and as de Man goes on in the appertaining footnote: "the similarity between anacoluthon and parabasis stems from the fact that both figures interrupt the expectations of a given grammatical or rhetorical movement. As digression, aside, "intervention d'auteur", or "aus der Rolle fallen", parabasis clearly involves the interruption of a discourse", 300.

[342] *Aesthetic Ideology*, 177-78.

[343] The irony of this statement is that it is a paraphrase of a sentence Schlegel quotes from Goethe, cf. *Aesthetic Ideology,* 181.

bler, for once, shows us his cards. By doing this we are made accomplices, sharers of responsibility for Richard's actions. How is it, one may ask, that we still remain safely seated, isolated in our stalls when the illusion we call stage performance is broken? Should not we accomplices interfere?

On the other hand, the truth-claim of the Aside has to remain an enigma. It is one thing to actualize the truth in a well-timed *apostrophe*, and another to thematize it in critical reflection. Unfortunately, the latter still dramatically lacks an Aside of its own.

BIBLIOGRAPHY

Primary sources:

Aeschylus, [*Works*] *In Two Volumes*, The Loeb Classical Library, ed. and trans. Herbert Weir Smyth, Cambridge, Mass., and London: Harvard University Press, 1963 (1922).

Chaucer, Geoffrey, *Troilus and Criseyde*, ed. John Warrington, London, 1974.

Euripides, [*Works*] *In Four Volumes*, The Loeb Classical Library, ed. and trans. Arthur S. Way, Cambridge, Mass. and London: Harvard University Press, 1958 (1912).

Homer, *Odyssey*, ed. J. C. Bruijn, C. Spoelder, Haarlem: H. D. Tjeenk Willink and Zoon N. V.

Kyd, Thomas, *Spanish tragedy*, London: Methuen, 1969.

Machiavelli, Niccolo, *The Prince*, trans. George Bull, London: Penguin Books, 1968.

Mirandola, Pico della, *Oration on the Dignity of Man,* trans. E. L. Forbes, in *The Renaissance Philosophy of Man*, eds Cassirer–Kristeller–Randall, Jr., Chicago, Illinois: University of Chicago Press, 1948.

Ovid, *Metamorphoses*, trans. Frank Justus Miller, London: Heinemann, 1916.

Shakespeare, William, *Coriolanus*, ed. Philip Brockbank, Arden edn., London and New York: Routledge, 1990 (1988); *Hamlet*, ed. Harold Jenkins, Arden edn., London and New York: Routledge, 1993 (1989); *King Lear*, ed. Kenneth Muir, Arden edn., London and New York: Routledge, 1993 (1989); *Macbeth*, ed. Kenneth Muir, London and New York: Routledge, 1994 (1988); *Richard the Third,* ed. Antony Hammond, Arden edn., London and New York: Routledge, 1994 (1988); *Sonnets*, ed. Katherine Duncan-Jones, Arden edn., London: Thomas Nelson and Sons Ltd., 1997; *Timon of Athens*, ed. H. J. Oliver, London and New York: Routledge, 1994 (1991); *Titus Andronicus,* ed. Jonathan Bate, Arden edn., London and New York: Routledge, 1995.

Sophocles, [*Works*] *In Two Volumes*, The Loeb Classical Library, ed. and trans. Francis Storr, Cambridge, Mass. and London: Harvard University Press, 1962 (1912).
Sophocles, *Ajax the Locrian*, The Loeb Classical Library, ed. and trans. Hugh Lloyd-Jones, Cambridge, Mass. and London: Harvard University Press, 1996.
Vives, Juan Luis, *A Fable About Man*, trans. Nancy Lenkeith, in *The Renaissance Philosophy of Man* (see Mirandola).

Secondary sources:
Ackrill, J. L., *Essays on Plato and Aristotle*, Oxford: Clarendon, 1997.
Adkins, A. W. H., *Merit and Responsibility: A Study in Greek Values*, Oxford: Clarendon, 1960.
Ancsel, Éva, *Az aszimmetrikus ember* [*The Asymmetric Man*], Budapest: Kossuth könyvkiadó, 1989.
Anscombe, G. E. M., *Intention,* Oxford: Basil Blackwell, 1963 (1957).
Aristotle, *Nicomachean Ethics*, The Loeb Classical Library, English trans. H. Rackham, Cambridge, Mass. and London: Harvard University Press, 1994 (1926).
Aristotle, *Poetics*, The Loeb Classical Library, ed. and trans. Stephen Halliwell, Cambridge, Mass. and London: Harvard University Press, 1995
Aristotle, *Rhetoric*, The Loeb Classical Library, trans. J. H. Freese, Cambridge, Mass. and London: Harvard University Press, 1967.
Aristotle, *Politics*, The Loeb Classical Library, trans. H. Rackham, Cambridge, Mass. and London: Harvard University Press, 1967.
Arrowsmith, William, "The Criticism of Greek Tragedy", in *Tulane Drama Review,* III/3. (March, 1959).
Austin, John L., *How to Do Things with Words,* ed. J. O. Urmson, Oxford: Oxford University Press, 1973.
Austin, Norman, *Meaning and Being in Myth,* University Park & London: The Pennsylvania State University Press, 1990.
Baldwin, T. W., *Shakspere's Five-act Structure,* Urbana: University of Illinois Press, 1947.

Barthes, Roland, *A szöveg öröme,* [*Le Degré zéro de l'ecriture,* 1953, *Le Plaisir du texte,* 1973], Hungarian trans. Babarczy E., Kovács S., Mihancsik Zs., Romhányi T. G., Budapest: Osiris, 1996.
Barthes, Roland, *Criticism and Truth,* trans. and ed. Katrine P. Keuneman, London: The Athlone Press, 1987.
Bate, Jonathan, *Shakespeare and the English Romantic Imagination,* Oxford: Clarendon Press, 1992 (1986).
Bate, Jonathan, *The Genius of Shakespeare,* Picador, London: Macmillan, 1997.
Bauman, Zygmunt, *Postmodern Ethics,* Oxford: Blackwell, 1995.
Belfiore, E. S., *Aristotle on Plot and Emotion,* Princeton: Princeton University Press, 1992.
Beöthy, Zsolt, *A tragikum* [*The Tragic*]*,* Budapest: Franklin-társulat, 1885.
Birenbaum, Harvey, *Tragedy and Innocence,* Washington: University Press of America, 1983.
Bloom, Harold, *Ruin the Sacred Truths,* Cambridge, Mass.: Harvard University Press, 1989.
Bloom, Harold, *Shakespeare: The Invention of the Human*, New York: Riverhead Books, 1998.
Booth, Stephen, *King Lear, Macbeth, Indefinition and Tragedy*, New Haven & London: Yale University Press, 1983.
Bowers, Fredson, *Hamlet as Minister and Scourge*, Virginia: University Press, 1989.
Bowers, Fredson, *Essays on Shakespeare and Elizabethan Drama in Honour of Hardin Craig*, Columbia: Richard Hosley, Missouri Press, 1962.
Bowra, Maurice, *Sophoclean Tragedy*, Oxford: Clarendon, 1965.
Bradbrook, M. C., *Themes and Conventions of Elizabethan Tragedy,* Cambridge University Press, 1969.
Bradley, A. C., *Shakespearean Tragedy,* London: Macmillan, 1993 (1904).
Bradshaw, Graham, *Shakespeare's Scepticism,* Ithaca, New York: Cornell University Press, 1987.
Bremer, Jones M., *Hamartia, Tragic Error in the Poetics of Aristotle and in Greek Tragedy*, Amsterdam: Adolf M. Hakkert, 1969.
Brereton, Geoffrey, *Principles of Tragedy*, London: Routledge & Kegan Paul, 1968.
Calarco, N. Joseph, *Tragic Being, Apollo and Dionysus in Western Drama,* Minneapolis: University of Minnesota Press, 1969.

Calderwood, James L., *Shakespearean Metadrama*, Minneapolis: University of Minnesota Press, 1971.
Calderwood, James L., *Shakespeare and the Denial of Death*, Amherst: University of Massachusetts Press, 1987.
Calderwood, James L., *To Be or Not To Be: Negation and Metadrama in Hamlet*, New York: Columbia University Press, 1983.
Calvin, John, *Commentaries XXIII*, trans. & ed. Joseph Haroutunian and Louise Pettibone Smith, London: SCM Press Ltd., 1958.
Calvin, John, *Institutes of the Christian Religion*, trans. Henry Beveridge, London: Clarke, 1962.
Campbell, Lewis, *Tragic Drama in Aeschylus, Sophocles and Shakespeare*, London: Smith Elder & Co., 1904.
Cassirer, Ernst–Kristeller, Paul Oscar–Randall, Jr. (eds), *The Renaissance Philosophy of Man*, Chicago, Illinois: University of Chicago Press, 1948.
Cavell, Stanley, *Disowning Knowledge*, New York: Cambridge University Press, 1987.
Charlton, H. B., *The Senecan Tradition in Rensaince Tragedy*, Manchester: Manchester University Press, 1946.
Cohen, Michael, *Hamlet in My Mind's Eye*, Athens and London: University of Georgia Press, 1989.
Coleridge, S. T., *Shakespearean Criticism I-II*, ed. T. M. Raysor, London: 1960.
Conacher, D. J., *Euripidean Drama, Myth, Theme and Structure*, Toronto: University of Toronto Press, 1967.
Conklin, Paul. S. (ed.), *A History of Hamlet Criticism 1601-1821*, London: Routledge & Kegan Paul, 1957.
Council, Norman, *When Honour's at the Stake*, London: George Allen & Unwin Ltd., 1973.
Cs. Szabó, László, *Shakespeare*, Budapest: Gondolat, 1987.
Culler, Jonathan, *Structuralist Poetics*, London: Routledge and Kegan Paul, 1975.
Culler, Jonathan, *On Deconstruction, Theory and Criticism after Structuralism*, Ithaca: Cornell University Press, 1982.
Cunliffe, John W., *The Influence of Seneca on Elizabethan Tragedy*, Hamden CT: Archon Books, 1965.
Danby, John, *Shakespeare's Doctrine of Nature*, London: Faber, 1949.
Dasenbrock, Reed Way (ed.), *Literary Theory after Davidson*, University Park: Pennsylvania State University Press, 1993.

Dávidházi, Péter, *The Romantic Cult of Shakespeare: Literary Reception in Anthropological Perspective*, London: Macmillan, 1998.
Davidson, Donald, *Essays on Actions and Events*, Oxford: Clarendon 1985 (1980).
Deleuze, Gilles, *Kant's Critical Philosophy: The Doctrine of the Faculties*, trans. H. Tomlison and B. Habberjam. Minneapolis: University of Minnesota Press, 1984 (1963).
De Graef, Ortwin, *Serenity in Crisis: A Preface to Paul de Man*, Lincoln and London: University of Nebraska Press, 1993.
De Graef, Ortwin, *Titanic Light*, Lincoln and London: University of Nebraska Press, 1995.
De Graef, Ortwin, "Sweet Dreams, Monstered Nothings: Catachresis in Kant and Coriolanus" (see Hadfield).
De Man, Paul, *Allegories of Reading*, New Haven and London: Yale University Press, 1979.
De Man, Paul, *Blindness and Insight*, London: Routledge, 1983.
De Man, Paul, *Aesthetic Ideology*, ed. Andrzey Warminski, Minneapolis, London: University of Minnesota Press, 1997.
Derrida, Jacques, *Writing and Difference*, trans. Alan Bass, London: Routledge, 1993 (1978).
Derrida, Jacques, *Margins of Philosophy*, trans. Bass Alan, Chicago: University of Chicago Press, 1982.
Derrida, Jacques, *Aporias*, trans. Thomas Dutoit, California: Stanford University Press, 1993.
Desmond, William, *Perplexity and Ultimacy*, Albany: University of New York Press, 1995.
Dietrich, B. C., *Death, Fate and the Gods*, University of London: The Athlone Press, 1965.
Dodds, E. R., *The Ancient Concept of Progress*, Oxford: Clarendon Press, 1973.
Dodds, E. R., *The Greeks and the Irrational*, Berkeley, Los Angeles: University of California, 1951.
Dodsworth, Martin, *Hamlet Closely Observed*, London & Dover: New Hampshire, 1985.
Dollimore, Jonathan, *Radical Tragedy*, Great Britain: Harvester Wheatsheaf, 1989.
Drakakis, John (ed.), *Shakespearean Tragedy*, London & New York: Longman, 1992.
Driver, T. F., *The Sense of History in Greek and Shakespearean Drama*, New York: Columbia University Press, 1960.

Easterling, P. E., "The End of an Era? Tragedy in the Early Fourth Century", in *Tragedy, Comedy and the Polis: Papers from the Greek Drama Conference* (Nottingham, 18-20 July 1990), eds A. H. Sommerstein, St. Halliwell, J. Henderson, B. Zimmerman, Italy: Levante Editori, 1993.
Edwards, Philip, *Shakespeare and the Confines of Art*, London: Methuen & Co Ltd., 1968.
Elam, Keir, *Shakespeare's Universe of Discourse: Language-Games in the Comedies*, Cambridge, London: Cambridge University Press, 1984.
Elam, Keir, *The Semiotics of Theatre and Drama,* London and New York: Routledge, 1990 (1980).
Eliot, T. S., *Elizabethan Essays,* London: Faber and Faber, 1934.
Eliot, T. S., *Essays on Elizabethan Drama,* New York: Harcourt, Brace & Co, 1956.
Eliot, T. S., *The Sacred Wood: Essays on Poetry and Criticism*, London: Methuen, 1960.
Elliot, G. R., *Scourge and Minister: A Study of Hamlet,* Durham, North Carolina: Duke University Press, 1951.
Elton, W. R., *King Lear and the Gods,* San Marino, California: The Huntington Library, 1966.
Exum, J. Cheryl, *Tragedy and Biblical Narrative,* Cambridge: Cambridge University Press, 1992.
Faas, Ekbert, *Tragedy and After,* Kinston and Montreal: McGill-Queen's University Press, 1984.
Fabiny, Tibor, "Catholic Eyes and Protestant Ears [The Conflict of Visuality and Aurality in a Hermeneutical Perspective]", in *Iconography in Cultural Studies: Papers in English and American Studies VII*, ed. Attila Kiss, Szeged: József Attila University, 1996.
Fabiny, Tibor, "The Eye as a Metaphor in Shakespearean Tragedy", in *Celebrating Comparativism,* eds Katalin Kürtösi and József Pál, Szeged, 1994.
Falck, Colin, *Myth, Truth and Literature,* Cambridge: Cambridge University Press, 1989.
Farley-Hills, David, *Shakespeare and the Rival Playwrights 1600-1606*, London and New York: Routledge, 1990.
Farnham, Willard, *The Medieval Heritage of Elizabethan Tragedy,* Oxford: Basil Blackwell, 1963.

Fawkner, H. W., *Deconstructing Macbeth: The Hyperontological View*, London and Toronto: Associated University Press, 1990.
Fisher, N. R. E., "Hybris and Dishonour", in *Greece & Rome XXIII*, Oxford: Clarendon Press, 1976.
Foakes, R. A., *Hamlet versus Lear*, Cambridge: Cambridge University Press, 1993.
Fontenrose, Joseph, *The Delphic Oracle*, University of California Press, 1978.
Frye, Northrope, *Fools of Time*, Toronto: University of Toronto Press, 1973 (1967).
Frye, Northrope, "The Koine of Myth", in *Myth and Metaphor: Selected Essays 1974-88*, ed. Robert O. Denham, Charlottesville: University Press of Virginia, 1990.
Frye, R. M., *The Renaissance Hamlet*, Princeton: Princeton University Press, 1984.
Gadamer, Hans-Georg, *Truth and Method*, trans. Gordon Barden and W. G. Doerpel, New York: Seabury, 1975.
Géher, István, *Shakespeare-olvasókönyv, [A Shakespeare Textbook]*, Budapest: Cserépfalvi, Szépirodalmi könyvkiadó, 1991.
Genette, Gerard, *Figures of Literary Discourse*, trans. Alan Sheridan. Oxford: Basil Blackwell, 1982.
Gill, Robin, *A Textbook of Christian Ethics*, Edinburgh: T&T Clark, 1995.
Gordon, Braden, *Renaissance Tragedy and the Senecan Tradition: Anger's Privilege*, New Haven: Yale University Press, 1985.
Granville-Barker, Harley, *Prefaces to Shakespeare*, London: B. T. Batsford Ltd., 1958.
Greenblatt, Stephen Jay, *Shakespearean Negotiations: The Circulation of Social Energy in Renaissance England*, Berkeley: University of California Press, 1988.
Greenblatt, Stephen Jay, *Learning to Curse*, London, New York: Routledge, 1990.
Greene, W. Ch., *Moira: Fate, Good and Evil in Greek Thought*, Cambridge, Mass.: Harvard University Press, 1944.
Grene, Nicholas, *Shakespeare's Tragic Imagination*, London: Macmillan 1992.
Hadfield, Andrew–Rainsford, Dominic–Woods, Tim (eds), *The Ethics in Literature,* London: Macmillan, 1999.
Hartman, Geoffrey H., "Shakespeare and the Ethical Question", *ELH* 63, Spring 1996.

Harsh, Ph. Wh., "Hamartia Again", *TPAPA* 76, 1945.
Hawkes, Terence, *That Shakespeherian Rag: Essays on a Critical Process*, London and New York, 1986.
Hegel, G. W. F., *Early Theological Writings,* trans. T. M. Knox, Philadelphia: University of Pennsylvania Press, 1948.
Hegel, G. W. F., *The Philosophy of Fine Art*, trans. F. P. B. Osmaston, London: G. Bell and Sons Ltd., 1920.
Hegel, G. W. F., *Vorlesungen über Aesthetic* III, in *Werke in zwanzig Banden 15*. Theorie Werkausgabe, Suhrkamp Verlag, Frankfurt, 1970. English trans. T. M. Knox, *Aesthetics, Lectures on Fine Art by G. W. F. Hegel*, Oxford: Clarendon, 1975.
Heidegger, Martin, *Lét és Ido* [*Sein und Zeit*], Hungarian trans. Mihály Vajda, Budapest: Gondolat, 1989.
Heidegger, Martin, *Der Ursprung des Kunstwerkes,* Stuttgart: Philip Reclam Jun., 1995 (1960).
Heidegger, Martin, *Basic Writings,* ed. David Farrell Krell, London: Routledge, 1996 (1978).
Heilman, R. B., *Tragedy and Melodrama: Versions of Experience,* Seattle & London: University of Washington Press, 1968.
Heilman, R. B., *This Great Stage: Image and Structure in King Lear,* Seattle: University of Washington Press, 1963.
Henn, T.R., *The Harvest of Tragedy,* London: Methuen & Co. 1956.
Hirsch, E.D. Jr., *Validity in Interpretation,* New Haven & London: Yale University Press, 1971 (1967).
Jackson, Leonard, *The Poverty of Structuralism, Literature and Structuralist Theory*, London: Longman, 1991.
Jaspers, Karl, "Vollendung der Wahrheit in Ursprunglichen Anschauungen", in *Tragik und Tragödie,* Volkmar Sander, 1971.
Japers, Karl, *Tragedy Is Not Enough,* trans. H. A. T. Reiche, H. T. Moore, and K. W. Deutsch, Boston: Beacon, 1952.
Jones, Emrys, *The Origins of Shakespeare*, Oxford: Clarendon, 1977.
Jones, Ernst, *Hamlet and Oedipus,* New York: Doubleday & Co., 1949.
Jones, John, *On Aristotle and Greek Tragedy*, London: Chatto & Windus, 1962.
Kállay, Géza, *Nem puszta szó* [It is not Words], Budapest: Liget, 1996.
Kálmán, C. György, *Az irodalom mint beszédaktus* [*Literature as Speech Act*], Budapest: Akadémiai Kiadó, 1990.
Kant, Immanuel, *Groundwork of the Metaphysics of Morals,* trans. H. J. Paton, London: Unwin Hyman, 1989.

Kant, Immanuel, *Critique of Practical Reason,* trans. Lewis White Beck, New York: Liberal Arts Press, 1956.
Kant, Immanuel, *Critique of Judgement,* trans. James Creed Meredith, Oxford: Clarendon, 1969.
Kant, Immanuel, *Religion within the Limits of Reason Alone,* trans. T. M. Greene and H. H. Hudson, New York: Harper and Row, 1960.
Kelly, Henry Ansgar, *Ideas and Forms of Tragedy from Aristotle to the Middle Ages,* Cambridge: Cambridge University Press, 1993.
Kerényi, Carl, *The Gods of the Greeks,* trans. from German by N. Cameron, New York: Thames and Hudson, 1992 (1951).
Kermode, Frank, *Shakespeare's Language,* London: Allen Lane, The Penguin Press, 2000.
Kerr, Walter, *Tragedy and Comedy,* London, Sydney, Toronto: The Bodley Head, 1967.
Kerrigan, John, *Revenge Tragedy, Aeschylus to Armageddon,* Oxford: Clarendon, 1996.
Kiefer, Frederick, *Fortune and Elizabethan Tragedy,* San Marino: The Huntington Library, 1983.
Kirk, G.S., *A Mítosz [Myth],* Budapest: Holnap kiadó, 1993.
Kitto, H. D. F., *Form and Meaning in Drama,* London: Methuen, 1956.
Kitto, H. D. F., *Greek tragedy,* London and New York: Routledge, 1993 (1939).
Klett, E. T., *The Meaning of Tragedy: Shakespeare and the Spirit of Euripides,* M.A. thesis, University of Birmingham, 1997.
Knight, G. Wilson, *Shakespeare and Religion,* London: Routledge & Kegan Paul, 1967.
Knight, G. Wilson, *Shakespeare's Dramatic Challenge,* New York: Barnes & Noble Books, 1977.
Knight, G. Wilson, *The Wheel of Fire,* London: Methuen & Co Ltd., 1949 (1930).
Knight, G. Wilson, *The Imperial Theme,* London: Macmillan, 1965.
Knights, L. C., *An Approach to Hamlet,* London: Chatto & Windus, 1970.
Kolakowski, Leszek, *The Presence of Myth,* Chicago: The University of Chicago Press, 1989.
Kott, Jan, *Shakespeare, Our Contemporary,* London: Routledge, 1994 (1965).

Krieger, Murray, "Tragedy and the Tragic Vision", in *The Tragic Vision,* ed. Holt–Rinehart–Winston, 1960.
Krook, Dorothea, "The Scheme of Tragedy", in *Elements of Tragedy,* New Haven & London: Yale University Press, 1969.
Krutch, Joseph Wood, "The Tragic Fallacy", in *The Modern Temper,* Harcourt: Brace and World, 1957.
Kuch, Heinrich, "Continuity and Change in Greek Tragedy under Post-classical Conditions", in *Tragedy, Comedy and the Polis* (see Easterling).
Laan, Thomas F. Van, *Role-playing in Shakespeare,* Toronto, Buffalo, London: University of Toronto Press, 1978.
Lacan, Jacques, *Ethics of Psychoanalysis,* ed. Jacques-Alain Miller, trans. Dennis Porter, London: Routledge Tavistock, 1992.
Laroque, Francois, *Shakespeare, ahogy tetszik* [*Shakespeare As You Like It*], Hungarian trans. Berecky Zs. Erzsébet, Budapest: Park kiadó, 1993.
Latte, Kurt, "Schuld und Sünde in der Griechischen Religion", *Archiv für Religionswissenschaft* 20. Leibzig und Berlin: B.G. Teubner, 1920.
Lattimore, Richmond, *Story Patterns in Greek Tragedy,* University of London: The Athlone Press, 1964.
Leech, Clifford, *Tragedy,* London and New York: Routledge, 1989.
Lerner, Laurence (ed.), *Shakespeare's Tragedies*, London, 1963.
Lesky, Albin, *Die Griechische Tragödie,* Stuttgart: Alfred Kroner Verlag, 1958.
Levin, Harry, *The Question of Hamlet,* New York: Oxford University Press, 1958.
Lewis, C. S., *Studies in Shakespeare,* London: Oxford University Press, 1964.
Liebler, Naomi Conn, *Shakespeare's Festive Tragedy,* London and New York: Routledge, 1995.
Lloyd-Jones, Hugh, *The Justice of Zeus,* Berkeley, Los Angeles, London: University of California Press, 1971.
Long, A. A., *Helenistic Philosophy,* London: Duckworth, 1974.
Lucas, F. L., *Serious Drama in Relation to Aristotle's Poetics*, London: The Hogarth Press, 1966.
Lucas, F. L., *Seneca and Elizabethan Tragedy,* New York: Haskell House Publishers, 1922.
Maár, Judit, *A drámai és elbeszélo szöveg szemantikai vizsgálata* [Semantic Analysis of Dramatic and Narrative Textuality], Budapest: Akadémiai Kiadó, 1995.

MacDowell, Douglas M., "Hybris in Athens", *Greece & Rome* XXIII, Oxford: Clarendon Press, 1976.
MacIntyre, Alasdair, *After Virtue*, London: Duckworth, 1994 (1981).
MacIntyre, Alasdair, *A Short History of Ethics*, London: Routledge, 1993 (1963).
Mack, Dietrich, *Ansichten zum tragischen und zur Tragödie*, München: Wilhelm Fink Verlag, 1970.
Mack, Maynard, *Killing the King*, New Haven & London: Yale University Press, 1973.
Mackie, J. L., *Ethics*, London: Penguin Books, 1990 (1977).
Mangan, M., *A Preface to Shakespeare's Tragedies*, London and New York: Longman, 1991.
Marcel, Gabriel, *Tragic Wisdom and Beyond*, trans. Stephen Jolin and P. McCormick, Evanston: Northwestern University Press, 1973.
Margeson, J. M. R., *The Origins of English Tragedy*, Oxford: Clarendon, 1967.
McGee, Arthur, *The Elizabethan Hamlet*, New Haven & London: Yale University Press, 1987.
McGrath, Alister E., *A Life of John Calvin: A Study in the Shaping of Western Culture*, Oxford: Blackwell, 1993.
McLuskie, Kathleen, "The Patriarchal Bard: Feminist Criticism and Shakespeare: *King Lear* and *Measure for Measure*", in *Political Shakespeare: New Essays in Cultural Materialism*, eds Jonathan Dollimore and Alan Sinfield, Manchester, 1985.
Miola, Robert S., *Shakespeare and Classical Tragedy: The Influence of Seneca*, Oxford: Clarendon, 1992.
Montano, Rocco, *Shakespeare's Concept of Tragedy*, Chicago: Gateway editions, 1985.
Moxon, R. Stewart, *The Doctrine of Sin*, London: George Allen & Unwin Ltd., 1922.
Muir, Kenneth (ed.), *The Sources of Shakespeare's Plays*, London: Methuen & Co. Ltd., 1977.
Muir, Kenneth (ed.), *King Lear: Critical Essays*, New York & London: Garland Publishing Inc., 1984.
Niebuhr, Reinhold, *Beyond Tragedy*, London: Nisbet & Co., 1938.
Niebuhr, Reinhold, *The Nature and Destiny of Man*, London: Nisbet & Co. 1944.
Nietzsche, Friedrich, *The Birth of Tragedy and the Genealogy of Morals*, trans. Francis Golffing, New York: Anchor Books, Doubleday, 1956.

Nietzsche, Friedrich, *Beyond Good and Evil,* trans. R. J. Hollingdale, Penguin Books, 1990.
Nilsson, M. P., *Greek Piety,* Oxford: Clarendon, 1951.
Norris, Christopher, *Deconstruction, Theory and Practice,* London and New York: Routledge, 1993 (1982).
Nussbaum, Martha C., *The Fragility of Goodness*, Cambridge: Cambridge University Press, 1993 (1986).
Olson, Elder, "The Elements of Drama: Plot", in *Perspectives of Drama* (see Rosenberg).
Osterud, Svein, "Hamartia in Aristotle and Greek Tragedy", *Symbolae Osloenses* 51-53, Oslo-Bergen-Tromso, 1976.
Parke, H. W., *Greek Oracles,* London: Hutchinson University Library, 1967.
Parker, Robert, *Miasma, Pollution and Purification in Early Greek Religion*, Oxford: Clarendon, 1983.
Pelican, Jaroslav, *Christianity and Classical Culture,* New Haven & London: Yale University Press, 1993.
Péterfy, Jeno, "A tragikum" [*the tragic*], in *Válogatott Muvek,* ed. István Sotér, Budapest: Szépirodalmi könyvkiadó, 1983.
Plantinga, Theodore, *Learning to Live with Evil,* St Catharines: Paideia Press, 1982.
Poe, Joe Park, "Heroism and Divine Justice in Sophocles' Philoctetes", *Mnemosyne,* Bibliotheca Classica Batava, E. J. Brill, 1976.
Poole, Adrian, *Tragedy: Shakespeare and the Greek Example*, Oxford: Basil Blackwell, 1987.
Prosser, Eleanor, *Hamlet and Revenge,* California: Stanford University Press, 1971.
Rabkin, Norman, *Approaches to Shakespeare,* USA: McGraw-Hill Book Company, 1964.
Reed, Robert, R., *Crime and God's Judgement in Shakespeare*, University Press of Kentucky, 1984.
Ricoeur, Paul, *Symbolism of Evil*, trans. Emerson Buchanan, Boston: Beacon Press, 1967.
Ricoeur, Paul, *Fallible Man,* trans. Charles A. Kelbley, New York: Fordham University Press, 1986.
Ricoeur, Paul, *Hermeneutics and the Human Sciences,* ed. and trans. John B. Thompson, Cambridge University Press, 1992 (1981).
Ricoeur, Paul, *From Text to Action: Essays in Hermeneutics*, trans. Kathleen Blamey and J. B.Thompson, Evanston, Illinois: Northwestern University Press, 1991.

Ricoeur, Paul, *Time and Narrative I-III,* trans. Kathleen Blamey and David Pellauer, Chicago: University of Chicago Press, 1984.
Ricoeur, Paul, *Oneself as Another,* English trans. Kathleen Blamey, Chicago: University of Chicago Press, 1992.
Riffaterre, Michael, *Semiotics of Poetry*, Bloomington and London: Indiana University Press, 1978.
Rist, J. M., *Stoic Philosophy,* Cambridge: Cambridge University Press, 1969.
Rorty, A. O. (ed.), *Essays on Aristotle's Poetics,* Princeton: Princeton University Press, 1992.
Rorty, Richard, *Contingency, Irony and Solidarity,* Cambridge: Cambridge University Press, 1989.
Rosenberg, Harold, "Character Change & the Drama", in *Perspectives on Drama* (see M. Rosenberg).
Rosenberg, Marvin, *The Masks of Macbeth,* Berkeley, Los Angeles, London: University of California Press, 1978.
Rosenberg, Marvin, "A Metaphor for Dramatic Form", in *Perspectives on Drama,* eds J. L. Calderwood and Harold E. Toliver, New York: Oxford University Press, 1968.
Ross, David, *Aristotle,* London: Routledge, 1995.
Rösler, Wolfgang, "Die Frage der Echtheit von Sophocles, Antigone 904-920, und die politische Funktion der attischen Tragödie", in *Tragedy, Comedy and the Polis* (see Easterling).
Rupp, E. Gordon–Watson, Philip F. (eds), *Luther and Erasmus: Free Will and Salvation*, Philadelphia: The Westminster Press, 1969.
Rusch, Ernst G., "Das Problem des Tragischen in Christlicher Sicht", in *Tragik und Tragödie,* Darmstadt: Volkmar Sander, 1971.
Rymer, Thomas, *A Short View of Tragedy,* London: A Scolar Press Facsimile, 1970.
Scheler, Max, "On the Tragic", trans. B. Stambler, in *Cross Currents* IV, 1954.
Schelling, F. W. J., *The Philosophy of Art*, trans. & ed. Douglas W. Stott, Minneapolis: University of Minnesota Press, 1989.
Schücking, Levin L., "Character and Action: King Lear" in *Shakespeare: The Tragedies,* ed. Clifford Leech, Chicago & London: University of Chicago Press, 1965.
Scofield, Martin, *The Ghosts of Hamlet,* Cambridge: Cambridge University Press, 1980.
Searle, J. R., *Speech Acts, An Essay in the Philosophy of Language,* Cambridge: Cambridge University Press, 1984 (1969).

Searle, J. R. (ed.), *The Philosophy of Language,* Oxford: Oxford University Press, 1971.
Searle, J. R. and Vanderveken, D., *Foundations of Illocutionary Logic,* Cambridge: Cambridge University Press, 1985.
Sewall, Richard B., *The Vision of Tragedy,* New Haven & London: Yale University Press, 1962.
Sík, Sándor, *Kereszténység és Irodalom* [Christianity and Literature], Budapest: Vigilia, 1989.
Spurgeon, Caroline F. E., *Shakespeare's Imagery,* Cambridge University Press, 1935.
Stachniewsky, John, *The Persecutory Imagination: English Puritanism and the Literature of Religious Despair*, Oxford: Clarendon Press, 1991.
Statman, Daniel (ed.), *Moral Luck,* State University of New York Press, 1993.
Steiner, George, *The Death of Tragedy,* London: Faber and Faber, 1961.
Stinton, T. C. W., "Hamartia in Aristotle and Greek Tragedy", *CQ* 25, 1975.
Stoll, E. E., *Art and Artifice in Shakespeare,* London: Methuen, 1963.
Storm, William, *After Dionysus: A Theory of the Tragic,* Ithaca and London: Cornell University Press, 1998.
Taylor, Gary, *Reinventing Shakespeare*, London: Hogarth, 1990.
Taylor, Gary, *Moment by Moment by Shakespeare*, Macmillan, 1985.
Tengelyi, László, *Kant,* Budapest: Kossuth Könyvkiadó, 1988.
Tengelyi, László, *A bun mint sorsesemény* [Guilt as Fate Experience], Budapest: Atlantisz, 1992.
Tengelyi, László, *Élettörténet és sorsesemény* [The Wild Region in Life History], Budapest: Atlantisz, 1998.
Tillyard, E. M. W., *The Elizabethan World Picture,* London: Chatto & Windus, 1967.
Tillyard, E. M. W., *Shakespeare's Problem Plays,* London: Chatto & Windus, 1950.
Verma, Rajiva, *Myth, Ritual & Shakespeare,* New Delhi: Spantech Publishers PVT LtD., 1990.
Vernant, Jean-Pierre, *Myth and Society in Ancient Greece,* trans. Janet Lloyd, New York: Zone Books, 1990.
Vernant, Jean-Pierre–Vidal-Naquet, Pierre, *Myth and Tragedy in Ancient Greece,* trans. Janet Lloyd, New York: Zone Books, 1990.
Vickers, Brian, *Towards Greek Tragedy,* London: Longman, 1979.

Vickers, Brian, *Appropriating Shakespeare,* New Haven and London: Yale University Press, 1993.
Weisinger, H., *Tragedy and the Paradox of the Fortunate Fall,* London: Routledge & Kegan Paul, 1953.
Wells, Stanley, *Shakespeare: a Dramatic Life,* London: Sinclair-Stevenson, 1994.
Whitaker, Virgil K., *Shakespeare's Use of Learning: An Inquiry into the Growth of his Mind,* San Marino: Huntington Library, 1953.
Williams, Bernard, *Ethics and the Limits of Philosophy,* London: Fontana Press, 1993 (1985).
Williams, Bernard, *Shame and Necessity,* Berkeley, Los Angeles, and London: University of California Press, 1993.
Williams, Raymond, *Modern Tragedy,* London: Verso, 1967.
Wilson, J. Dover, *What Happens in Hamlet,* Cambridge: Cambridge University Press, 1935.
Wilson, F. P., *English Drama 1485-1585,* Oxford: Clarendon, 1990.
Wimsatt, W. K., *Hateful Contraries: Studies in Literature and Criticism,* Lexington: University of Kentucky Press, 1965.
Wittgenstein, Ludwig, *Filozófiai vizsgálódások* [*Philosophische Untersuchungen*], Hungarian trans. Katalin Neumer, Budapest: Atlantisz, 1992.

INDEX

action, 5-7, 14, 18-19, 30, 32-33, 36, 38-39, 42, 45, 47-48, 51-53, 55, 58-64, 66, 68, 72-73, 76, 79, 81-83, 85-91, 95-97, 99-100, 104, 107-108, 111-112, 114, 117-120, 123-124, 126, 129-144, 146, 148-150, 153, 155, 157, 158-170, 195-196; inaction, 7, 40, 120, 130, 132-135, 138-139, 142, 144, 146-150, 168; passivity, 68, 129-130, 132-135, 139, 142-144, 166; plot, 186, 195
Adkins, A.W.H., 17, 185
Aeschylus, 11, 26, 40, 63, 184, 187, 192; *Agamemnon*, 28; *Eumenides*, 25-26, 29, 41, 89, 92, 128; *Libation-Bearers*, 23, 26, 40; *Orestes*, 25-26, 28-29, 39, 89, 93, 120, 128, 167; *Persians*, 37, 82; *Prometheus*, 39-40, 132-135, 144, 166; *Seven Against Thebes*, 26
agency, 7, 126, 134, 149, 158-159, 161-164, 169-170
alterity, 125, 171-172; internal alterity, 172
Anscombe, G.E.M., 158-160, 162, 185
areté, 17
Aristotle, 6-8, 11, 16, 17-20, 27, 30-33, 36-38, 66, 80-87, 89, 94, 96-98, 104, 111, 113, 123, 127, 130-131, 136-138, 167, 185-186, 191-193, 195-197; *anagnórisis*, 23, 25, 29, 31, 34, 41, 86, 92, 125; *katharsis*, 6, 31, 83, 94-95, 110, 123-124, 127; *mimesis*, 45, 107, 131, 135; *Nicomachean Ethics*, 8, 17, 19, 30, 32, 37, 83, 135; *peripeteia*, 31, 41, 86; *Poetics*, 16-17, 27, 31-33, 36, 66, 80-87, 94-98, 130, 135, 167, 185-187, 193, 196

aside, 44, 117, 165, 175-179, 181-183
Austin, J.L., 150-153, 155-157, 166, 185; illocution, 152; infelicities, 151-152; performatives, 150-153, 155; perlocution, 151; speech acts, 7, 133-134, 142, 144, 149-150, 152-157, 166-167

Bauman, Zygmunt, 9-10, 186
Bradley, A.C., 77, 111, 186

Calvin, John, 47, 50-51, 59, 187, 194; *deus absconditus*, 51, 63, 145; *Institute*s, 50-52, 59, 187; predestination, 52, 63, 68, 108, 126, 132
catachresis, 67, 181, 188
Cavell, Stanley, 77, 105, 111, 187
chance, 68
character, 6-7, 12, 16-17, 21, 46, 55, 61-78, 83, 89-90, 98-101, 103-128, 131-132, 136, 138, 140-141, 143-144, 167, 171, 177-178, 180, 182, 196; dividedness, 6, 66-67, 70-71, 74, 76, 79, 98-99, 101, 104, 112, 117, 132
Chaucer, 48, 121, 184
Christian tragedy, 5, 14, 50, 59, 62-63
conflict, 189
contextualism, 6, 106, 110

Davidson, Donald, 158-163, 187-188; pro attitude, 158, 160
deconstruction, 7, 175, 179-180, 182, 187, 195
defilement, 24-25, 28-29, 41-42, 58, 59, 72, 99, 101, 126, 171
delusion, 91-92, 94-102, 125-126
De Man, Paul, 181-182, 188; *Aesthetic Ideology*, 182, 188; *Allegories of Reading*, 182, 188
Derrida, Jacques, 153, 178, 188

Elam, Keir, 131, 137, 178-179, 189
Else, G.F., 30, 80, 84, 94-95
Elton, W.R., 51, 70, 77-78, 95, 189
emplotment, 82-83, 85-87, 95, 97, 113
endurance, 41, 56, 78, 146, 148

éthos, 7, 17, 165-168, 170
Euripides, 12, 24-26, 29, 35, 40, 80, 85, 97, 110, 114, 146, 184, 192; *Alcestis*, 146; *Andromaché*, 83; *Bacchanals*, 39, 96; *Electra*, 27, 40; *Hippolytos*, 27; *Ion*, 24, 26; *Iphigeneia in Aulis*, 12; *Iphigeneia in Taurica*, 24, 26; *The Madness of Hercules*, 27; *Medeia*, 24; *Phoenician Maidens*, 39

fate, 6-7, 9, 11, 21-24, 26-27, 28, 32, 34-36, 38, 42, 49, 53, 54, 56, 60, 62-65, 67-69, 74, 76, 82, 89, 92-94, 96-97, 100, 108, 122, 124, 126, 130-132, 137, 160, 172, 188, 190, 197
felix culpa, 47-51
finitude, 13, 19, 56, 77, 93-96, 99, 103-104, 110, 127
folly, 38, 54-57
fortune, 192
Frye, Northrop, 83, 106, 190

Gadamer, Hans Georg, 65, 94, 129, 190
Greek tragedy, 5-11, 14, 16, 20, 22-34, 37, 39, 40-43, 47-48, 50-53, 59, 61-65, 67-68, 70-71, 73-74, 76-78, 80-81, 83-84, 86-87, 89-95, 97-98, 104-105, 107, 110-111, 115-116, 120-121, 123, 125-126, 128-131, 136-138, 143, 146, 167, 170-172, 175, 184, 192; *hamartia*, 17, 24, 30-35, 41-42, 55, 86, 98, 186, 191, 195, 197; *hybris*, 24, 31, 35, 36-42, 126, 133, 144, 166, 190, 194; *kakos*, 24, 26, 28, 30, 40, 42; *miasma*, 24-26, 28, 30, 37, 41-42, 126, 195; *moira*,34, 63; myth, 5-7, 14-16, 20-23, 28, 32, 38, 42-43, 48, 52, 55, 62, 69, 71, 81-83, 85, 87, 94, 97, 104, 107-108, 110-112, 115, 117, 123, 126, 131-132; *phthonos*, 27, 34-35
guilt, 88, 197

Halliwell, Stephen, 27, 82, 185, 189
Hegel, G.W.F., 6, 8-9, 11, 64, 81, 86-90, 93, 95, 107, 191; *Aesthetics*, 64, 86, 191; *Phenomenology of Spirit*, 88; *Philosophy of Fine Art* , 90; reconciliation, 23, 27, 29, 41, 56, 87-90, 92-93, 96, 164
Heidegger, Martin, 122, 129, 191
Heilman, Robert B., 66-67, 70-72, 97, 130, 191
Homer, 38, 69, 82, 184; *Odyssey*, 69, 184
honour, 36, 53, 60-67, 75-76, 165, 168-170, 186-187

identity, 63, 112-122; narrative identity, 6, 112-116, 119-123; nature, 54, 58, 68, 71-72, 75, 99, 187, 194; role, 70-71, 73; tragic identity, 6-7, 62, 78, 105, 110, 120-126, 128
irony, 25, 69, 164-165, 169, 176, 181-182, 196

Jaspers, Karl, 31, 49-51, 191

Kant, Immanuel, 8-10, 67, 188, 191, 192, 197
katharsis, 6, 31, 83, 86, 94-95, 110, 123-124, 127
Kelly, Henry Ansgar, 130, 192
Kitto, H.D.F., 82, 192
Kyd, Thomas, 52-53; *The Spanish Tragedy*, 52, 184

Lattimore, Richmond, 39, 133, 193
Levin, Harry, 76-77, 100, 193, 196
Luther, Martin, 47, 51, 88, 196; servile will, 62

Machiavelli, Niccolo, 45-47, 184
MacIntyre, Alasdair, 6, 19, 47, 85, 113-114, 120, 122, 194
melodrama, 5, 23-24, 26, 28, 53, 62, 66-67, 81, 90, 92, 97, 101, 105, 110, 120, 128-130, 191
mimesis, 45, 80, 107, 131, 135, 175, 179, 180-182; and semiosis, 181; ungrammaticality, 181
Mirandolla, Pico d., 43, 184
morality, 8-10, 12, 50, 59

Nagel, Thomas, 9-10

INDEX

nature, 12, 18, 25, 43, 47, 50-51, 53-60, 62, 67-68, 70-78, 80, 87-88, 91, 95, 99, 107, 124-125, 127, 131, 154, 159-160, 165, 167-170, 187, 194
necessity, 11, 18, 27, 40, 54, 57, 59, 65, 68-70, 82, 95, 108, 113-114, 116-117, 120, 126-127, 131-132, 134, 136, 138, 160
Nietzsche, Friedrich, 8, 178, 181, 194-195
nihilism, 144-145, 166
Nussbaum, Martha, 10-11, 171, 195

Ovid, 12, 52, 110; *Metamorphoses*, 12, 52, 110, 184

parabasis, 181-182
paralysis, 130, 132-133, 135, 138, 142-144, 146, 148, 166
pathei mathos, 6, 63, 70, 79, 123, 124, 127
pathos, 65, 87, 89-90, 95
Pavis, Patrice, 178
Pfister, Manfred, 178
Plato, 33, 85-86, 185
poiesis, 85, 113, 116, 175, 179, 181
Pride, 24, 35-36, 39-42, 58-61, 75, 99, 126, 133, 148
prohairesis, 17-18, 167

recognition, 21, 32-34, 53, 55-59, 73-74, 77, 86, 91-94, 96, 98-101, 121, 123-127, 137-138, 146-147
reflection, 15-16, 65, 132
Reformation, 47; inherent deprivation, 47, 51
revenge, 26-28, 34, 37, 40, 42, 52-53, 59-62, 66, 68, 73, 75-77, 98, 100, 102, 109, 111, 120, 123, 134, 142, 144-145, 148, 165, 169, 173, 192, 195
Ricoeur, Paul, 6, 7, 19, 21, 28, 29, 49, 51, 85, 96, 112-116, 118-120, 122, 125, 128-129, 131, 135, 158, 171, 195-196; *Fallible Man*, 19, 195; *idem*, 113, 118; *ipse*, 113, 118; *Oneself as Another*, 7, 85, 112, 115, 125, 158, 196; sameness, 105, 112, 113-114, 116-119;

selfhood, 7, 57, 97, 112-116, 118-119, 123, 170-171; *Symbolism of Evil*, 21, 29, 135, 195; *Time and Narrative*, 114-115, 119, 135, 196
Riffaterre, Michael, 179-181, 196
Rorty, A.O., 85-87, 196

scepticism, 111, 144, 166, 182, 186
Schelling, F.W.J., 6, 8, 64-65, 196; *The Philosophy of Art*, 65, 196
Schlegel, Friedrich, 181-182
Searle, J.R., 152-153, 155, 157, 196, 197
self-constitution, 7, 92, 115, 171; and authentication, 96; delusion, 91-92, 95-102, 125-126; self-formation, 120-121, 128, 132; self-distanciation, 30, 71, 74, 76-77, 125, 133
Seneca, 11-12, 187, 190, 193-194
Shakespeare, William, 3, 6, 11-12, 31, 34, 45, 55, 60, 63-71, 73, 76-78, 82, 97, 100, 106, 109, 111, 120, 143, 165, 175-176, 178-179, 186-187, 189-198; *A Midsummer Night's Dream*, 139; *Coriolanus*, 61, 67, 74-75, 188; *Hamlet*, 7, 12, 45, 46-47, 51-54, 59-61, 66-69, 73-77, 100, 102, 106, 107, 109, 111, 117, 120-121, 123, 132-134, 136, 138, 140-146, 148-150, 153-166, 168-172, 184, 186-196, 198; ghost, 67, 100-111, 120, 141, 144, 156-157, 169, 172; readiness, 76-78, 121, 168; *Julius Caesar*, 62, 175; *King Lear*, 51, 54-55, 68-72, 77-78, 95, 102, 109, 116, 120, 125, 127-128, 137, 139, 184, 186, 189, 191, 194, 196; ripeness, 55-57, 76-78; *Macbeth*, 47, 53-54, 58-60, 65, 68-69, 71-72, 74, 77, 97, 99-101, 105, 107, 124, 140-141, 143, 171-172, 177, 184, 186, 190, 196; weird sisters, 172; *Measure for Measure*, 140, 194; melodrama, 97, 101, 105, 120; *Much Ado About Nothing*, 139; *Othello*, 101, 139; *The Sonnets*, 58, 69-70; tragedy, 6-7, 14, 43, 47-48, 50, 52, 59, 61-68, 70-71, 73,

78, 97, 105, 111, 120, 126, 129, 138, 171; tragic, 49, 52, 55, 56-57, 59, 62, 71, 103, 126; *Richard the Third*, 61, 97, 98, 104, 172, 175, 180; *Timon of Athens*, 104; *Titus Andronicus* , 61, 66, 97, 101, 120, 128, 184; *Twelfth Night*, 139, 143
shame, 198
sin, 62, 194
Sophocles, 11, 25, 31, 34, 65, 83, 90, 123, 185, 187, 195-196; *Ajax*, 39, 83, 95-96, 185; *Ajax the Locrian*, 83, 185; *Antigone*, 35-36, 39, 65, 94-95, 196; *Electra*, 26-27, 39-40; *Oedipus at Colonus*, 25, 34, 41, 89-90, 92-93, 96; *Oedipus Tyrannus*, 25, 41, 65, 90, 92, 96, 105, 128; *Philoctetes*, 89-90, 93, 195
Stoll, E.E., 106, 197
Strawson. P.F., 152-153

Tate, Nahum, 55
teleology, 23, 26-27, 32, 34, 42, 53, 61, 63, 91-93, 96-97, 130, 131; *telos*, 5, 23-24, 27-28, 34-35, 52-54,
56-57, 59, 63, 65-66, 79, 81, 83-86, 90-93, 95-97, 124, 130-132, 136-137; differential teleology, 91; *teleute*, 84
Tengelyi, László, 3, 9, 20, 122, 124, 197
tragic, 5-8, 10-12, 14-17, 20, 22, 24-29, 31-42, 48-53, 55-64, 66, 69-72, 74, 76, 78, 80-83, 86, 89-101, 103-105, 107-108, 110-112, 115, 117-126, 128-130, 135-138, 143, 146, 162, 167, 171, 195
tukhe, 11, 27

Vives, Juan Luis, 44-45, 185

Weisinger, Herbert, 50, 198
Williams, Bernard, 9-11, 198
Wilson, Rawdon, 77, 106-110, 140, 192, 198
Wimsatt, W.K., 30, 95, 198